Understanding Mental Illness and its Nursing

Second Edition

K.L.K. TRICK, MB, BS, LRCP, MRCS, DPM

Late Consultant Psychiatrist, St Crispin Hospital, Northampton;
Consultant Psychiatrist, St Andrews Hospital, Northampton

and

S. OBCARSKAS, SRN, RMN, RNT

Late Principal Tutor, School of Nursing, Littlemore Hospital, Oxford;
Area Nursing Officer, Salop.

Pitman Medical

First published 1968
Second edition 1976
Reprinted 1978

Catalogue Number 21 3599 81

Pitman Medical Publishing Co Ltd
PO Box 7, Tunbridge Wells,
Kent, TN1 1XH, England

Associated Companies

UNITED KINGDOM
Pitman Publishing Ltd, London
Focal Press Ltd, London

CANADA
Copp Clark Ltd, Toronto

USA
Fearon Pitman Publishers Inc, California
Focal Press Inc, New York

AUSTRALIA
Pitman Publishing Pty Ltd, Carlton

NEW ZEALAND
Pitman Publishing NZ Ltd, Wellington

ISBN: 0 272 79385 X

Text set in 10/12 pt Monotype Times New Roman, printed by letterpress,
and bound in Great Britain at The Pitman Press, Bath

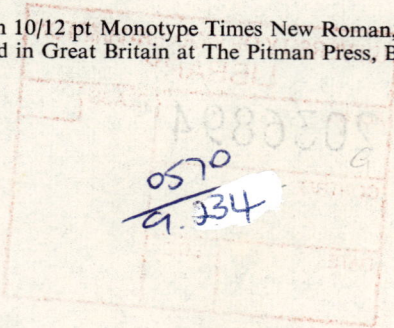

Contents

Preface to the 2nd Edition

Since the first edition of this book was written a new syllabus for the final examination has been drawn up (1974) and aspects of sociolgy are now included. A chapter has been added, outlining some areas where psychiatry and sociology have common ground.

There have been few striking advances in psychiatric treatment since the first edition was written. Following the rapid strides made with the introduction of the phenothiazines, and the anti-depressant drugs there has been a period of consolidation and reappraisal. Psychiatry has been under constant attack from those who propound theories grouped together as 'anti psychiatry'. Their criticism is usually shrill and ill-informed yet if it prevents us from becoming complacent it will have been of some value. Unfortunately, it has not infrequently influenced young people suffering from severe mental disorders into refusing treatment that could be of benefit to them.

In the last few years there has been a wholesale and expensive reorganisation of the social services (following the Seebohm report) and of the National Health Service. These changes are dealt with in Chapter 18.

Psychiatric nurses have begun to play a much more extensive rôle in the community and a new section on this aspect of their work has been included in this edition.

Whatever changes may occur in the future, the basic requirement for all work with psychiatric patients will remain: tolerance, compassion and respect for other human beings.

K.L.K.T.
S.O.

Preface to the 1st Edition

Descriptions of mental illness in textbooks tend to dehumanise the picture, so that the nurse is unable to recognise the patients whom she meets in her day to day work as having anything in common with those described in books. On the other hand, those texts designed to cover the nursing aspects tend to deal in generalities rather than with the specific problems arising in the different conditions. For this reason, the case histories contained in this book are written more as short stories than in the conventional case report style. These case stories are followed by conventional descriptions of the illnesses. In this way it is hoped that the nurse will be able to relate the living person to the conventional ways used to describe their behaviour.

While this book is designed primarily to meet the needs of the student mental nurse, it is planned in such a way as to be suitable for others who have to deal with the mentally ill, either in the course of their professional work or because they have sick relatives. With the increasing emphasis on community care of the mentally ill, more and more people are having to cope with problems that were previously the province of the mental nurse, and they require help, both in understanding the nature of the illness and the way in which they should respond to the patient.

It is hoped that this book will encourage the reader to try to understand not only intellectually, but also emotionally, the fears, anxieties, and agonies that the patient may be experiencing, for only then will it be possible to accept, at all times, the patient as a human being who needs love and respect.

We would like to acknowledge the help given to us by Miss A. Cocker while Tutor at Littlemore Hospital and to Miss M. Wenger of Pitman Medical Publishing Co. Ltd, whose comments have been of great value.

K.L.K.T.
S.O.

Part One

Patients and Illnesses

The people described in the case stories are not based on any one living person but are made up of facets drawn from many patients

1 The Neuroses

Three Illustrative Stories

1. 'It's really got beyond a joke,' said the attractive young woman who had been referred by her GP to the psychiatric clinic, 'I just cannot go out on my own even to post a letter. Recently,' she continued, 'I can hardly bear to be alone in the house, and my husband is losing time from work because of it. We cannot afford it, because we need his overtime to help pay for the car and the washing machine.'

'When did you first have this trouble?'

'Well, soon after we moved to the new house, that was about eighteen months after my little girl was born. Of course I've always been a bit highly strung, but never as bad as this.'

'What was the first thing you noticed?'

'It was in the supermarket; I was getting the shopping, with Carol my daughter, and suddenly I felt as if I was going to faint. I felt so panicky that I just left the basket and pushed my way out of the shop. I tried again the next day, but as I walked along I began to get so scared I might pass out that I began to perspire and my heart was pounding away. I thought I was going to die, so I had to turn back.'

'You felt all right in the house?'

'Yes, at first, but recently I've been getting these feelings at home, and when I get into a state I'm convinced something dreadful is going to happen to me, and so I have to have someone to stay with me.'

As she and the doctor discussed the problem certain points emerged. At first she had insisted that she had no real worries, but she gradually began to talk about her uncertainties and fears. She had led a rather sheltered life as a child, and had always been protected because she was thought to be 'nervous'. Her marriage had not started too well, as she was very ignorant of sexual matters and at first had experienced a number of difficulties in this aspect. She had become pregnant but miscarried at three months and had been very

3

upset, feeling that in some way she was a failure as a mother. However, she had conceived again quite soon, and following the birth of the child they had moved from her mother's house to a new estate where she knew no one and where she had no one to ask for help with the problems of dealing with a new baby. The child frightened her, it seemed so vulnerable and she felt so ignorant. Each time it cried at night she was sure it had some serious illness. Soon she could hardly sleep, even when the child was quiet. She felt so tired and tense that she began to avoid her husband's love-making, and finally he had stopped making any advances. She then became convinced he must have a girl friend, and the day before her first panic attack they had had a row when she had accused him of infidelity.

2. A patient lay on the examination couch in the Casualty Department seeming rather indifferent to her surroundings, but perfectly alert and aware of what was going on around her. 'She just says: "I don't know" to everything we ask,' said the staff nurse. 'All we know is that she was wandering around in the graveyard, and one of the grave diggers thought she looked a bit lost, so he asked her if she was looking for a particular grave, and she just started to cry and kept repeating, "I don't know". He called the police and they brought her here. She had an envelope in her handbag and the police have gone to see if they can find a relative or someone who knows her.'

The casualty officer examined her and could find no evidence of injury or physical disease to account for her amnesia. He arranged for her admission to the psychiatric unit to await further information.

Some hours later a worried young man arrived at the ward and having seen the patient said, 'Yes, that's my wife. Whatever is wrong with her, Doctor? Why doesn't she recognise me?' The doctor reassured him that his wife was not seriously ill, and that the most likely explanation was that her loss of memory was the result of some severe emotional stress.

'I cannot imagine what is worrying her,' said her husband.

'Well, the first step is for us to know some background details,' said the doctor, and in the course of the next hour or so the following details were obtained.

Ann was an only child of rather elderly parents who doted on her. She had been a bright child, made friends easily, and tended to be the leader of her group. Her school reports often contained phrases such as: 'Bright but needs to work harder.' 'Could do better, but tends to lose interest'. Her school days were punctuated by days when she was away ill with vague complaints of stomach-ache or vomiting attacks, and her parents began to realise that these illnesses seemed to occur when there was something happening that Ann wanted to avoid.

She had many boy friends, but her friendships did not last long, and she was considered to be rather a flirt. She and her husband met at a dance and married after six months courtship. They had been married for almost two years and she had continued to work in a local shop. They talked about having a family, but she had wanted to wait for a few years, so that they could 'have a good time' first. They were buying their own house, and ran a small car, but had no real financial worries, nor any other obvious problems.

A further interview with Ann produced no more information, as she continued to say, 'I don't know' and 'I cannot remember' to every question.

It was decided, in view of the acute onset of symptoms, to try to get her to talk by giving her an intravenous injection of sodium amytal. Under the influence of the drug, she began to cry, and gradually the cause of her distress emerged.

For some months she had been having an affair with the manager of the shop at which she worked and her period was now two months late. She had concluded that she was pregnant, and after days of worrying had finally decided to kill herself by jumping in the river. She had set off, but had wandered into a cemetery on the way, and vaguely remembered someone asking her if she was looking for a particular grave. At this point she felt as if her mind had gone blank.

A pregnancy test showed that she was not, in fact, pregnant, and with some encouragement she told her husband all about her affair. He took the news remarkably calmly, and apart from insisting she gave up her job, made no conditions about having her home.

3. 'I've had to give up my job', the young bearded man said. 'I just couldn't get started you see. I'm a driving instructor, and I keep the firm's car at home. Each morning I get in and start up and am just going to back out of the drive when I think: what if a child is playing behind the car? I have to get out and check. At first I could then

drive off, but now when I get back in I think that perhaps in the time it's taken me to get into the car, a child has come along and is out of sight by the back wheels. I know it's stupid and ridiculous, but I could not bring myself to reverse out, so I had to back into the drive, and for a while it was all right, but then I began to think about children running out in front of me, and so I have to drive slowly enough to always be able to stop. As you can imagine this doesn't make me the ideal driving instructor.'

'Do you have any other difficulties?'

'Well,' he said, after a few minutes thought, 'I have this thing about washing; I always worry that I might have some germs on my hands which will get into the food and harm my wife and little boy. I take ages to wash my hands and sometimes have to go back and do them again, because the towel might have been dirty.'

In reply to questions, he told the psychiatrist of his childhood, and how strict his parents had been and the emphasis they had placed on cleanliness. He recounted a scene he had witnessed on one occasion when his younger brother had wet the bed when he was supposed to be pot trained. His father had been extremely neat and tidy and had insisted on his sons being the same. Although they were rarely beaten, there was always the threat of punishment in the air. When he went to boarding school, he found things little different, and had tried to avoid getting into trouble by taking the greatest care over his work. His work was often held up as an example to the other boys, which did not endear him to them.

He had started work in an office, but had lost his job because his constant checking and rechecking of his work made him too slow.

He then found employment in a dairy, working the machine which filled the bottles. This seemed rather an unskilled task in view of his intellectual ability, but he explained that the bottles moved on automatically as soon as he pulled the lever, and he was thus prevented from checking whether or not the top was properly in place. After a few months, however, he found the job too boring and had left to become a driving instructor.

The doctor arranged for him to attend the out-patient clinic regularly, to allow him to discuss his problems, and to try to reach a better understanding of himself; in addition, the doctor prescribed some capsules of chlordiazepoxide which helped to reduce the patient's anxiety to a more tolerable level.

The Neuroses

The neurotic illnesses can best be understood by regarding them as the individual's attempt to deal with feelings of anxiety. Attempts that have failed and, in failing, have created fresh problems of their own.

Anxiety has been described as 'fear spread thin', and it is a normal and necessary part of being alive. Without it one's ability to survive in a hostile environment would be much diminished. It acts as a warning that the well being of the person is threatened, and increases his alertness and ability to respond to the danger. Anxiety is experienced as a feeling of apprehension, 'as if something dreadful is going to happen'. This mental state is accompanied by a series of physical changes in the body. These are mediated by activity of the sympathetic nervous system, and by the release of adrenaline from the suprarenal glands into the blood. This, in turn, produces alterations in various body systems that are designed to prepare the body for severe physical effort, such as running away or standing and fighting. This is referred to as the 'fight or flight response'. The changes that occur can be listed as follows—

1. *Circulation*

Both the rate and force of the heart's contraction is increased, raising cardiac output. This is accompanied by a rise in blood pressure.

The blood vessels in the skin constrict so that the person looks pale. The blood supplying the gut is also greatly reduced. The vessels supplying the skeletal muscles and the heart are dilated to increase the blood supply to these areas.

2. *Lungs*

The muscular coat of the bronchioles relaxes so that the diameter increases and the resistance to the flow of air through the lungs is reduced. The mucous secretion is also reduced. This is experienced as a dry mouth, and may lead the person to lick his lips frequently.

3. *Muscles*

The tone of the skeletal muscles is increased and may be felt as bodily tension, which may lead to aches and pains in various parts of the body, or may give rise to a general feeling of physical exhaustion.

The muscles of the intestines relax and their rhythmic contraction (peristalsis) is reduced.

In the skin, the small muscles, arrectores pili, which cause the hair to stand on end, constrict. In fur-covered animals this leads to an apparent increase in size, and improves the heat loss during activity. In hairless man it has no useful effect, but gives rise to that state of the skin usually called 'goose pimples'.

4. *The Eyes*

The pupils of the eyes dilate, and the lids retract.

5. *The Liver*

The conversion of glycogen, stored in the liver, to glucose is increased, thus making available to the muscles a source of energy.

These bodily changes are a useful preparation for dealing with problems by desperate physical effort, but for modern civilised man relatively few situations can be resolved in this way. It is not socially acceptable to thump your boss on the nose or to run like a hare when your mother-in-law enters the room.

When the problem cannot be resolved in a direct way, the feeling of anxiety may persist and the person will then attempt to lessen it in a variety of ways depending on his personality and previous experience. The type of situation that gives rise to anxiety also depends on the patient's personality and life experience, and the psycho-analytic explanation is that present situations arouse anxiety because they resemble and revive conflicts that existed between the child and its close relations during the early years of life, and which were not satisfactorily resolved at that time. The 'behaviourists', however, place less emphasis on early experiences, and consider that the patient has learnt to respond to a certain situation with anxiety. If this experience is repeated a number of times, the anxiety may become aroused by factors that happen to be associated with the original event in a quite casual way. This anxiety may be provoked long after the actual causal event, and persist as an unnecessary and distressing habit.

This difference in theory leads to a rather different approach to treatment, which is discussed later.

The methods by which people attempt to deal with persistent anxiety can be grouped into three broad clinical groups, but it is important to remember that in practice, features of each group can be seen in the individual patient, both at the same time and at different times, in the illness. It is also important to remember that the patient, or his relatives, seek help only when the method has failed, and that in some circumstances 'neurotic' symptoms enable a person to carry on leading a comparatively normal life under considerable stress.

The clinical patterns can be considered under the headings of (a) anxiety states, (b) hysteria, and (c) obsessional neurosis. Reactive depression is considered under the general title 'Depression', and the condition of anorexia nervosa considered on page 11, under the heading 'Anorexia Nervosa'.

Anxiety States

The patient may complain of feeling tense and anxious, but is usually unable to give a reason for his feelings. The reason is often fairly obvious when looking at the patient's life situation, but at times the basis of the anxiety may be deeply hidden. The direct complaint of anxiety is comparatively unusual, for most patients have attempted to deal with it in various ways and, also, many feel that it is not the sort of complaint they can offer to their doctor, or one that he will respect. Thus, the anxiety may give rise to secondary symptoms, probably the most common being headaches. These arise as the result of increased tone in the muscles of the neck which cause pressure on the nerves supplying the scalp. Thus, the typical tension headache starts in the neck and runs up over the top of the head. It may be described as a 'pressure' or 'like a knife in the top of my head'.

Other patients become aware of the bodily changes associated with anxiety, and this leads to even greater anxiety with a further increase in symptoms. Thus, the patient feels her heart beating faster and louder, and becomes convinced that her 'palpitations' are the first sign of an impending heart attack.

Others find the increase in respiratory effort frightening and are convinced that they cannot breathe. A frequent complaint is the fear of fainting. The patient experiences a sinking sensation in the stomach, racing pulse, a cold sweat, and slight shaking of the limbs, this combined with a feeling of approaching doom, convinces her that she is about to faint or even die. The experience may occur when she is in a crowd, out shopping, or on a bus, and she is rapidly convinced that it will occur each time she repeats the activity she was engaged in. The next time she goes out, her level of anxiety is already high, so she again experiences the physical changes described, and her belief in the association between the activity and the 'fainting feeling' is reinforced. The stage is now set for the 'house-bound housewife' syndrome, as she avoids the activities she associates with her panic attacks, by remaining in her house as far as is possible.

This attaching of anxiety to specific events or situations is also seen in the so-called phobic states. In these conditions the original anxiety is displaced on to a particular object or situation, and thus it may not interfere too much with normal life. A fear of dead bodies would not be a great problem for the average housewife, but it could be tiresome for an undertaker.

Hysteria

Hysteria and hysterical are used in a number of different ways, and the resulting confusion has led to the suggestion that the name be discarded. This is unlikely to happen, so it is important to try to recognise the different ways in which the words are applied.

'Hysterical' is used as a description of a personality type. The person so described seems to have the need to appear more than they really are, as if they were playing a part in which they have become totally immersed. They are able to change roles quickly (and often make good actors!). At one moment they may see themselves as a tragic victim of fate, while a little later, under different circumstances, they see themselves as successful, popular, and irresistible. Their grasp of truth may be tenuous, and they may soon come to believe their own untruths. Their emotional life is shallow: they flirt but cannot love, and as if to compensate, they exaggerate their emotional response. Thus, everything is fabulous and wonderful, or devastating and shattering.

Such people may never develop hysterical symptoms but, if exposed to stress, are more prone to do so than some other personality types, and the condition is more likely to become chronic.

Hysterical Symptoms

These are symptoms of mental or physical disorder that arise as a result of stress, and which help the patient in some way to deal with it. While the symptoms can mimic any condition known to medicine, they generally represent some loss of function of part of the body or the mind.

The stress may be real: a soldier in the front line under heavy fire may unconsciously convert his very understandable fear into a symptom such as blindness or loss of memory, which leads to him being sent back from the front.

Another form of real stress is an organic illness. The patient may be suffering more pain than is realised, or may have a particular fear of some condition; if he feels he is not being given sufficient help or understanding, he may exaggerate his symptoms even further, or develop additional symptoms, which do not fit in with the picture of his condition. Such patients are sometimes said to show 'functional overlay'.

Unconscious anxiety can arise as a result of conflict between the primitive drives of the individual and the dictates of society, or of conscience. If the individual is unable to resolve this conflict realistically, he may resort to some form of defence mechanism. Conversion and dissociation are two such techniques, and their use may lead to the development of hysterical symptoms. This condition is often referred to either as hysteria or conversion hysteria. The patient usually presents with the complaint of loss of function of some part of the body or mind.

Mental symptoms presented by the patient may be any of the following:

1. Amnesia—the patient has 'lost' his memory.
2. Fugue states—the patient does not know where he is or what he is doing.
3. Unconsciousness, trance states, or fits—the functions of the brain are lost completely for varying lengths of time.
4. Pseudodementia—brain function appears impaired as in a dementing illness, but the patient tends to give appropriate answers.

The following physical symptoms may be presented:

1. Motor symptoms—the patient loses the use of one or more limbs, or can no longer stand still, balance, walk, or run, etc.
2. Sensory symptoms—feeling is lost in some part of the body. The area affected usually doesn't correspond to the nerve supply of the part.

3. Special senses the—patient may lose the function of any or all of the special senses, becoming blind, deaf, or unable to taste or smell.
4. Loss of sexual function—frigidity on the part of the woman and impotence on the part of the male, may be a hysterical symptom.

Anorexia Nervosa

Conversion hysteria has become much less common in recent years, but anorexia nervosa has, in contrast, become less of a rarity, perhaps as a result of all the pressures on people to diet and become slim.

Anorexia nervosa is the name given to a syndrome seen mainly in young women. It was first described by Sir William Gull in 1868. The illness consists of a refusal by the patient to eat. As a result, she loses weight, until she may resemble the victim of a concentration camp. In spite of this extreme emaciation, she may retain a surprising degree of vigour and activity until the terminal stage, when extreme weakness confines her to bed. Along with the weight loss there is almost invariably cessation of menstruation and other physical changes including low temperature, low blood pressure, slow pulse, and the growth of downy hair on parts of the body which are normally hairless.

The diagnosis of anorexia nervosa is made only in the absence of other physical or mental illness. Whether it is a disease in its own right, or a manifestation of hysteria or obsessional neurosis is debatable. The underlying cause of the condition varies, but commonly the sufferer has some considerable difficulty in accepting her sexuality. The illness usually first develops within seven years of the onset of puberty. Frequently it follows an attempt at dieting to lose weight. The desire to lose weight may arise from a wish to prevent the development of secondary female sexual characteristics—especially the breasts. Other patients explain that they feared they had become pregnant, not as a result of intercourse—for most sufferers have had no sexual experiences—but in some way which reflects their sexual ignorance. They associate being pregnant with being fat, and hope that by getting rid of their flesh they will get rid of the imagined pregnancy.

Many of these patients have an obsessional personality and their behaviour has a ritualistic quality. Some fluctuate between periods of starvation and periods of compulsive over-eating. The patient rarely seeks help, being brought along by anxious relatives, and is often uncooperative with treatment. They seem to derive a certain satisfaction from contemplating their skeletal bodies, and often go to extreme lengths to avoid taking food. Their lying and cheating in this matter, and occasional episodes of stealing, is in marked contrast to their honesty and puritanical behaviour prior to the onset of the illness.

Treatment is directed at resolving the patient's fears of growing up, and sorting out her ideas about 'fatness', combined with restoring her to normal body weight. This usually requires in-patient treatment. For part of the time in hospital the patient may have to be confined to bed, and to get over her resistance to treatment she is usually given moderate to large doses of chlorpromazine. In order to stimulate her appetite and to utilise to the maximum the food she takes, modified insulin treatment may also be used.

The relationship established between the patient and the nursing staff is a vital factor in treatment. On the regime described, most patients gain weight, but if a relapse is to be avoided, continuing support has to be provided after the patient has been discharged. The illness has an appreciable death rate, both from intercurrent illness and from suicide.

Obsessional Neurosis

In these conditions the patient tries to control his anxiety by persistently repeating certain thoughts or acts. Initially, this diminishes his anxiety, but if the anxiety persists the patient develops a compulsive need to increase his ritual, until the repetition of the thoughts or actions begins to interfere with his life to such an extent that the symptoms themselves give rise to secondary anxiety.

The clinical picture may be dominated by obsessional thoughts, obsessional acts, or obsessional fears. Such symptoms may occur in other psychiatric illnesses as part of the patient's defence mechanism, and for the diagnosis of obsessional neurosis to be made the patient must experience a feeling of compulsion to perform the ritual, which he attempts to resist, recognising the absurdity of his behaviour.

Compulsive thoughts may take the form of *persistent doubting*. The patient is unable to convince himself, for example, that he has locked the door, put the cat out, or turned off the gas, and has to go downstairs to check; no sooner has he returned to bed than his doubt returns and he has to check once more. Other patients complain that obscene words keep coming into their mind and they may feel an almost irresistible urge to stand up in church and shout Anglo-Saxon expressions at the congregation.

Obsessional acts may be the result of such thoughts, but also exist in their own right. They may involve special routines concerned with washing or dressing and often have to be repeated a certain number of times. These rituals are closely linked with the 'magical' games children play—like not treading on the cracks between paving stones. The magical quality of ritual may also be seen in various religious ceremonies.

Obsessional fears are often associated with both acts and thoughts. The patient may be obsessed with ideas about dirt, and the harm this may cause. This may lead to her developing elaborate washing rituals, which she may also expect other members of the family to carry out. Fears of aggressive acts towards their loved ones may lead them to lock up all knives and other sharp instruments.

The obsessional neuroses represent an extension of the features of the obsessional personality. A degree of obsessionality can be a desirable character trait, making the person conscientious, reliable, and careful, but it is often associated with a tendency to set too high a standard in work and personal behaviour, a degree of rigidity in attitude which makes any change difficult to accept, and an inability to tolerate criticism. Many such people experience great difficulty in dealing with, and accepting, their aggressive feelings. People with this type of personality are not only liable to develop obsessional states, but are also more liable to depressive illnesses, particularly in middle age.

The treatment of patients with an obsessional neurosis consists in reducing their anxiety with drugs such as chlordiazepoxide (Librium) and, if there are any features suggesting depression, treating this with antidepressant drugs. Psychotherapy is supportive in nature, as any attempt at a more analytic approach is not only difficult because of their inability to stop censoring their thoughts, but also may arouse such strong feelings of guilt that the patient becomes severely depressed and may attempt suicide.

Treatment and Nursing Care of Neuroses

The great majority of people with neurotic illness can be treated as out-patients, with a combination of psychotherapy and drugs if required. Some patients need more support and will attend as day-patients, while a minority will require admission either for a prolonged period, or for a short time to help them through an acute crisis. Admission is avoided in general because entering hospital may help the patient escape from the problem that is causing the illness, without doing anything to solve it. Thus, the patient may feel perfectly well in hospital, but will experience a return of symptoms as soon as discharged. The aim of treatment is to help the patient understand the reasons for the illness, and to help him or her find some other way of dealing with it. Sometimes it is possible to give practical help in resolving patients' difficulties by adjusting their environment. For example, a woman who is worried by an inability to manage the housekeeping may improve if her husband is persuaded to take over the responsibility. Usually, it is not as simple as that, and a combination of practical help and psychotherapy are necessary. Specific consideration of psychotherapy is the subject or a later chapter, but one aspect is especially important in regard to patients with neurotic problems who are in-patients or day attenders. This is the handling of acute emotional crises—a technique sometimes referred to as 'psychiatric first aid'.

Psychiatric First Aid
The principles of psychiatric first aid can be summarised thus:

1. The nurse must remain calm and in control of herself and the situation;
2. She must be prepared to spend time with the patient even if other activities have to be temporarily neglected;
3. She must listen patiently to the patient;
4. She must reassure the patient;
5. She must attempt to help the patient find an occupation that distracts him from endless preoccupation with personal problems;
6. The patient may require sedation.

1. *Calmness.* The nurse may often feel irritated, or even angry at the demands made upon her by an anxious patient, particularly if the patient demonstrates her need by some form of dramatic acting-out behaviour, or by constantly demanding to see a doctor. However, nothing is gained by losing one's temper with the patient, as any hostile reaction on the nurse's part merely increases the tension and anxiety of the patient, and may also affect other patients in the ward.

2. *Time*. The patient must feel that the nurse is genuinely interested in her and wants to help. She will not feel this if the nurse is obviously wanting to get on with some other task. The nurse must remember that time spent with the patient at this moment may make all the difference to the progress the patient makes, and if the situation is mishandled, the patient may be worse than when originally admitted.

3. *Listening*. The patient should be invited to go with the nurse to a quiet place and to talk about her problems and the way she feels. The art of listening is one of the most important aspects of psychiatric nursing. It involves being sufficiently emotionally involved with the patient to be able to remain interested, yet being sufficiently detached to take an objective view of what the patient is saying.

4. *Reassurance*. In formal psychotherapy reassurance is avoided as it tends to confirm the patient in patterns of neurotic behaviour, but during an acute emotional crisis it is essential that the patient be supported in this way. Reassurance means much more than telling the patient that everything will be all right. It is partly the calm attitude of the nurse—demonstrating to the patient that all is not lost. Verbally the nurse should explain in simple terms some of the reasons for the patient's symptoms—especially if the patient's anxiety is giving rise to physical symptoms such as palpitations. A brief explanation of the relationship between anxiety and the bodily changes produced can be very helpful.

5. *Occupation*. After listening and talking to the patient it may be possible to involve her in some activity that helps to distract her from her emotional problems. The most satisfactory occupations are those in which the patient is of use or service to someone else, in order that she can see some justification for the job, beyond her own needs.

6. *Sedation*. Occasionally, the patient is unable to respond to the approach suggested, and remains distraught. Even the old stand-by of a 'nice cup of tea' may fail to work its customary charm. The patient may then require a sedative drug such as sodium amytal, valium or librium, which should be administered on the doctor's instructions.

The nurse's attitude to neurotic patients must be a blend of sympathy and optimism—not minimising the patient's difficulties, but conveying the conviction that the problem is not insoluble.

Observation of the patient should include an assessment of situations which seem to make the patient anxious or upset, as well as situations in which the patient seems better. Such observations may help to throw light on the psychological factors involved in the illness. Often, patients deny emotional problems, particularly if a close relative is involved, but they reveal the source of their anxiety by their behaviour when that person is present. Careful note should be made of anything suggesting an increasing depression that might lead to a suicidal gesture. Increasing agitation or panic must also be observed as, in the earlier stages, this can be diverted into more useful activity than is possible when a crisis has arisen and the patient has been overwhelmed by anxiety.

The relationship of the nurse to the patient may be of overriding importance in determining the recovery of the patient. The nurse has to avoid increasing the patient's dependence, while at the same time not giving the patient a feeling that she is being rejected.

One of the most important aspects of the nursing care is arranging a day that meets the needs of the patients. The patients, in general, are physically fit and perfectly in touch with their surroundings. They require three main activities:

1. time for discussion of their neurotic problems;
2. occupation or entertainment that provides a distraction from themselves and their symptoms;
3. occupation that allows them to feel of use to others.

1. *Time for Discussion of their Problems.* This may take the form of individual sessions with the doctor or nurse, or group discussions involving some or all of the patients in the unit. The actual form of group or individual therapy used will depend on the technique of the person leading the group. When insufficient opportunity is provided for patients to discuss their symptoms and problems with the staff, they will tend to do so among themselves. This may be of benefit, but, equally, may lead to increased anxiety and the perpetuation of false beliefs. To issue notices forbidding patients to discuss each other's symptoms serves little useful purpose. Given enough time for discussion, and with the rest of the day filled with interesting and rewarding activity, few patients will feel a pressing desire to keep on about their symptoms.

2. *Occupation and Entertainment to Provide Distraction.* Unlike some of the patients with psychotic illness, the patient with neurotic symptoms does not usually require training in a new trade, nor the

re-establishment of work habits. The aim of occupational therapy is to provide a relief from boredom and preoccupation with symptoms, to stimulate new and old interests, and to enable the patient to derive satisfaction from creating something. The actual form of task will depend on the patient, his skills, and his illness, and is best selected by discussion with a trained occupational therapist. The nurse must help the patient to see that such activities form as important a part of treatment as do his drugs and his group therapy. By working with the patient in the ward, or in the OT Department, the nurse will foster a relationship and increase her opportunity for making valuable observations on the patient's behaviour and personality.

3. *Occupation of Service to Others*. Many patients with neurotic symptoms feel they are useless or unwanted. Part of their treatment must be the restoration of their self-respect. Others have become so preoccupied by their own needs and wishes that they are unable to modify their behaviour to meet the demands of others. In both cases they have to be helped to work with, and for, other people. In so doing they may learn that through giving and serving they obtain greater and more lasting satisfaction than in any pursuit of their own ends. Such routine ward activities as cleaning, bed-making, washing up can be dull chores, or they can become useful tasks which help the patient to recover.

2 Psychopathy and Sexual Disorders

Illustrative Story

'He must be mad. No one in his right senses would do a thing like that,' said the landlord of The Bull. He was talking about a case reported in the local paper in which a young man had stolen a motor car, driven it at great speed, and finally crashed it, almost killing himself. This act was not so unusual, but the aspect that gave rise to the landlord's comment was that this event had occurred while the young man was awaiting trial for exactly the same offence, committed a few months previously.

The court had taken the same view as the landlord and had remanded the defendant while a medical report was obtained.

When Peter came into the room, he smiled broadly at the psychiatrist, and shook him warmly by the hand.

'So you're the head-shrinker who is going to get me off the hook?' was his opening remark.

'I've been asked to prepare a report for the court about you,' the psychiatrist replied.

'Right,' said Peter. 'I suppose you want to know whether I-loved-my-mother-and-hated-my-father, and all that kind of rubbish.'

'No, just your history.'

'I was illegitimate, and my mother brought me up—if that's what you can call it. Most of the time I was just dumped with relatives while she worked—as a model. At least, that's what she called herself. Anyway she seemed to earn quite a lot! I never found out who my father was—not that I care much.

'Yes, I was quite bright at school—when I was there that is. More often than not I pushed off and hung about the town. I left when I was fifteen and worked on the buildings. Two days after starting I had a fight with the foreman—he lost two teeth and I lost my job. I had quite a few jobs after that, couldn't stick any of them for long.

19

I'd get into a row with the other men, or turn up late, or just get fed up.

'Recently? Oh, recently I've been working a racket with a chap in a garage, knocking off cars, doing them up and selling them. No, I wasn't on the job when I pinched the car I crashed. It was just sitting there and I thought how nice it would be to do a ton in it down the motorway, so I got in and then this E-type tried to pass me, so I try to carve him up and suddenly I get wheel wobble, next thing I'm sitting up in bed covered in plaster and this nurse is asking me if I've had my bowels open.'

'Did you consider that you might kill yourself or someone else?'

'No, not really, in any case, so what! I've got to die some day, and no one's going to care whether its today or when I'm ninety.'

'Were you drunk at the time?'

'No, for once I wasn't. I'd arranged to meet this girl see, and we were going on to some party, but I wasn't drunk at the time. Sure I drink, anytime I feel like it. Sometimes I get drunk, other times I don't. Drugs? Yes, purple hearts, and reefers at times. I've tried H and C but I didn't dig it. Why do I take them? Because it gives me a kick.

'Yes, I've had plenty of women. It's OK, but when they go all emotional on you it gets to be a drag so you move on.'

'What about homosexual relationships?'

'I'm no queer, but I've let them pick me up occasionally, and gone back to their place; after a few drinks I've beaten them up and taken their wallets. They can't go singing to the law can they?'

'I got nicked once though, but first offence so they put me on probation. I used to go and chat to this bloke once a week and tell him what a good boy I'd been. At the time I was living off this bird —old as the hills she was, but loaded.'

At the end of a long interview the psychiatrist wrote his report. He said he could find no evidence of any psychotic illness, and that Peter was of above average intelligence. He had no neurotic symptoms, but in view of the history it seemed that Peter was of psychopathic personality within the definition of the Mental Health Act of 1959. While the prognosis was poor, it was unlikely that he would be improved by being imprisoned, and if the court so directed, he would be accepted for treatment in the mental hospital.

In due course the court accepted this advice and Peter was ordered to be admitted to the hospital under Section 4 of the Criminal Justices Act.

The unit to which he was sent was run on the principle of a 'therapeutic community' (q.v.) and Peter was expected to attend the various meetings that took place. At first he treated them as somethingof a joke, and delighted in goading other patients into being aggreesive towards the staff. He lost no opportunity of trying to provoks the staff himself, and he seemed to find the degree of tolerance shown almost as difficult to accept as he had, previously, found the restrictive attitudes of normal society. On those occasions when he exceeded the limits of the community's tolerance his behaviour was discussed at the meetings and an attempt was made to show him that not only was such behaviour unsuccessful in achieving what he wanted, but that it was unnecessary, in that a more satisfactory solution to his problems could be reached by discussion.

Over the months there was little overt change in his way of life. At times he seemed better able to control his impulsiveness, at others he would lose control and do something foolish. He finally found a job and was allowed to work from the hospital. After a period of time it was decided that as he had kept his employment for longer than almost any previous work, he could leave the hospital and try, once more, to adjust to the demands of society.

Psychopathy

The word psychopath is used very loosely, not only by the general public, but also by people concerned in the management of such problems. In America, an attempt was made to change the name to *sociopath*, to emphasise that it was their behaviour in relationship to society that was disturbed, but this name has not caught on widely in Europe. In the 1959 Mental Health Act, psychopathic disorder was defined as, 'a persistent disorder or disability of mind (whether or not including subnormality of intelligence) which results in abnormally or seriously irresponsible conduct on the part of the patient, and requires, or is susceptible to, medical treatment'.

Psychopathic personality is recognised by the behaviour of the patient throughout his life history. The person with a psychopathic personality seems to be unable to experience the normal emotions of love and affection. It is as if he was emotionally tone deaf and thus unable to understand the effects of his behaviour on others. Because of this inability to empathise with others he lacks the emotional response of guilt, except in a superficial and short-lasting way. He seems unable to delay satisfying his needs and desires in order to fit in with the requirements of society. As a result, his behaviour tends to be impulsive and inadequately motivated, and he fails to learn from previous experience. Thus, his life story often reveals a poor work record, with constant changes of job without good reason. He may have committed criminal acts, committed with little forethought, for very little profit, and with a minimum attempt at avoiding the consequences. The punishment which followed appears to have had little effect.

His sexual activities reflect the same lack of real emotional involvement, being indiscriminate and short-lasting. He may well at times indulge in homosexual practices, often for financial gain, while at other times consorting with female prostitutes. As a consequence, a history of venereal infection is not uncommon. His attitude to drink and drugs also shows a lack of concern for the future. He may become addicted, or in other cases, indulge in sporadic bursts of heavy and uncontrolled drinking. In his relations with other people, he reveals his basic self-centredness, which may be expressed by his lack of concern for their welfare, or by his actual physical violence toward them.

Violence may be a striking feature of the history; the normal person, however frustrated he may feel, is restrained from giving expression to his feelings because he realises the possible effects it will have on others and the feeling of guilt and remorse he will suffer later. In the psychopath no such checks exist and, therefore, he tends to act out his feelings of aggression in physical violence. In some ways the psychopath resembles the small child who, when denied the granting of his every wish at the very moment of desire, flies into an uncontrolled temper tantrum. The closeness of this simile is shown by certain findings in the study of the aetiology of this condition.

Aetiology

The causes of psychopathic personality development seem to lie in early childhood. Genetic factors are difficult to assess, as the parents not only pass on their chromosomes, but also tend to reduplicate the kind of environment in which they also spent their own early years. The following factors have been considered to play a part.

1. *Brain Damage.* A number of studies have suggested that there is a higher incidence of a history of brain damage in psychopathic personalities than in the normal population. Many investigators claim that a high percentage of such people have abnormal EEGs (electro-encephalograms), some with specific abnormalities but others showing features usually seen in the recordings of children rather than adults.

2. *Parental Separation.* The role of broken homes and separation from one or both parents has been stressed in the causation of psychopathy to an extent not justified by the facts. However, there is some evidence that for normal personality development to occur it is necessary for the child to have contact with a normally loving mother, or mother-substitute, at least during the first two years of life. It is necessary to stress the normally loving mother, as physical absence is not the only way in which a child can be deprived of a mother figure. A woman who is unable to give love to, or receive love from, a child as a result of mental illness or personality may also fail to meet the child's needs.

Treatment of Psychopathy

That no completely successful treatment of the problem of psychopathic personality disorder has yet been devised is clear from the range of methods currently employed, and the feelings of helplessness often expressed by those willingly or unwillingly faced with dealing with such people.

All the usual forms of physical treatment have been tried without any confirmed benefit. Individual psychotherapy has occasionally produced good results but is, in general, difficult and somewhat unrewarding, as the psychopath often has little motivation to change his ways, and only uses the therapist to avoid the consequences of his acts.

Group psychotherapy and therapeutic community methods have been tried with some success, notably at the Henderson Hospital, though the patients admitted to the unit are to some extent selected on the basis of being likely to improve, i.e., the more severe cases are excluded.

At the other extreme are units with the emphasis on maximum security, run on very authoritarian lines. Such units have the advantage that, in general, the person sent there has to stay for a prolonged time and thus benefits not only from any treatment given, but also undergoes a normal process of maturation with the passing of time. Many psychopaths tend to improve naturally as they grow older.

While some special units have been established for their treatment, at present such people are usually admitted to the wards of ordinary mental hospitals, where they tend to create a problem out of all proportion to their numbers. These problems are related to the following facets of their behaviour.

1. *Tendency to Escape from Treatment.* They do this by absenting themselves from the hospital, by withdrawing from ward activities, and by demonstrations of hostile or violent behaviour.

2. *Manipulation of Staff and Patients.* They are often adept at playing off one member of the staff against another, using threats, flattery, and lies to do so. They persuade other patients to join them in their antisocial acts, or use them as a smoke screen to hide their own activities.

3. *Impulsiveness.* This, and their need to test the community's tolerence to the limits, leads to repeated incidents of vandalism, suicidal attempts, or verbally aggressive outbursts which produce a high level of anxiety among the staff and other patients.

4. *Apparent Freedom from any Signs of Illness in the Usual Sense.* This, plus their lack of remorse or gratitude, tends to arouse the feeling in the staff that the psychopath is 'on to a good thing' and that it is they who are the stupid ones for facing up to their problems and responsibilities, exercising self-denial and conforming to the conventions of society. As a result of this feeling the staff become ambivalent toward the patient, recognising in them facets of their own personality which they are forced to deny, while at the same time secretly wishing to behave in the same way. This ambivalence makes it much easier for the psychopath to manipulate the staff.

It is obvious that whatever type of treatment is employed, the problems described must be recognised and dealt with. Thus, the following general principles can form the basis of treatment.

The person with an extreme degree of psychopathic personality, affectionless, ruthless, and explosively violent, cannot be treated except in a situation of maximum security. Anywhere else, his behaviour and potential danger creates too great a problem, the staff becoming anxious both for their own safety and for the possible consequences should the patient escape from hospital. In the resulting state of tension, no one, least of all the patient, can function effectively.

The less-severe psychopath requires the same type of training as a spoiled child. It is probably better that he be placed under some form of legal control which can be used to prevent him from opting out of treatment as soon as it presents any difficulty for him. He must then be treated in such a way that he knows clearly the limits to which the community will tolerate his behaviour. Any irresponsible or destructive acts must be discussed with him as soon as possible, and the consequences of such acts by way of lost privileges and social disapproval should be brought home to him. Equally, it is essential to reward any evidence of increased social responsibility, both verbally in public and by the granting of privileges. Throughout treatment he must feel that those concerned in his management do not reject him as a person, even when they are displeased with his behaviour. His attempts at manipulation should be pointed out to him, and he should be helped to see that while his childhood may explain *why* he acts as he does, it does not absolve him from responsibility for his actions.

In order to put these principles into action it is necessary to organise the setting in which treatment occurs in such a way that everyone is clearly aware of what is happening, and where events can be examined critically and constructively without the barriers to communication that exist in most institutional settings. For this reason, some form of therapeutic community setting is probably best suited to the needs of both staff and patient. The features of such a setting, and the nurse's role in it, are discussed later.

SEXUAL DISORDERS

The sexual relationship is probably the most intense and emotionally charged relationship between human beings. The aim of this relationship in biological terms is to achieve the fertilisation of the ovum by the sperm in order that a new individual may result, thus helping to preserve the species. The act of genital union has the capacity for giving rise to intense pleasure, associated with a powerful release of tension; this is referred to as an orgasm. So, in the narrowest sense, the purpose of sexual activity is to produce off-spring. However, the process has become overlaid and interwoven with a wide range of secondary activities and emotional factors not related to the primary aim.

The methods employed to achieve or heighten the satisfaction of an orgasm are so diverse that it is almost impossible to divide them into normal and abnormal, but as a working rule it can be said that sexual behaviour becomes abnormal when:

1. it involves practices that result in one of the partners inflicting physical or mental damage on the other;
2. some activity other than sexual union is *always* substituted for intercourse as a means of achieving orgasm; or
3. the partner chosen is of the same sex.

Sexual deviations rarely occur in isolation. They generally form part, either cause or result, of a neurotic disorder, reflect a psychopathic personality, or are the result of some other underlying psychiatric disorder.

That sexual activity can be the cause of so much anxiety and resulting neurotic behaviour is due to the interplay of several factors. First, until recently the subject was taboo in 'polite' society—not only was the practice of it limited by severe restrictions (in theory, if not in practice), but even discussion of the subject was frowned upon. Second, prior to the development of efficient forms of contraception, intercourse carried a high risk of unwanted pregnancies. Third, the fear of acquiring venereal infections. This factor is related, in part, to the confusion between sex and dirt. This, in turn arises partly because of Nature's economic approach to the subject in her combination of sexual and excretory function in the same organs, or in closely related areas of the body. Finally, the restriction placed on incestuous relationships by most societies has led to a separation between the early emotional relationship of a child with its parents and siblings, and its emerging sexual feelings.

Due to these factors the child soon learns to associate feelings of guilt with the whole subject of sexual activity, an idea that has been reinforced by the teachings of some religious organisations. The child who is overburdened with restrictions, punishments, and admonitions on this subject is likely to find it difficult to achieve normal sexual relationships as an adult.

The main ways in which sexual problems express themselves are as follows:

1. failure to achieve or allow intercourse and derive pleasure from it;
2. substitution of other practices for intercourse;
3. substitution of different objects as means of sexual gratification in place of a partner of the opposite sex;
4. substitution of a partner of the same sex for one of the opposite sex.

Failure to Achieve Orgasm During Intercourse

In males this condition is called impotence, and usually reflects a failure of the man to achieve or maintain erection of the penis. A variation of this is premature ejaculation in which the man reaches his climax before, or immediately after, achieving penetration.

Impotence may be due to some physical cause, but much more frequently it is due to anxiety. There are many reasons for the anxiety, including unconscious guilt feeling, fears of castration, incest fears and the like, but one of the commonest sources of anxiety is previous failure. Most men fail to achieve satisfactory intercourse at some time, but if they have some basic doubt about their virility such a failure may assume great importance. The next time they attempt intercourse they are plagued by fears of failure, and their state of anxiety leads to their downfall. This rapidly leads to a vicious spiral of increasing anxiety and consequent failure.

In woman, failure to achieve intercourse or to derive pleasure from it, in situations which society considers suitable, is referred to as frigidity. There may be a physical cause, but usually this condition arises from ideas of guilt, fear of being hurt or injured, or anxiety about unwanted pregnancies. It is important to remember, however, that both males and females show a wide range of capacity for sexual enjoyment. So much emphasis is placed these days on the quality and frequency of sexual performance that it almost assumes the characteristics of an event in the Olympic Games. People whose capacity is limited may be made to feel inferior and a failure. There is no measure of normal sexuality. Problems arise only when the sexual needs and abilities of partners do not match each other.

Loss of interest in sexual activity may form part of the general diminution in drive of patients with depressive illnesses. Impotence may also arise as a side effect of some drugs used in the treatment of

depression. Reluctance to take part in sexual activity is not infrequently the reason that finally brings people to seek medical aid for
their emotional illnesses.

Substitution of other Practices for Sexual Intercourse

Under the restrictions of society, most people at some time in their
life relieve their sexual needs by some activity other than intercourse.
The commonest method is masturbation (self-stimulation). This is
in no way abnormal, nor does it, in itself, lead to any physical or
mental damage. It can, however, be a problem in two ways. First,
it may give rise to a sense of severe guilt and anxiety in a person who
has been taught that it is harmful or wicked. Second, in people who
find intercourse difficult or threatening, it may become a substitute
for the actual performance. This, in the case of a married person
may create problems for the partner.

Excessive masturbation, often performed without regard to social
conventions may be one symptom of schizophrenia, dementing
illnesses, or subnormality. It occasionally forms part of an obses-
sional-compulsive ritual.

Transvestism. In transvestism, the person derives sexual satisfaction by dressing up in clothing of the opposite sex. The actual
putting on of the clothes often has a ritualistic quality, and patients
not infrequently deny sexual pleasure from the act, claiming that it
provides a release from general tension and anxiety.

Sadism. Sadism gets its name from the Marquis de Sade who wrote
numerous books describing sexual activity in which the pleasure was
mainly derived by the infliction of pain. In most love-making there
is a slight sadistic element, but in pathological forms the person can
achieve orgasm only by inflicting severe pain or injury upon his
partner. Such a need may lead to the sufferer murdering or mutil-
ating his sexual partner.

Masochism. This is the opposite side of the coin to sadism, though
both tendencies may exist in the same person. In this condition,
orgasm is achieved as a result of suffering pain or humiliation. The
subject may demand to be beaten, punched, whipped or kicked.
Others indulge in self punishment, often including tying themselves
up. Such practices may result in the accidental death of the subject.

Exhibitionism. This is a condition in which sexual satisfaction is
derived by a man through exposing his genitalia to a woman.
Usually, the pleasure results from the shock and fear with which the

woman responds, and the subject would be terrified by any overt sexual response on the woman's part. Some exhibitionists restrict their activity to revealing themselves to small children. Very few such people progress to any form of actual sexual assault, and they represent more of a nuisance than a danger.

Voyeurism. In voyeurism, sexual satisfaction is derived from watching other people, either in a state of nudity or while indulging in sexual activity. This condition represents an extreme form of behaviour which most people find sexually stimulating to some degree. The person involved may become a Peeping Tom, and come into conflict with the law. In many cities the needs of such people are catered for by strip clubs of varying degrees of respectability.

Substitution of an Object for a Sexual Partner as the Source of Satisfaction

In normal life, certain aspects of a woman are regarded as being especially sexually exciting, and even items of female clothing may have a stimulating effect. For some people, however, these partial features become of special importance, and they can achieve sexual satisfaction merely by looking at, or handling these objects. The objects chosen are often articles of female clothing, leather articles, or some form of fabric such as silk, velvet, or fur. The importance of the feel of the object may be stressed by the patient.

Substitution of a Partner of the Same Sex—Homosexuality

Both men and women may choose partners of the same sex in preference to a partner of the opposite sex. Probably everyone at some stage of their development experiences a strong attraction towards someone of the same sex. Such feelings are often referred to as 'crushes' or 'hero-worship' and need provoke no anxiety in the parents. However, in some cases, usually where there is a faulty relationship between the child and its parents, the individual is unable to pass beyond this phase and persists in this type of relationship in adult life. There is very little evidence to support the idea that homosexuality is due to genetic factors. Environmental causes predominate, the emotional influences to which the person is exposed in early childhood being particularly important.

The word 'homosexuality' is used in a loose way to describe a wide range of behaviour, and it might be more helpful if it was restricted to those who are unable to form a mature sexual relationship with a member of the opposite sex, and as a result are predominately concerned with forming relationships with their own sex. Occasional homosexual acts are relatively common between men who are mainly heterosexual. Such acts may occur because there are no women available, as in prisons, boarding schools, mental hospitals and the like. Other people indulge in such episodes as part of their psychopathic pattern of behaviour, and usually do so for financial gain rather than sexual satisfaction.

Persistent homosexual behaviour, however, reflects a basic immaturity, and often arises from deepseated fear of the opposite sex, rather than a positive desire for the same sex. The family backgrounds of homosexuals frequently show similar patterns. In males, there may be a history of the father having little affection for his son, or even being actively hostile. The growing boy is unable to relate to his father and is thus deprived of a satisfactory male image on which to model himself. As a result, he may have doubts about his own masculinity, or may even decide to be as unlike his 'male' father as possible.

This kind of relationship with the father is often combined with a very close relationship to the mother, who seems to use the son as a substitute for an unsatisfactory husband. The boy may find himself unable either to meet the demands of such a relationship or to break free from it. As a result he may develop a fear of women as people who both deprive him of his masculinity and also bind him to them with emotional ties. He may come to feel that men are less threatening objects for affection.

Female homosexuals rarely seek treatment for their homosexuality, usually coming to the doctor because of depression or anxiety arising from the stresses and strains of their current relationship. Male homosexuals, also, more often present with secondary symptoms rather than because they wish to change their basic interests. Sometimes they seek treatment because they are being prosecuted, or fear that they will be caught soliciting. The fact that male homosexual practices were illegal until 1967 greatly increased the sufferers' guilt and anxiety.

Treatment of Sexual Disorders

Where these represent a facet of neurotic or psychotic illness, treatment is directed at the underlying disorder. In all cases, the condition is usually associated with some degree of guilt, anxiety, and depression. The person is often ashamed of his practices and thoughts and may feel himself to be an outcast. The fact that someone can listen to his story and not reject him by moralising may prove of considerable benefit. More specific treatment directed at removing the symptom may be tried.

Aversion therapy has been used with some success in cases of transvestism and of fetishism. It has been claimed to help in some cases of homosexuality. Some men who persistently expose themselves have been helped to control their habit by reducing their sexual drive, using female hormones. The results of this treatment tend to be unpredictable, and it depends on the patient co-operating by taking the tablets regularly. In general, some form of psychotherapy is attempted.

There can be few more fatuous pastimes than attempting to treat a homosexual patient in a ward which contains only male (or female) patients. It corresponds to treating a drug addict in a pharmacy! To improve, the patient has to learn to form a new kind of relationship with members of both sexes.

Due to ingrained attitudes towards sex, many otherwise rational and mature people respond with repulsion and horror to those who practice some form of deviant sexual behaviour. Such an attitude cannot help the patient. Many people with sexual disorders already consider themselves as disgusting and undeserving of human love. Hostility and rejection pushes them further into their guilt and isolation. On the other hand, calm acceptance of them as persons, in spite of their deviation, can help them considerably. The reassurance that they are not unique, and can be tolerated by 'normal' people, forms the first step in their treatment.

At some stage a nurse will probably meet a patient (or a member of the staff!) who will suggest some form of homosexual relationship. There is no purpose in a violent rejection. Explain to the patient that while you are glad that he or she feels sufficient confidence in you to want such a relationship, you do not want such a relationship, nor do you feel that it would be of benefit to the patient. Such incidents should be reported in staff meetings, and it is probably better to avoid an over-exclusive relationship with that patient in the future—without rejecting him. In general, a nurse should not form an exclusive one-to-one relationship with any patient, nor should patient/staff relationships involve seeing each other alone outside the hospital setting. The consequence of so doing can be the development of a relationship which neither the patient nor the nurse can handle.

Some homosexuals have a high degree of talent and creativity; by exploiting these facets of their personality, the nurse can help them to become an accepted and valued member of the hospital community. This may diminish their sense of isolation and abnormality.

3 Alcoholism and Drug Addiction

Three Illustrative Stories

1. 'I don't think I can take much more of it', she said, stifling a sob. 'Sometimes I think it's my fault, then sometimes I feel he is deliberately destroying himself and us. I have managed to keep things going so far, but it is getting impossible. He has lost his job now, and yet he still expects to be able to buy a bottle of whisky a day.

'I never know where he is, and when he is out I expect to have a phone call saying he has been in an accident. When he is home it's like hell. The slightest criticism and he flares up into a terrible rage. He has started knocking me about in front of the children, and it terrifies them. He says it's because I won't sleep with him; I won't because he just wants to use me. There is no love in it—anyway I'm terrified I'd get pregnant. Then he starts accusing me of having a lover.

'I've told him if he doesn't get treatment I'm leaving him. That's why he has come today—he doesn't think there is any problem. I keep telling myself he cannot help it, that he is ill, but sometimes, I wonder.'

2. 'Get them away from me', she could hear her voice screaming. A feeling of panic overwhelmed her. She flung herself from the bed and tried to hide in the next room, but it was too small and full of hanging bodies that tried to grasp and smother her. She fell to the floor, pulling at the bedclothes, her hands shaking violently, and the sweat pouring from her. The bedspread, grasped in her hand, turned into a snake and writhed around her. She screamed, and a barber in a white coat entered the room to cut her throat with an open razor.

The nurse said, 'I'll help you back into bed. It is no use trying to hide in the wardrobe you know. As soon as you're back in bed I'll give you an injection and something to help you sleep.'

3. 'Drink's no problem for me Doc', he said. 'How much have I had this morning? Oh, about half a bottle of brandy! I could do

without though. Only last week I didn't touch a drop for a whole day. I work as well as I ever did—perhaps I take a bit more time off than I used to, but a man's entitled to ease up a bit. It's not as if I get drunk you know—carry it like a gentleman—always have, always will. Only trouble I get is indigestion; thought I'd got an ulcer, then, last week, I had this vomit when I brought up a lot of blood. That's why I thought I'd come for a check up—nothing to do with being an alcoholic, I assure you.'

Addiction

From earliest times man has used various preparations to produce changes in his mental state either in an attempt to make life more enjoyable or to induce experiences of mystical quality as part of religious ceremonies. Tobacco and alcohol are so commonly used as to be almost universal. In Asia the use of marihuana and opium is widespread. The use of more powerful and dangerous drugs appears to be an increasing social problem in the West. In particular, drugs such as the amphetamines, heroin, and cocaine, and hallucinogenic drugs like LSD (lysergic acid diethylamide) are increasingly taken by teenagers for 'kicks'. With the less powerful substances like alcohol, comparatively few of the many millions who take it suffer any marked ill effects, but with the more potent drugs, relatively few who start taking them avoid eventual physical or mental damage. This, in part, is related to the fact that these drugs produce in the individual a state of tolerance; that is, after having the drug for some time the body becomes resistant to its effects, so that a bigger dose has to be taken to achieve the previous pleasurable state. Not only does the body become tolerant, it may also become dependent on the drug to the stage where, if the drug is stopped, the body responds by developing severe symptoms—the so called 'withdrawal state'. The nature of the symptoms depend on the particular drug used. In order to avoid these symptoms, and to satisfy the body's craving for the drug, the person can no longer limit his use of the substance.

Strictly, the word addiction implies these three facets: loss of control, active craving, and physical dependence, though it is often used in a much looser sense. Because of this rather artificial limitation, it has been suggested that it is better to use the term 'drug dependence', in order to include people who cannot stop using the drug for emotional reasons, but who are not yet suffering physical damage from it, as well as those who have progressed to the stage of physical dependence.

An alcoholic may be defined as a person who is suffering physical, mental, or social damage as a result of his inability to control his intake of alcohol. The reasons why an individual drinks excessively can be summarised as follows (a combination of such factors may occur).

OCCUPATIONAL AND SOCIAL

In some jobs there is a much greater opportunity and encouragement to drink than in others. For example, workers in the brewing industry, commercial travellers, and sailors tend to drink either in the course of their work, or because drink is cheap. In certain societies, notably in wine-growing countries like France, alcoholic liquids are taken in comparatively large amounts throughout the day by a high percentage of people. The result of this prolonged high intake over many years is more often physical damage than mental or social.

DUE TO UNDERLYING MENTAL DISORDER

Neurotic Conditions. A person who is suffering from tension, anxiety, or depression may find his symptoms relieved by taking alcohol. As this does nothing to relieve the cause of the anxiety he finds he has to keep drinking to avoid his symptoms returning. Gradually he develops tolerance and has to increase his intake; at this stage he may start to develop physical symptoms, or his social situation may deteriorate because of the time and money he is spending on drink. This, during periods of awareness, increases his anxiety or depression and leads to yet further drinking.

Psychotic Illness. The schizophrenic patient or the severely depressed may resort to alcohol for similar reasons as the neurotic. The person with organic brain damage may lose control of his drinking as part of his general falling off in judgement, so that alcoholism becomes added to the previous problem.

Psychopathic Personality. The abuse of alcohol may reflect the inability of the person to delay immediate gratification of his wishes, his inability to learn from previous experience, and his failure to appreciate emotionally the effects of his drinking on his friends and relations. In such cases the alcoholism may take the form of episodes of excessive drinking which are separated by periods of abstinence or normal social drinking. These episodes almost always have a damaging effect socially, usually leading to loss of work, the squandering of savings, and sometimes prison sentences for drunkenness or violence. They may be followed by withdrawal symptoms of various kinds and, as the episodes occur more frequently, lead to the development of dependence and craving.

CONSEQUENCES

The ways in which the person suffers as a result of excessive drinking can be considered under the following headings.

Physical. Many of the physical changes resulting from chronic alcoholism are due to the poor diet of the patient, both to save money for more drink and because of the gastritis the drink causes. Alcohol, particularly when taken as spirits, has direct action on the stomach and stimulates the secretion of hydrochloric acid. The chronic hyperacidity may lead to the development of peptic ulceration, and many alcoholics bear the scar of a partial gastrectomy.

Liver disease may occur, taking the form of a biliary cirrhosis which, in turn, may lead to the veins at the lower end of the oesophagus becoming varicose. This, in turn, may result in haemorrhage from the thin-walled vessels. The spinal nerves supplying the limbs may be damaged because of interference with Vitamin B metabolism, producing weakness of muscles and impaired sensation in the areas supplied by the affected nerves.

Mental. The mild degrees of intoxication are familiar to most people. The inhibitory effects (alcohol is *not* a stimulant) act first on the higher centres, so that self criticism becomes reduced and the person acts more freely and with less self-restraint. He considers himself to be more efficient, but objectively he is less so—hence the dangers of driving after drinking. As the alcohol level rises, the inhibitory effects spread to lower centres of the brain with consequent impairment of motor activity; finally, the vital centres become affected and consciousness becomes impaired, progressing from stupor to coma, or even to death. Dead drunk can be literally true.

Social. It is difficult when writing of the social repercussions of chronic alcoholism to avoid sounding like a Victorian temperance pamphlet, for the situation has much melodrama, and provokes moralistic responses. Watching the gradual disintegration of a perhaps previously successful husband and father into a shambling wreck, hated and despised by his family, moves one both to sorrow and anger. At first, he becomes more impulsive and irritable, rows flare up from trivial beginnings, which perhaps stems from his underlying guilt. Gradually, his capacity for self-pity dominates and he becomes self-centred, self-justifying, and untruthful. His mood of bonhomie and euphoria turns to one of violent anger at a word of criticism, or to one of maudlin sentimentality at a word of commiseration. Gradually, as brain damage occurs (due mainly to his failure to eat an adequate diet) memory fails, personal habits deteriorate, and dementia supervenes.

The physical and mental deterioration are usually matched by a downhill social course. He loses his job; all financial resources are sacrificed to obtain drink. He forgets his responsibilities towards his family, and blames them for his misfortune. They, in turn, suffer abuse, violence, poverty, and social stigmatisation. Relatively few children reared in such a home manage to achieve a satisfactory level of mental health in later life.

Alcoholic Psychoses

Alcoholic Hallucinosis. After, or during, a spell of particularly heavy drinking, some people start to hear noises, although their awareness of their surroundings remains normal. The sounds heard may be simple noises such as bells ringing, a fire crackling, or a whistle blowing. Sometimes voices are heard, usually abusing or accusing the patient. The condition usually clears fairly rapidly when alcohol is stopped, but is likely to recur when the patient drinks. It may lead to a paranoid development.

Delirium Tremens. This condition may occur in a chronic alcoholic following an unusually heavy drinking bout, or may be precipitated by an injury following a fall, or pneumonia due to exposure, occurring during a drunken episode. It usually starts with increasing restlessness and a refusal to eat, the patient begins to misinterpret his environment, shadows become terrifying monsters, the pattern of the bedclothes becomes loathsome animals. Hallucinations usually occur, and are often of a frightening nature. Rarely, they may take the form of diminutive figures who dance or perform plays which the patient finds entertaining (so called Lilliputian hallucinations).

The patient is confused as to time, place and person, and is extremely restless. Physically he may show evidence of anxiety; pale, sweating, with a rapid, often weak, pulse. He may have a marked tremor of the hands and, frequently, of the tongue; speech is slurred and indistinct, and epileptiform fits may occur. Usually symptoms subside in three to ten days, but death may occur from heart failure, pneumonia, cerebral oedema, or status epilepticus. Some cases go on to develop a Korsakoff's psychoses, while others later show a paranoid development.

Korsakoff's Syndrome. This condition consists of a failure of recent memory which the patient covers up by inventing accounts of recent events (confabulation). The mood is usually euphoric, and he is very suggestible. In extreme cases one is able to give the patient a blank sheet of paper from which he will read aloud, when asked. This condition is not specific to alcoholism and is due to interference with Vitamin B metabolism. It may occur in uraemia, following head injury, or as part of a nutritional deficiency.

Wernikes Encephalopathy. This condition is also due to Vitamin B deficiency but it is the brain stem that is affected rather than the cortex. The mental symptoms are those of confusion associated either with nystagmus, paralysis of some of the eye muscles, or other cranial nerve lesions.

Treatment of Alcoholism

Many people advocate the establishment of special units dealing only with alcoholics and other drug addicts. The advantage of these units is that the staff develop special skill and experience in handling such patients. The initial response of many people to the alcoholic is one of contempt, hostility, and moral condemnation, a response that makes it unlikely that the staff will be able to help the patient. The social aspects of the problem are vital in planning treatment, and the services of a skilled social worker are essential. The existence of units of this kind seems to encourage alcoholics to seek treatment before they have reached the level of social and personal deterioration that usually leads to their unwilling admission to hospital. This means that the prognosis tends to be better in a special unit.

The treatment almost always starts off with the patient being admitted to hospital, in order to effect some control on the availability of alcohol. It consists of dealing with any physical or mental symptoms resulting from excess alcohol, and then aiding the patient to abstain by the use of such drugs as Antabuse, and providing group or individual psychotherapy in an attempt to help him see the reasons for his drinking more clearly, and to find a more satisfactory method of solving these problems.

Antabuse (Disulfiram). The effect of this drug is to slow down the process by which the body breaks down alcohol. As a result, the intermediate products between alcohol and carbon dioxide and water persist for much longer in the body. One of these substances is acetaldehyde. When present in appreciable amounts in the blood it produces a series of unpleasant reactions including flushing, a pounding headache, and a sensation of choking. In severe reactions the patient may collapse and be profoundly shocked. Serious or markedly unpleasant responses can be terminated by giving 1 gramme of ascorbic acid by intravenous injection.

The purpose of the drug is to demonstrate to the patient that while he continues to take it he will not be able to derive any satisfaction from taking alcohol. This may help him refrain from at once turning to his old standby. Before the patient is started on Antabuse, a test of his response is carried out, both to decide on the dose he requires and to demonstrate to him the effect of drinking while taking the drug.

Abstem has similar properties and is used in the same way.

Aversion Therapy. The principles of this form of behaviour therapy are discussed in Chapter 16. In this particular case, the patient is given alcohol and an injection of apomorphine, which produces vomiting. This is repeated until a reflex is established and the patient becomes nauseated by the taste and smell of alcohol in the absence of the apomorphine. The treatment is repeated at intervals to reinforce the reflex; and is so unpleasant that to submit himself to it the patient must be very keen to stop drinking. It is not without risk, as profound dehydration and collapse can occur from repeated vomiting.

Psychotherapy. Group psychotherapy is widely employed in treating alcoholics. The sharing of a common problem means that, while they may criticise one another, the members of the group are not able to be scornful or humiliating. Each person in the group is helped to see how his actions affect other people. Those in the group who have been able to abstain provide encouragement for the others. Finally, discussion between patients helps to clarify some of the reasons for their behaviour and assists in finding new ways of tackling problems.

Alcoholics Anonymous. In 1935, an organisation in America was started to help alcoholics by establishing groups of sufferers. At their meetings the members subject themselves to self-examination, admit their failures, and try to help each other and atone for past misdeeds. The groups provide support and practical help to the alcoholic, both at meetings and by a personal relationship between the new member and his 'sponsor', who is an alcoholic who has stopped drinking.

Nursing Aspects

Nursing aspects involve the problems of managing acutely disturbed patients, psychopathic personality disorders, and the physically ill, plus the special techniques involved in the various forms of behaviour therapy. These are discussed in the appropriate chapters.

Drug Addiction

Four Illustrative Stories

1. 'We have a man in the ward, on whom we would like a psychiatric opinion,' said the eye surgeon to the consultant psychiatrist as they sat for lunch. 'He came in with ulcers on his eyes which were extremely painful; so much so that we had to give him pethedine to ease the pain. We couldn't think how he had developed the ulcers, but finally he admitted that he had produced them himself by jabbing a burning cigarette-end into his eyes. He says he is addicted to pethedine, and his usual source of supply has failed, so he thought up this method of obtaining it. He also claims he wants to come off pethedine, and would like treatment.'

Later, the patient told the psychiatrist that he had become addicted to the drug following a severe injury, when pethedine had been used to control the pain. After only a few days he had begun to enjoy the drug for its own sake, and had claimed to be in pain long after his injuries had ceased hurting.

He had worked as a seaman, and in many parts of the world it was fairly easy to obtain supplies comparatively cheaply, but in Britain it was difficult—and very expensive. All his wages were spent on buying the drug, and he had begun to steal in order to get more money. He agreed to enter hospital to undergo withdrawal of the drug. However, after a few days on a reduced dose, he climbed out of a window and absconded.

2. 'Don't be chicken, take a drag, man, it's cool, real cool.'

Reluctantly, Robin took the half-smoked clumsily rolled reefer and inhaled nervously. Nothing happened, so he took a deeper breath. Still nothing changed. The noise of the pop group continued to beat against his brain; the sting of smoke pricked at his eyes, and the jerking twitching mass of teenagers still surged around the table at which he sat.

He took a third puff, and his head swam and he heard a ringing in his ears. 'It's like floating', he said. He suddenly felt confident and happy and had an intense urge to dance. He was sure that no one in the room could dance as he was going to. As he stood up he swayed slightly, but he was soon flinging himself about in a frenzy of twisting and shaking, shouting and talking to the girls who briefly figured as his partners. Not many minutes later, as he thought, he returned to the table where his friend sat.

'You were really high, man, wayout', said his friend. 'You've been swinging for hours.' Robin looked at his watch and was amazed to find that more than two hours had passed since he had smoked the hemp-filled reefer. He felt tired and relaxed, but very hungry.

Some months passed, Robin was now buying a regular supply of hemp from his friend, but the effects of smoking it were no longer so satisfying. He mentioned this to his friend who said, 'If you really want kicks, man, you need H and C, but that will cost you.' 'But they are dangerous, they can kill you', said Robin. 'Sure', said his friend, 'but you've got to go some day. When the bomb drops, you'll pay, so why not choose your own way.'

3. Joan had made her choice six months ago. Many of her friends took LSD—they claimed it helped their painting or their writing. It demonstrated their freedom from convention; their superiority to all the 'peasants' and 'squares' by whom they considered the world to be populated.

She had taken LSD for some time, hoping that the 'psychedelic' experiences would help her painting. However, the effects were not all she had hoped for and she became increasingly depressed. One day a friend had suggested that she should try heroin. At first, she had injected it beneath the skin, but as her tolerance for the drug increased, she had started injecting it into a vein—'mainlining' as her coaddicts called it. Within a few months, her life had become dominated by her need for a 'fix'. The drug gave her short periods of release. She felt calm and happy after an injection, but in a few hours she felt depressed and irritable, lacking the energy to do anything.

Now she sat in a dirty public lavatory, fumbling in her bag for the syringe, the spoon, matches, and the precious drug. There was a ritualistic quality to her preparations which seemed almost as important to her as the effects of the drug. At last, she jabbed the needle into a vein, the blood swirled into the syringe, and as she pressed the plunger, the drug entered her bloodstream. She no longer bothered to measure accurately the dose she gave herself. Her pulse began to slow down as the drug took effect, and she began to feel drowsy and relaxed, the room began to spin and she suddenly felt sick, but before she could stand, darkness engulfed her, and she slid to the floor, the syringe rolling from her fingers. She was found, some hours later, when the lavatory attendant checked why the door was still locked.

The verdict at the inquest was 'death by misadventure'.

4. 'They talk about me. I can hear them outside my room, and people look at me in the street.'

'Why should they do that?' asked the doctor.

'I don't know, but they have been doing it for some months now.'

'I see you have been on night duty for almost two years now.'

'Yes, I'm night sister at the Royal Infirmary.'

'Did you find it difficult to adjust to night work?'

'Yes, at first I couldn't sleep in the daytime, so I had to start taking sleeping tablets, then I found I couldn't stay awake at work.'

'So you started taking amphetamine', said the doctor.

He had thought, from her complaints, that she was suffering from paranoid schizophrenia, but now he realised that the most likely explanation of her recent symptoms was a paranoid psychosis, due to amphetamines.

'Yes', she said, 'I started taking them about a year ago. I had to take more and more, to get the same effect. At first my own doctor prescribed them for me, but when he refused I began to let myself into the hospital pharmacy on the pretext of getting drugs for patients. When it comes to light, I shall be struck off the register.'

Until recent years, drug addiction was a small problem in Great Britain, but recently the number of people involved has been increasing at an alarming rate. For a long time the problem was mostly confined to members of the nursing and medical profession, for whom access to dangerous drugs was relatively easy. Some addicts were unfortunately started on their habit by the over prescription of powerful pain-killing drugs during the course of painful illness. Now, however, a different group of people are becoming involved. Teenagers, and even young children, are starting to take addictive drugs as part of the search for new experiences, and as a sign of revolt against the standards of their elders. As the habit spreads, the social condemnation of drug-taking becomes less effective. Drug-taking becomes the 'done thing', and the youngster who refuses becomes 'odd man out'. Thus, a practice that was usually confined to people of grossly abnormal personality has begun to spread to people whose personality is relatively normal, or not even developed.

Some people claim that drug-taking is a legitimate way of improving one's life, and equate it with smoking or drinking. Few such people can have seen the results of addiction to drugs, or they would not talk such nonsense. The addictive drugs fall into four groups, which will be discussed separately. All of them can produce addiction in a relatively short time. All can lead to the mental, physical, and social destruction of the individual.

Pain Killers (Analgesics)

A number of powerful drugs exist which are capable of controlling severe pain. Unfortunately, they also tend to induce a state of euphoria in which the patient feels free from worry, anxiety, or depression.

Morphine. This is derived from the sap of the oriental poppy. The crude extract is called opium, about 10 per cent of which is morphine. In therapeutic doses, morphine relieves even severe pain, and induces a mental state of calmness and well-being. A toxic dose produces rapid loss of consciousness, with depression of respiration, and may result in death. Heroin is a derivative of morphine, and is even more powerful. Both produce addiction, partly through their euphoriant effect, and partly because of the unpleasantness of the symptoms produced when the drug is stopped.

Withdrawal Symptoms. These begin within twenty-four hours of stopping the drug, reaching a peak in about seventy-two hours. The patient feels anxious, depressed and restless: sleeplessness usually occurs, and he may develop confusion with terrifying hallucinations. Physical symptoms, such as muscle cramps, rise in temperature and blood pressure, nausea, vomiting, and diarrhœa may also occur.

Pethedine. This drug produces similar results to morphine but addiction may be acquired even more quickly.

Cocaine. Usually this is taken by subcutaneous injection, or in the form of snuff, and is often combined with heroin (known as H and C). The drug produces a state of excitement, and in large doses leads to hallucinations and delirium. Under its effects the subject feels sociable, alert, witty, and full of bright ideas, but when the effect wears off he becomes depressed and lethargic. When the drug is withdrawn, some people experience a curious sensation which they describe as 'feeling as if insects were creeping about under the skin' (formication).

Pep Pills. These are drugs which have the effect of combating fatigue, stimulate activity, and induce a feeling of confidence and happiness. They have the side effect of reducing appetite, and have been widely used to assist in slimming. They were also used to help people remain awake for long periods during battle and similar situations. At one time they were used in the treatment of depression. Most are derived from amphetamine and related compounds. Overdose leads to restlessness, irritability, tremor, rapid pulse, and raised blood pressure. Chronic overdosage can produce a clinical picture indistinguishable from acute schizophrenia—the diagnosis may be confirmed by testing the urine for amphetamine, and by the resolution of the illness when the drug is withdrawn.

Sedative Drugs

Such preparations are taken to combat insomnia, and may be used in combination with pep pills. The barbiturates are the commonest type. Chronic barbiturate poisoning resembles hypomania, the patient being restless, over-talkative, irritable, and unsteady on his feet. An acute overdose produces unconsciousness, leading to death, and taking these drugs is the most popular method of attempting suicide. Sudden withdrawal of the drug may produce epileptic fits or a delirious state.

Hallucinogenic Drugs

These are drugs that induce hallucinations and other changes in perception. Mescaline and lysergic acid diethylamide (LSD) are two such drugs. They produce their characteristic mental changes in very small doses. The changes include euphoria, or depression, changes in behaviour, visual hallucinations, delusions, depersonalisation, and derealisation. In susceptible personalities such experiences may form the starting point of a psychotic illness, even if the drug is not continued. LSD appears to enable the subject to have access to some events otherwise buried in their subconscious, and it has been used as an abreactive drug.

Treatment of Drug Addiction

Treatment of the patient who is addicted to drugs falls into two parts: the withdrawal of the drug, and an attempt to help the patient find a more satisfactory way of life.

The handling of the withdrawal state can be accomplished only in a hospital. The addict dreads the suffering entailed in giving up the drug and, in the absence of support and supervision, is likely to obtain supplies of his drug by theft, deceit, lies, or bribery. The drug may be discontinued immediately, or withdrawn gradually. In either case, skilled and constant supervision by trained staff is essential. There is no advantage in allowing the patient to suffer the full misery of the withdrawal symptoms, and it is usual to tide him over this period by some form of sedation, using chlorpromazine, or even modified insulin. During this time the patient's blood pressure, pulse, temperature, and fluid balance must be carefully observed.

Rehabilitation of the patient is the most difficult aspect. Access to the drug must be avoided. In the case of doctors and nurses, this means finding some other employment; in patients who have been associating with other drug-takers, it may require a change of job and residence. The patient has to be helped to find some other way of dealing with the frustrations of life, and this may require prolonged psychotherapy.

4 Manic Depressive Illness

Three Illustrative Stories

1. Edward put down his pen and carefully blotted the note he had written. He propped it against the photograph of his wife, who had died four years previously at the early age of forty-eight.

He crossed the room, and locked the door, he checked that the window was tightly closed, as he did each night before going up to bed, but instead of switching off the light, he turned on the gas fire and, taking a cushion from the chair, he lay down on the floor with his head close to the fire. He closed his eyes and prepared to die.

'Why don't we drop round and see your Uncle Ted before going home, as we are so close?' asked Fred's wife.

'He'll be in bed by now, and anyway he hardly speaks when you do go to see him,' replied Fred.

'It is only ten o'clock, and it might cheer him up. You know how lonely he is since your Aunt died.'

'Oh, well, if you insist,' said Fred, signalling that he was going to turn right.

The house seemed to be in darkness from the front, and Fred was all for going home without knocking, but his wife said she thought she could see a light in the kitchen. They went to the back door and knocked. Getting no answer, Fred tried to peep through a chink in the curtain, but all he could see was a pair of legs stretched out on the floor, the rest of the body being hidden by a table. Desperately trying to control his feeling of panic, Fred said, in a slightly shaking voice, 'I think he has had an accident. You had better ring for an ambulance while I try to get inside.'

His wife responded with surprising calmness and hurried off to the telephone box, which she knew was about a hundred yards away. Fred examined the window, and with a skill that might have aroused the suspicion of the police had they witnessed it, broke a pane of glass, and leaning in, opened the catch. As soon as he did so he smelt the gas. He vaulted into the room, turned off the fire, and, holding his breath until he thought he would burst, he struggled to unlock the door. At last the cold night air swept in, and after taking a deep gasping breath he began to pull his uncle into the fresh air. The old man was still breathing, but only just. The ambulance arrived and the driver began giving Edward oxygen.

Some hours later he opened his eyes, and when he realised he was still alive he began to weep.

'I've an old chap who tried to gas himself. He's very depressed and I'm worried he'll have another go', said the houseman on the telephone to the psychiatrist. 'Can I transfer him to your hospital?'

When he arrived in the psychiatric hospital, Edward sat in bed refusing to speak, but not resisting physical examination, which revealed no organic illness. He showed no interest in his surroundings, and would not eat or drink without constant persuasion.

The next morning, having satisfied himself that Edward had recovered fully from the effects of the gas, the ward doctor arranged for him to have ECT that afternoon. 'He will not sign the consent form so we shall have to get his nearest relative to do it', said the doctor.

After six treatments spaced out at two a week, Edward was much better and began to talk freely about the way he had felt. He was no longer sorry to be alive, and thought that the future might still hold something for him. He became very friendly with one of the staff nurses and told her a great deal about his life and the events leading up to his attempted suicide.

All his life he had tended to have mood swings; for some weeks he would feel optimistic and full of energy, tackling new schemes and having many bright ideas, then without warning he would feel frustrated and hopeless, all his interests and activities would suddenly seem stupid and pointless, and he would sit around at home doing little or nothing. However, fairly soon this mood would again give way to one of optimism, and he had to learn to live with himself when he was both 'up' or 'down'.

After his wife's death he had felt lonely and unhappy for some months, but had got over it in about a year. Some twelve months before his attempted suicide he had entered one of his 'down' phases, but this time it had persisted, and as the months went by he had sunk deeper and deeper into misery and despair.

He felt he must have some serious physical illness, and this was confirmed for him by his loss of appetite and weight. Life meant nothing for him and he could see only a future of increasing pain and infirmity. He had finally decided to cut the process short.

2. 'Please help me, don't let me die. You won't kill me will you? I know I've been wicked, I deserve to die, but help me, please help me.'

A white-haired woman in her late fifties, clung to the doctor's arm as he entered the ward. He reassured her, and for a few moments she sat down, but was soon pacing up and down the ward, wringing her hands and shaken with soundless sobs. A nurse entered the room, and at once Miss Smith clung to her, seeking the reassurance that brought her such short-lived comfort.

'I see Miss Smith is still very agitated,' said the doctor, reaching for her case notes from the cabinet in sister's office.

'Yes,' said sister, 'she is very restless and constantly asks for help. She has had four ECTs, but is only slightly better so far.'

'Has she any relatives?'

'Only a sister who lives in Scotland, and they rarely see each other.'

'Miss Smith still works?'

'Yes, she is a private secretary at one of the ministries. I gather it's a very responsible job, and she coped with it very well until a month or so ago. She is one of these ultra efficient women, and seems to have little interest outside her work. I understand her boss has just retired and a new man has taken over, so I expect her routine has been altered a little.'

After some discussion the doctor decided she should have further ECTs, and increased her dose of *Amitriptyline* to 50 mg t.d.s. Gradually, over the next month Miss Smith became more settled and less depressed. She was able to take part in a small group, where she started to talk about some of her difficulties. She told how she had been strictly brought up, with a great emphasis on cleanliness and tidiness, and how guilty she had felt if she ever failed to keep to the high standards she set herself. She explained how difficult it was for her to adjust to any new ways and how upset she became if anything unexpected happened. She had felt very threatened by her chief's retirement, and his replacement's new methods. The thought of her own job coming to an end, and the consequent loss of status and interest had made her feel even more anxious and depressed. She had started to find it difficult to concentrate on her work, so that it took her longer; consequently she worked longer hours and became more tired. Her tiredness made her inaccurate so that the work had to be repeated. Gradually she had lost her grip, and the nightmare spiral of increasing demand and diminishing ability had reduced her to a state of exhaustion. She felt like a child again, expecting a terrible punishment for a sin she did not understand.

3. 'Whatever is wrong with me?' Ann asked herself. 'I must stop shouting at the children; they are not really very noisy, but when they shout it goes right through me.'

With a gesture of weariness she pushed a strand of hair back from her face, and tried to summon enough energy to start preparing the evening meal for her husband. She knew that when the meal was served she would just pick at it. For weeks she had not really wanted to eat and had just forced it down to keep her husband from worrying about her.

'If only I could have a decent night's sleep,' she thought, 'perhaps I wouldn't feel so tired.' For the past month or so she had been waking up at three or four in the morning and, instead of being able to turn over with a sigh of relief and go back to sleep, she had lain awake, her mind churning over the various problems that she had, which in reality were not great but in the early hours loomed like mountains. She had begun to dread the mornings, and no longer looked forward to a new day. She had lost her zest for everything, and had started to make excuses to avoid joining in any family outings her husband might suggest. She was worried, too, that her feelings for him had changed, she no longer welcomed his love-making, but avoided it by pleading she felt too tired.

As she sat thinking how different she felt from her usual gay and active self, she suddenly felt overwhelmed by a feeling of utter despondency; life meant nothing to her, she might just as well be dead. She began to cry, but her tears brought little relief.

When her husband came in she was still sitting there, wearing her working clothes, her hair unbrushed, and no meal was ready. His first reaction was annoyance at having to deal with an emotional crisis after a tiring day at the office, but he realised this was more than some temporary upset that his wife would 'snap out of'.

'What is it, darling?' he asked, putting his arm around her shoulders. 'What is upsetting you?'

'I don't know,' she replied, starting to cry again. 'It's stupid really, I've everything I want, yet I just wish I were dead.'

'Why don't you get off to bed,' he said, 'and I'll bring you a warm drink, and get the doctor to come round and see you.'

At first Ann was most reluctant to allow the doctor to call, but eventually she agreed. After listening to her symptoms, and asking about her family history, the doctor gave her a sedative and went downstairs to talk to her husband.

'Your wife has a depressive illness,' he said, 'but it is not too severe at present, so I want to see if we can treat her with drugs. If she hasn't improved in about three weeks, I'll ask a psychiatrist to see her.'

He handed her husband a prescription which was only just decipherable as Imipramine 25 mg three times a day.

At first, Ann felt no better in spite of taking the tablets regularly, but after about ten days she began to feel less like crying, and seemed to have more energy. When her doctor asked her if the tablets had bothered her in any way she said, 'Well, my mouth has been a bit dry, and I sometimes feel hot and flushed, but it is worth it to feel so much better in myself.' She continued taking the tablets for two more months, then, after reducing the dose, her doctor said she could stop them. She continued to feel perfectly well, and, as she put it, 'my old self again'.

Symptoms of Depression

The primary symptom in depression is the change in mood, yet this is often not the principal complaint of the patient, who may present a whole range of symptoms suggesting physical illness rather than a mental disorder. The patient may be ashamed of feeling depressed, as if it is a sign of weakness on his part, and therefore he must offer the doctor a more respectable sort of illness. People of obsessional personality who set themselves high standards of behaviour are particularly prone to present in this way. Other patients are very aware of the secondary physical features of their illness and may hardly realise that their mood is one of depression, so they complain of insomnia, constipation, tiredness, loss of energy, and the like, rather than their feeling of hopelessness and misery. The diagnosis of a depressive illness is often only made as a result of careful inquiries into whether the patient has certain symptoms apart from those of which they spontaneously complain.

Clinically, it is possible to divide depressive illness into two main groups, but in practice it is often very difficult to decide in which group an individual patient should be placed. These two groups are called reactive and endogenous depression.

Reactive Depression

As its name implies, reactive depression is a change in mood arising from events happening to the individual, and the features of the illness are similar to the normal grief reaction we all experience as a result of the loss of someone, or something, for whom we have strong feelings of love or affection. Thus, the patient can usually understand and explain why he feels as he does, and will date the onset of his illness from a particular event. He feels sad and fearful, and may derive benefit from crying. He is preoccupied with thoughts concerning his loss, and there is often an underlying anger and resentment, usually directed at other people rather than at himself, with a tendency to blame them for his loss. He feels worse towards evening, and may find it difficult to get off to sleep, but usually once asleep, he will remain so for the whole night. He can usually be cheered up at least for a time, and be able to respond to company. While he may lose his appetite, and become constipated, the physiological changes are usually slight.

Endogenous Depression (arising from within)

While the illness may be precipitated by some external event, it can arise without any obvious cause, so that patients often say, 'I've nothing to be depressed about'. The feeling of sadness seems to differ in some way from the normal response to unhappy events, and it is almost always accompanied by a number of physiological changes. Patients may weep, but frequently they complain that 'crying doesn't help', or 'I've gone beyond tears'. Not only does the patient feel low in spirit, but there is a general lowering of interest in, and desire for, almost all former interests. Thus, food no longer holds any pleasure and may become actively disliked. Hobbies and pastimes are neglected, and even reading a newspaper or watching a television programme becomes too much of an effort. They are unable to concentrate and may find it difficult to make even quite simple decisions. While they remain at work these difficulties make it impossible for them to get through their normal amount of work. This, in turn, leads to the work accumulating, which increases their sense of guilt and hopelessness, so that they become even more depressed. They, and their families, often feel that it was overwork that caused the illness, but almost always the true course of events is the one just outlined.

The patient may complain that his mind keeps on turning over the same problem or morbid thought, and that he cannot concentrate because of these fixed ideas, which are often concerned with death. He may ponder on the death of friends or relatives, and may wish that he, too, was dead. This state of being 'half in love with easeful death' may progress to the actual wish to commit suicide, and the patient may make plans for so doing, or carry out an attempt. He may become so preoccupied with morbid thoughts, and find life so unrewarding that he becomes withdrawn to an extent that he merely sits, unspeaking and almost unmoving. In extreme cases the patient may pass into a state of depressive stupor, which, clinically, is very similar to the condition that occurs in some patients with catatonic schizophrenia.

Not all patients show this reduction in activity or *motor retardation* as it is called; some show the opposite state in which, while their mood is depressed and their appetites diminished, they become physically over-active and restless and extremely agitated. This type of depression is quite often seen in people who have their first attack of depression in middle age, and who have a rather rigid and obsessional personality prior to their illness. This type of depression is sometimes called '*involutional*' because of the time of life at which it occurs. Many patients with this type of illness express delusional ideas, which arise from the feelings of hopelessness and misery and in some ways represent the patients' attempt to explain to themselves why they feel so awful and life seems so horrible.

The delusions generally fall into one of four types: (*a*) delusions of guilt or unworthiness, (*b*) delusions of poverty, (*c*) hypochondriacal delusions, (*d*) nihilistic delusions.

1. *Guilt and Unworthiness.* The patient may feel that the misery he is experiencing is a form of punishment and will seek events in his past life that could justify such a reward. He may become convinced that it is the result of some quite trivial misdeed that he performed many years ago, and will either seek constant reassurance on this score, or

insist that he richly deserves his punishment and will refuse treatment on the grounds he does not deserve to be helped.

Some patients, who perhaps favour a slightly more grandiose explanation for their present sufferings, will become convinced they must have committed some enormous and unspecified crime. They talk in terms of 'committing the unforgivable sin' of 'killing God', or 'things too foul to mention'. Others claim they have killed their nearest and dearest, and persist in this claim even in the prescence of those whom they state to be deceased.

2. *Delusions of Poverty.* The patient insists that he is bankrupt and cannot support himself or his relatives, although his bank manager may produce evidence to the contrary. This type of delusion may indicate the lifelong preoccupation the patient has had with making money, and its loss represents the greatest disaster he could imagine.

3. *Hypochondriacal Delusions.* Many depressed patients present originally with complaints of physical illness, especially pain, but if the underlying depression is recognised, the patient is able to relate, in time, his original symptoms to the alteration in mood. However, some patients become preoccupied with the physical accompaniments, and develop the conviction that there is some alteration in their body. A frequent delusion relates to constipation and loss of appetite, which are almost invariably present. The patient talks about his bowels being blocked and the food rotting inside him. (Quite a few such patients have undergone exploratory operations.) In their more extreme forms these ideas merge with those relating to death, and nihilistic delusions may be expressed.

4. *Nihilistic Delusions.* The patient becomes convinced that part of him is dead or has been destroyed. He will talk about 'being dead from the waist down', or 'my bowels have rotted away', or 'my brain has been destroyed'. The ultimate nihilistic delusion is the idea that he is already dead.

Aetiology

Inheritance plays an important part in the aetiology of depressive illness, but the actual mode of inheritance has not yet been established beyond doubt. Endogenous depression is more common in people of short, stocky build, and occurs more frequently in women than men, in a ratio of three to two. Several types of personality are associated with depressive illness. These are:

Cyclothymic Personality. People of this personality experience mood swings throughout their lives, unrelated to circumstances. Their mood fluctuates between elation and depression, and rarely persists in one phase for more than a few days or weeks.

Obsessional or Anankastic Personality. These people are rather rigid, conformist, and anxious. They seek security by leading ordered organised lives, and may resort to various forms of ritual behaviour. They are particularly prone to develop an agitated depression during the involutional period of their life.

Precipitating Events

1. *Physical.* A depressive illness may be triggered off in susceptible individuals by a variety of physical illnesses, influenza being a well-known example. Certain drugs, notably hypotensive agents, may also precipitate depression which does not respond on stopping the drug.

Childbirth and the physical changes of the menopause are also potent factors in precipitating depression.

2. *Emotional.* A wide range of emotional experiences has been described as causative factors in depression of an endogenous type. They share a common feature—the loss of a loved object, which may be a person, an animal or inanimate object, or an abstract concept such as status, or authority.

Treatment of Depression

Since the advent of electro-convulsive therapy (ECT) and the anti-depressent drugs, it has become possible to treat the majority of patients outside hospital. The factors likely to lead to admission rather than out-patient treatment are as follows:

1. *A High Suicidal Risk.* This or, more rarely, the danger of the patient harming other people can lead to admission. However, although anyone who is depressed is a potential suicidal risk, it is not necessary or desirable they should all be admitted to hospital. To some extent it is possible to estimate which patients are the most likely to attempt to kill themselves. The presence of one or more of the following features increases the likelihood:

(*a*) Previous suicidal attempt.
(*b*) Family history of suicide.
(*c*) Preoccupation with suicidal thoughts and plans.

d) Old age.
e) Few family or social ties.
f) No strong religious convictions.
g) Agitation or restlessness rather than retardation.

The risk of homicide rather than, or as a preliminary to, suicide is most likely when the patient has some close relatives who are dependent on him or her. The most frequent circumstance is probably the mother who becomes depressed following childbirth and decides that the world is such a dreadful place that she cannot bear to leave her children behind. Patients with marked depressive delusions of poverty, guilt, or unworthiness may also decide that their relatives should be spared the sorrows of this life. However, of the large numbers of people who become depressed very few commit murder.

2. *Unsuitable Home Environment.* If depression is obviously being caused by events in the patient's environment it may be beneficial for the patient to be taken into hospital for a period while attempts are made to modify the causative factors.

3. *Other Medical Conditions.* Depressive illness is not infrequently precipitated by other physical illnesses, and these may either require hospital treatment in their own right, or may increase the risk of out-patient treatment of the depression. Having made the decision whether the person is to be treated at home or in hospital the choice of which form of treatment used will depend on the severity of the disease and the extent to which external factors are playing a part in producing the disease. Patients who show few physiological changes, and who relate the onset of their illness to some specific happening, who feel worse towards evening, and find it difficult to get off to sleep, do not usually benefit from ECT, and are also said to respond better to drugs of the mono-amine oxidase type, though this is far from certain. On the other hand, patients who show marked loss of appetite and weight, with early waking, and increased symptoms in the morning, tend to do better with drugs such as imipramine (Tofranil), and if their symptoms are severe they may require ECT.

ECT is more likely to be used in those cases where there is:

1. A high suicidal risk.
2. Marked retardation or agitation.
3. Refusal of food, and associated weight loss.
4. Failure to respond to anti-depressant drugs.

The use of drugs and ECT in the treatment of depression is described in a later chapter.

Nursing Care of Depressed Patients

The principles involved in the nursing care of the depressed patient are those enumerated in Chapter 15: observation, care, and the forming of a therapeutic relationship. In this section an attempt is made to point out the special problems, and the areas of particular importance related to depressive illness.

Observation

It has been pointed out that many patients suffering from a depressive illness do not show the classical features of the condition, and present symptoms suggestive of other illnesses. Therefore, the diagnosis may be missed unless subtle indications are noted and recognised by the nursing staff who are in close contact with the patient for long periods. The features listed below should be looked for and commented upon. In patients not thought to be primarily depressed, the presence of the following symptoms may suggest the need to review the diagnosis:

1. Episodes of weeping unrelated to the patient's immediate situation, especially if the patient thinks he is unobserved.
2. Refusal or avoidance of food, and the reason for such refusal should be noted.
3. Difficulty in making simple everyday decisions, in a person who can normally act decisively.
4. Disturbance of sleep pattern, based not on the patient's statements but on accurate observation.
5. Loss of weight without obvious cause.
6. Suicidal ideas, expressed to the nurse or to other patients.
7. Suicidal attempts or preparations for such attempts by hoarding tablets, asking other people to purchase aspirins, etc, or attempts to obtain sharp instruments.
8. Attempts to avoid observation by making for empty rooms, cupboards, and the like.

Observations directed at assessing the patient's progress should not only include obvious changes in mood, but the subtler points concerning his ability to take interest in his surroundings, to relate to other people, and to take part in activities. A careful note should be made of physiological changes such as improved appetite, gain in weight, and normal bowel habit. The observation of the patient immediately following ECT is especially important, as in the early stage of treatment a transitory improvement may occur which indicates that it is worth continuing treatment even though some hours later the patient seems no better.

In any illness the outcome depends to a large extent on the previous personality of the patient, and a major part of the treatment must be directed to boosting those aspects of the patient's personality that are likely to help his recovery and subsequent health, while modifying those features that are perpetuating the illness. To plan such a therapeutic programme a detailed knowledge of the patient's personality must be built up, and this depends on accurate observation of the patient's responses to a variety of circumstances. The nurse should notice and record the patient's attitude to his relatives, and their response to him. His general attitude to staff and other patients should be described, avoiding such clichés as 'co-operative', which can mean anything from total dependency to active participation in ward activities. The patient should be encouraged to describe activities he previously found interesting as well as those that have proved a burden to him.

An attempt should be made to discover the ways in which the patient has dealt with stress throughout his life, so it is important to know in some detail about his childhood, schooling, work record, marriage, and his relationship with his wife, children, and workmates. While the psychiatrist will attempt to obtain much of this information, the nurse can often supplement it because of the much greater contact she has with the patient and the opportunity this provides for informal discussion and observation. The nurse should not attempt to probe beyond the point where the patient is prepared to talk, but should wait until the patient feels ready and able to discuss it further.

The degree of nursing care necessary depends on the severity of depression. The patient who is stuporous or withdrawn and retarded to the extent of being unable to look after himself will require nursing in bed, at least until treatment has lifted the level of depression. During this phase, attention will be directed to maintaining an adequate diet and fluid intake, preventing the development of pressure sores, and guarding against the other complications of bed rest, described in another chapter.

The less retarded patient may require help with feeding, dressing, and toilet activities, but every attempt should be made to encourage the patient to carry out these functions himself. It requires more skill and patience to help the patient help himself that it does to merely *do* things to the patient: if institutionalisation is to be avoided, this skill must be developed. It is important with the depressed patient to ask him to do only a little more than he feels able to do—if the demand is too great, his failure to achieve it will only lead to an increase in his depression.

With depressed patients it may be difficult to persuade them to take an adequate diet. When a patient is refusing to eat, an attempt must be made to discover the reason for his refusal. It may be based on delusional ideas, as previously described, or it may stem from the physiological loss of appetite. In the latter case, every attempt should be made to tempt the patient with small attractive dishes, particularly those which in the past have been his particular favourites. It may be necessary to supplement the diet with vitamin preparations and Complan. The patient must be weighed at least once a week.

Constipation frequently complicates depression. In the young, this is not of great moment; but in the elderly it may give rise to secondary problems such as bleeding or prolapsed piles, prolapse of the rectum due to straining, faecal impaction, or incontinence (*see* Chapter 11 on psycho-geriatrics). It may be necessary for patients to have laxatives such as Senokot or Dulcolax and, in extreme cases, a gentle enema. However, laxatives should not be given indiscriminately, and the patient should be encouraged not to dwell on the state of his bowels.

Relating to the Depressed Patient

In order to relate to a depressed patient, the nurse must be able to put herself in the patient's place, and to try to view the world as it appears to the patient. In this way the nurse learns that the patient's behaviour is not motivated by a desire to be stubborn or difficult, but arises as a consequence of the feeling of hopelessness and dread.

The aim of the relationship during the stage of marked depression is to provide continuing support for the patient's faint hope that recovery is possible. Thus, reassurance should be given, however often it is sought for, and however little effect it seems to have, for refusal or rejection will confirm the patient's worst fears. Patients should not be told to 'pull themselves together' or to 'snap out of it', which is equivalent to telling someone with a broken leg that all they need to do is walk on it. The nurse should avoid being too gay or boisterous, as the patient cannot respond and feels more depressed by contrast. There is little point in trying to disprove, by logical argument, the patient's ideas of guilt or unworthiness; instead, it should be explained that these thoughts and feelings are part of the illness, and that as the patient gets better they will be seen in better perspective. The best reassurance the patient can have is to feel that the nurse respects him as a person and does not regard him as an outcast or as one who lacks moral courage.

Mania: Illustrative Story

'I'm delighted to meet you, its a pleasure to talk to a professional man, an educated man like myself. I was at Oxford you know, and Cambridge; been to all the colleges. I studied science and biology, Latin and astronomy. There's not many people better educated than me. That's why they have given me this job as a spy you know, because of all the languages I can speak, parlez-vous, sprechen der deutche, parlalo italiano, and seven others.'

As he paused for breath the Doctor said: 'I wonder if you would stick to just English, and perhaps you would like to sit down.'

The patient paused for a moment in his restless wandering, and put down the ashtray he had just picked up.

'Ah yes,' he said. 'I should rest, I've not slept for two days. Too busy, I've got to get this deal fixed—it will make millions. No one else could carry it through. It is a good job I feel so well, otherwise I wouldn't have the strength to do it.'

'Why have you come to hospital if you feel well?'

'To help, of course; know how busy you are; can save you time, reorganise, cut down, speed up. Time and motion expert. This gentleman (pointing to the mental welfare officer) suggested I came; happy to oblige; can't stop of course, too busy.'

The mental welfare officer filled in the background details. He had been called to the local car factory by the works' doctor, because the patient, who worked in the assembly shop had begun to attach the bonnets to the cars without any regard to the appropriate colours. Black cars were coming off the line with yellow bonnets, green cars with blue ones, and the whole place was in chaos. The patient had never behaved like it before, but had had ECT in the past, when he had been severely depressed.

The patient was diagnosed as suffering from mania, and he was treated with a tranquillising drug on which he gradually became quieter and less restless.

Symptoms

Mania and hypomania are the opposite of depression, and some patients suffer from alternate episodes of the two states, sometimes with only short intervals of normality between them. Other patients have only an isolated episode of either depression or mania, and any combination can occur.

In hypomanic states the symptoms are less marked than in mania, but there are no hard and fast boundaries, between the two states. The patient's mood is raised, he feels cheerful, confident, and supremely fit and able. Nothing is impossible, but if he is frustrated he may become irritable and aggressive.

His mind is working very rapidly so that fresh ideas pour in, sometimes so quickly that his speech cannot keep up with them. These ideas seem to be dictated largely by events occurring around him, unlike the excited schizophrenic whose thoughts are more influenced by personal internal ideas and beliefs. Thus, the hypomanic patient is easily distracted, constantly altering his thoughts in response to external stimuli. As he talks he is influenced by the words he uses, so that he makes puns or strings together words that sound alike but mean different things, so that his conversation resembles that of certain comedians, who use this technique deliberately. In milder states such patients can be amusing and stimulating, but after a time they tend to become tiresome and irritating. They, in turn, find their more sombre acquaintances slow, boring, and stolid, so that they become irritated and angry. During such episodes their judgement is impaired and they may act in a financially irresponsible way, giving money away, taking on debts or writing cheques that cannot be met. This may cause great difficulty for their families.

The manic patient is extremely restless and may often be noisy and aggressive. He cannot stop to rest or sleep, and, if not treated, progresses into a state of exhaustion, dehydration, and malnutrition, which may prove fatal. Treatment is by use of tranquillising drugs— Haloperidol (Serenace) being claimed to be especially effective. Lithium salts are also used in some cases, and in severe states ECT may be given to restore the mood to normal.

Nursing Aspects of Mania and Hypomania

The patient suffering from mania may be in grave physical danger, as his persistent over-activity is not only exhausting in itself, but by preventing him sleeping, and even from taking an adequate amount of fluid and food, leads to a state of physical collapse. The patient may die as a direct result, or, more often, by developing some infectious disease because his resistance is so much reduced. For this reason, the patient must be adequately sedated, and then nursed in a quiet atmosphere, providing as little stimulation as possible.

The hypomanic patient often proves a most difficult nursing problem. In small doses his company may be entertaining and stimulating, but his nonstop activity, his interfering in everyone's business, and his incessant chatter soon prove extremely wearing. Additionally, his elated mood can rapidly change to one of aggressive irritability if he is thwarted in any of his plans.

The nurse must find suitable outlets for the patient's excessive energy, and she must accept the fact that his interest will soon flag, and new activities have to be found to keep him occupied. He should be given as much physical exercise as possible, but competitive situations should be avoided. Somewhat monotonous tasks may be more sedating than those that require concentration. Hypomanic patients require fairly firm handling, but there is no purpose in 'bullying' them. The more pressure that is put on them in one direction, the harder they move in the other.

5 The Schizophrenias

Four Illustrative Stories

1. Peter's advent came as rather a surprise to his parents, who had reconciled themselves to a childless marriage. His mother was forty when he was born and she had very mixed feelings about coping with a small baby at her time of life. Peter's father, however, had no such misgivings—here at last was the son he had wanted for so long. He could not do enough for the baby, he washed him, fed and changed him, and virtually excluded his wife from having anything to do with the child.

As Peter grew, his father tried to be everything to him, brother, friend, father and mother, all in one, but by the age of eleven, it was obvious that Peter was not going to be all that his father had desired. Instead of the tough, sports-loving boy his father had wanted, Peter was shy, sensitive, and quiet. Although he was quite healthy, he was thin and tall with narrow shoulders.

At school he was good at lessons, but had few friends, and suffered more than his fair share of teasing and bullying. In the evenings he would remain at home reading, and hardly ever went out with his contemporaries. When he was sixteen he left school, having passed five GCE subjects at 'O' level, and started work in a bookshop. At first he seemed quite happy, but gradually his mother noticed that she was having to call him several times before he would get up in the morning, and that he was taking an age to get dressed. The result was that he was late for work on a number of occasions and, finally, he was sacked from his work. He seemed to be very little bothered by this, and made little effort to find a new job. He remained in bed until mid-morning, lounged around in the afternoon, and retired to his room again straight after the evening meal. His parents thought he was worrying about something but he was not prepared to answer their tentative inquiries. In fact, on several occasions he lost his temper and swore at them, using words his mother had never guessed he knew.

After some weeks they persuaded him to see their family doctor. Peter said there was nothing wrong with him, apart from feeling a bit tired, and so the doctor gave him a tonic. A few days later his father took Peter to the theatre in an attempt to get him 'to snap out of it', as he put it. Throughout the first act Peter seemed very tense and anxious; he kept moving in his seat, and turning round to stare in a hostile and suspicious way at the people sitting in the row behind. During the first interval, when his father was thinking of going for a drink, Peter suddenly stood up, said he was going home, and began to push past people with little or no concern for their comfort. Embarrassed, the father hurried after his son and caught up with him in the car park. By then, Peter was shaking and crying, and appeared extremely upset. In the car his father asked him what was the matter, and he replied that it was the people in the row behind who had been talking about him, saying: 'He is the one they mentioned on the TV—you know the homosexual.' His father was completely bewildered by this turn of events, and as soon as they got home he sent for his GP who came round, gave Peter a sedative, and told his father that he would arrange an appointment at the psychiatric clinic which, luckily, was held the next day in the outpatient's department of the local hospital.

It was with difficulty that his father persuaded Peter to see the psychiatrist. At first Peter's attitude was hostile and withdrawn, but gradually he began to describe his experiences during the past few months. He had found increasing difficulty in getting his mind to work in the normal way. It seemed as if he had fewer ideas in his mind, and he would often lose track of his thoughts, so that his mind would go blank. Sometimes, after a second or two he would pick up the thread, but at other times a quite different idea would present itself. He felt that performing quite routine tasks like washing and dressing had become difficult because he no longer performed them automatically, but had to think deliberately of each step in their performance.

He began to feel that the world had changed in some way he could not clearly describe, except to say that it felt menacing and frightening. One day he suddenly had the idea that all these feelings were due to a group of people who were determined to make him into a homosexual. They all knew about him and could read his thoughts. They sent messages to each other, and to him, over the television, and seemingly quite ordinary phrases in broadcasts referred specifically to him. He heard people talking about him as he passed, and sometimes he heard a voice calling him a homosexual, when no one else was about. He had been too frightened to tell his parents about these feelings and ideas, and had tried to avoid people as much as possible. He thought he might be ill, but for most of the time he was convinced that his experiences were actually occurring outside his own mind.

It was decided to admit him to hospital for treatment and observation, and he reluctantly agreed to come in as an informal patient. In hospital, he was at first unsettled and his behaviour was impulsive and unpredictable. On several occasions he ran off home but came back with his father some hours later. Gradually, under the influence of the phenothiazine drugs he was having he became more settled and began playing a more active part in the ward meetings and social evenings. He decided he would like to work in the carpentry shop and showed an unexpected talent for using his hands.

After some three months, his symptoms had almost entirely gone, and he was considered fit to leave hospital. He was anxious to continue doing carpentry, and it was arranged that he went to a Government Training Centre some fifty miles from his home. This meant he had to live in a hostel, and it was felt that he might benefit from being away from the emotionally charged setting of his home. Arrangements were made for him to attend a local psychiatric out-patient clinic, where his progress could be judged and his drugs adjusted as the need arose.

2. The Sunday morning quiet in the village street was suddenly shattered by the sound of breaking glass and the shrill cries of an elderly lady who had just thrown a brick through the window of her next-door neighbour. 'That will teach you not to interfere with me', she yelled, as the startled occupants rushed out. 'You dirty devils, you ought to be in jail', she continued.

By now doors and windows were opening all along the street, and small groups were gathering. 'It's that strange old woman from number seventeen', people muttered. 'I knew she was mad', some remarked. The old lady still stood screaming abuse at her bewildered neighbours, while a small deputation debated whether to send for the police, the doctor, or the fire brigade. Finally, they decided in favour of the constable, who arrived in due course on his bicycle, perspiring freely, and clearly not overjoyed at this inter-ruption. He was soon surrounded by a crowd of people all offering contradictory accounts of what had happened, and even more conflicting advice on how he should deal with the situation.

The old lady continued to shout, but no one paid much notice to the substance of her complaint. At last the policeman decided to take the old lady and the nextdoor neighbour to the comparative peace of the local police station where he obtained the following story.

According to the neighbour, they had always been friendly to the old lady and her husband, until the latter died some eighteen months previously. They had always thought the old lady rather unsociable, and they had been struck by the comparative lack of emotion she had shown when her husband died. Not only had she not worn mourning, but she seemed to have spent some of the insurance money on some garishly bright clothes that did not seem very suitable either for her age or her state of bereavement. In the subsequent months she had become almost a total recluse and had ignored their invitations to drop in for tea, or an evening meal. Recently, they had noticed her wandering about in the garden muttering to herself, and occasionally shaking her fist in their direction. Late at night they had been disturbed by noises, which sounded as if she was dragging furniture about. In spite of these events, they were taken completely by surprise by the window-smashing and the torrent of abuse to which they had been subjected.

The constable now turned his attention to the old lady who had been given a cup of tea and was stroking the police station cat. 'You'll have to speak up, I'm a bit deaf', she said. She gave her name and address correctly, told him she was seventy-four years old, and that her husband had died on the 12th of November, eighteen months ago.

'Why did you throw a brick through this gentleman's window?' he inquired.

'To stop him shining those X-rays through my bedroom walls' she replied.

'X-rays?' he said, in a puzzled voice.

'Yes' she said, 'he shines them on my private parts when I'm in bed, and last night he tried blowing gas under the floorboards, so that he could break in and rape me.'

The policeman was accustomed to hearing some pretty bizarre

stories from clients accused of various crimes, but even he felt that this story was not very likely, and his doubts were confirmed by a glance at the neighbour's face, which bore an expression of outraged credulity, beyond the acting ability of a Royal Academy graduate.

'Yes' he said, and 'Yes' again, while he sought for inspiration.

'Aren't you going to arrest that man?' the old lady asked.

'Well, no' said the constable. 'I think I'd better get your doctor to see you.'

'Whatever for?' she asked.

Pretending to humour her, the constable replied that if she claimed she had been gassed they would require a medical report.

When her doctor had examined her, he rang the local psychiatric hospital to see if one of the consultants would come over to see the old lady. However, no one was available and the duty doctor advised the GP to call in the Mental Welfare Officer so that if they agreed she required hospital treatment, because she was a danger to herself or others, she could be detailed in hospital against her will, for a period of seventy-two hours observation.

The Mental Welfare Officer finally arrived and agreed that she needed to be detained. As she refused to enter hospital of her own free will, he and the GP completed a recommendation under Section 29 of the 1959 Mental Health Act. The old lady was persuaded to get into the mental welfare officer's car, and driven, still protesting, to the psychiatric hospital.

The duty doctor had considerable difficulty in persuading the old lady to allow him to examine her physically, and she was reluctant to talk about anything other than the iniquities of her neighbours and her desire to return home. Slowly he managed to find out some of her background history, and it was obvious that her memory and intellectual function were not impaired, apart from her difficulty in hearing.

There was nothing out of the ordinary in her early history and she seemed to have led a fairly normal married life, though she had never much liked going out and seemed to have been prone to take offence with only trivial provocation.

Shortly after her husband had died she had started to experience tingling sensations in her skin, and especially in her genitalia. She became convinced that this was the result of rays being shone on her. She also heard her neighbours plotting to break into her home, and often at night had heard sounds of people trying to force the doors and windows. Because of this she had barricaded herself in her bedroom by piling furniture against the door and window.

She kept insisting on leaving hospital, and in order to detain her for a further period she was examined by one of the consultants and by her own doctor, who then jointly filled in a form applying for her further compulsory detention in hospital for twenty-eight days, under Section 25 of the Mental Health Act (q.v.).

She was started on Stelazine (Trifluoperazine) and, because she kept spitting the tablets out, she was given it in syrup form. Gradually, her delusions began to diminish, and she no longer complained of hearing voices. She was fitted with a deaf-aid which made it much easier for her to establish contact with the nursing staff and patients. She decided that she did not want to return to her own home and a place was found for her in an old peoples home run by the county council. She sold her house, and moved directly from hospital to her new home.

3. Joan was well known by sight to everyone who worked in the psychiatric hospital where she had been a patient for about two years. They had all seen her walking to the hospital shop, and had noticed the curious habit she had, of walking ten paces forwards, stopping, and then taking three paces back.

She had been admitted from a ward of the general hospital when she was twenty-eight years old. She had been found by her landlady, lying in bed apparently unconscious, and had been taken to the casualty department as an attempted suicide. The casualty officer could find no evidence of overdosage, of injury, or any other physical cause for her state. She was not, in fact, unconscious in the usual sense, but lay rigid in bed not responding to any form of stimulus, However, if her arm was raised she would keep it in the same position for hours, and even held her head off the pillows for far longer than would normally be possible. She was completely mute, and actively refused to eat, changing from passive stillness to ferocious resistance when an attempt was made to feed her.

Psychiatric opinion was sought and she was transferred to the psychiatric hospital where she was given electro-convulsive therapy as rapidly as it could be arranged. She had a treatment every day for three days, and was also given chlorpromazine (Largactil) by intra-muscular injection, as she refused to take anything by mouth. Gradually, she emerged from her stuporose state and would reply in monosyllables to questions, though she still offered no spontaneous remarks. She began to eat and would take her tablets without complaint. ECT was continued at twice weekly intervals, and after six treatments Joan was a great deal better.

Her mother had been contacted and visited the hospital, though it was several hours' journey by car from her home. From the mother a full history was obtained.

Joan was the last of three children, and her childhood had been quite normal until the age of fifteen when her mother felt she had changed in some way. She had gradually become more withdrawn, and her friends stopped asking her out when they found their invitations were not being accepted. She had become moody and seemed to spend much of the time day-dreaming. Her mother noticed that she developed certain mannerisms, and that her movements took on a rather stilted form. There were days when she seemed very restless and would pace up and down. Trivial things would provoke her into a towering rage in which she seemed to lose control of herself, and she would be left shaking and frightened by the violence of her emotion. This had gradually passed away and her parents felt that it had been a phase of more than usually difficult adolescence. They then noticed that her emotional responses seemed rather shallow, as if she was putting on an emotional show without really feeling very strongly the emotions she portrayed.

At the age of twenty she had an acute episode of extreme restlessness and had to be admitted to a psychiatric hospital where she was given ECT and drugs, and recovered in about three months. She had remained well until the episode which had led to her present admission.

A maternal uncle had suffered from a similar illness and had spent many years in a psychiatric hospital, where he had eventually died.

4. Old Bill, as everyone called him, had a sly and knowing look about him. He was much given to beckoning with his finger, winking, and nodding, in a way which implied that he knew a great deal more than people gave for, him credit and that it would take an excessively early bird to put anything across on him. His conversation also gave the impression that at any moment he was going to reveal some vast and cataclysmic truth, but the moment never quite arrived. On closer acquaintance it became evident that the superficial profundity was only a reflection of a total lack of coherence or logic in his speech.

His real lack of profundity was clearly demonstrated by his life history. The seventh son of an itinerant tinker, he had followed in his father's wandering footsteps until arrested one day for stealing a bottle of milk. While he had been kept in the cells his family had moved on. He never found them again, and had not tried very energetically. From then on he had drifted from place to place, from job to job, and more lately from psychiatric hospital to psychiatric hospital. He seemed quite content with his lot, and seemed little moved by what fate had dealt him. His mood was usually one of optimism unmatched by his circumstances, and he often expressed fanciful schemes that he never found sufficient energy to put into practice. He was brought to the psychiatric clinic by a probation officer who felt that something might be done to improve Old Bill's mental state and turn him into an active and responsible citizen.

Symptoms
Superficially, the cases described seem to have little in common, yet all were diagnosed as forms of schizophrenia. Though some people think of schizophrenia as being one disease, it is probably best considered as a term used to cover a number of different clinical pictures, probably arising as a result of a variety of different causes, but having certain kinds of symptoms in common.

The name schizophrenia was first used in 1911 by Eugene Bleuler, and he considered that, for a diagnosis of schizophrenia to be made, the patient must show at least some of the following features:

1. disturbance of thinking,
2. disturbance of emotions,
3. disturbances of volition,
4. disturbances of motor behaviour,
5. accessory symptoms (e.g. hallucinations and delusions).

Disturbance of thinking. Thinking can be divided into two forms:

1. Goal-directed thinking—thinking that is directed to problem-solving and decision-making.
2. Phantasy thinking—day-dreaming or autistic thinking, in which logic and reality play little part and in which the individual gratifies his needs and desires in his imagination, unhindered by the actual situation in which he finds himself.

Schizophrenic patients often demonstrate difficulty in performing the first kind of thinking, and show a marked tendency to replace it by the wish-fulfilling thinking of the second kind.

The difficulties experienced are of various sorts, and it is helpful, in remembering the nature of these difficulties, to consider goal-directed thinking as having many of the characteristics of a stream (we often refer to a patient's 'stream of thought'). Thus, it has velocity, volume, and content; sometimes it flows between high straight banks, while at others it meanders about in shallow ill-defined channels. Some or all of these characteristics may be altered in schizophrenia. The 'volume' may be reduced or increased, so that the patient may complain that he has no ideas (poverty of ideation). He says his mind is blank, won't work, or when the ideas are increased he may say: 'My mind is too full', 'I can't stop my mind', or 'My mind is muddled' (pressure of thought).

The patient often tries to find explanations for these sensations and may project his difficulties onto his environment, so that he may claim that someone is interfering with his thoughts, taking his mind away, or, conversely, putting ideas into his mind, making him think certain things. He may further suggest ways in which people could achieve this, and the methods suggested tend to reflect the social and educational background of the patient. Thus, he may talk of black magic, or wireless waves, X-rays, or atomic radiation, and (since the late 1950s) of messages from Sputniks.

Velocity is a combination of speed and direction, and some patients find that while they seem to have the same number of ideas in their mind they can no longer arrange them in logical sequence, so that they lose the thread of their ideas, and this is reflected in their speech. They may start to answer a question but suddenly break off and are silent for a varying amount of time (as if the stream had run into a dam, and was trying to get round or over it). Sometimes they will continue the same idea, at other times when they resume speaking they refer to a different problem. This difficulty is called *thought blocking*, and various types are described.

The content may be abnormal in two ways. The patient may express false beliefs, which are not in keeping with his background (delusions), or he may use words in a way which differs from their normal usage, sometimes inventing new words (neologisms) in an attempt to describe the sensations he is experiencing, or the thoughts and emotions he is having.

A number of investigators have suggested that the characteristic disorder of thinking in schizophrenia is a failure to select the relevant associations from those which do not apply in the particular circumstances. Thus, if the patient has many associations related to a particular idea he will not be able to sort out the important from the unimportant, and he will wander from one aspect to another so that his answer is disjointed, diffuse, and difficult to follow. This is sometimes called 'over inclusive thinking' and may be demonstrated by certain sorting tests (q.v.).

Other patients seem unable to think abstractly; it is as if their thoughts run between high banks, and can not deviate from the original course. Their thinking has been called 'concrete', and it can be demonstrated by asking them to explain proverbs in their own words. They tend to use the same words as in the original, and cannot generalise the meaning of the proverb to other circumstances.

Disturbance of emotion (affect). In the early stages of the disease, the patient may respond to the strange sensations and difficulties he is experiencing by becoming anxious or depressed, and may be considered to have an anxiety state or a depressive illness. Throughout the illness episodes of depression or elation may occur, but the characteristic affective changes in schizophrenia are 'flattening' and/or incongruity.

In 'flattening' there is gross reduction in the amount of emotional reaction to situations, so that the patient seems unmoved by events involving him. Incongruity of affect means that the emotional response is out of keeping with the situation. Thus, the patient may giggle fatuously when told that a close relative has died; and may seem quite cheerful while describing the dreadful tortures that his persecutors are making him suffer. Such abnormal emotional responses can occur in conditions other than schizophrenia and are not diagnostic if taken in isolation.

Disturbance of Volition. Volition may be thought of as a combination of ambition and will-power; that is, both the wish to achieve something and the ability to stick at the task until it is completed. In schizophrenia there is often a loss of volition, and patients may complain that their will-power has gone. Frequently, they refer to this as feeling depressed or tired. Many who do not complain of these feelings demonstrate the failure of volition by their habit of staying in bed, their inactivity, their failure in competitive situations, their poor work performance, and their inability to translate into practice the many plans they have for the future.

Disturbance of Motor Behaviour. Some schizophrenic patients show greatly increased motor activity, being extremely restless, and at times, violently aggressive. At other times they may show the completely opposite picture in which motor activity is reduced to an absolute minimum and the patient lies mute and immobile, responding only to painful stimuli. This condition is known as catatonic stupor, and if untreated may lead to the death of the patient. The patient may exhibit mannerisms (q.v.) or stereotypes (q.v.). They may have abnormalities of posture, such as waxy flexibility (*flexibilitas cerea*), in which the limbs are kept in any position the examiner places them until they are rearranged. The reasons for these abnormal movements are not known for certain. Often they seem to have some symbolic meaning for the patient, but similar states can be seen in cases of organic brain damage in which there is no psychological factor. These symptoms seem to be much less common than they used to be. The reason for this is not clear, but may be related to earlier and more effective drug treatment.

Accessory Symptoms. The terms hallucination and delusion have been defined in Chapter 13. Their presence is not essential for a diagnosis of schizophrenia, and they may occur in almost any psychiatric condition.

1. *Hallucination.* Auditory hallucinations are one of the commonest symptoms of schizophrenia. The patient may describe them and may recognise them as hallucinations, or he may deny that he hears voices, but his behaviour leads one to suspect that he is hallucinated. He may stare at a spot with his head cocked as if he is listening to something; he may laugh or shout in response to the voice, or he may be violent or aggressive as a result of instruction from his hallucinations. The messages are often abusive in nature, and sometimes take the form of a dialogue in which one voice accuses while the other defends the patient; one may tell him to kill himself or carry out other violent suggestions while the other instructs him not to. Patients sometimes claim that the voices are not outside but within their own head; this condition is referred to as 'pseudo-hallucination'. One special form of hallucination is the patient hearing his own thoughts repeated aloud (*echo de pense*).

Hallucinations of the other senses also occur, and olfactory ones are not uncommon. The patient may experience unpleasant smells which are interpreted as poisonous gas, or they may feel that the smell is arising from them, and that other people are aware of it and commenting on it. Some of the complaints of sexual interference may arise from hallucinations of touch arising from the skin and genitalia.

Visual hallucinations are comparatively rare in schizophrenia, though they may occur in states of ecstasy. Functional hallucinations may occur, in which the hallucination is only experienced at times when the patient is receiving genuine stimuli at the same time. Thus, one patient only heard her voices while the noise of the flushing lavatory could be heard.

2. *Delusion.* In the early stages of their illness, many schizophrenic patients experience a strange mood in which they feel that their environment has changed in a way they do not understand and cannot easily describe but which is extremely menacing, so that they feel tense, anxious, and perplexed.

While in this state they may experience a 'delusional perception'. That is, they see some quite ordinary object or event, but suddenly believe that it has a special significance for them. Thus, a patient saw that the carpet had been moved an inch or two while he was out of the room, and 'knew' instantly, that this was a sign that he was going to be killed.

Others suddenly have a delusional idea: they declare that they are God, or the King of Siam. These delusions that arise abruptly in the patient's mind, fully developed and not reflecting the mood of the patient, are called primary delusions (apophanous).

Secondary delusions are those that arise as a result of other abnormal experiences, and may be thought of as the patient's attempt to explain or justify the experiences he has suffered, or the situation in which he finds himself. Thus, the delusions are frequently persecutory, or grandiose, or a combination of the two. A patient having olfactory hallucinations may believe that his neighbours are trying to gas him, and their reason for so doing is that he is really an extremely rich and important person. The content of the delusion often reflects the patient's need for respect and affection, and may be an attempt to compensate for his feelings of unimportance and inferiority, as well as accounting for his abnormal experiences.

The patient's delusions may be well organised and logical, or they may be poorly developed and contradictory. They may be held with great emotional strength so that the patient becomes distressed if they are challenged, or they may have little affective loading.

Classification

Bleuler classified schizophrenia into four main types. They are still referred to, although it is often difficult to place a patient in a particular pigeon hole—the same patient may show different clinical features at different times. The four types are:

1. *Simple.* Lack of volition and shallow emotional response are the main features of this type, and the more florid and bizarre symptoms are not present. This type of patient may drift into crime or prostitution or take to the road.
2. *Hebephrenic.* Thought disorder is the main symptom in this group and the illness usually develops insidiously before the age of thirty. Such patients often appear 'silly', and may be overactive and hilarious.
3. *Catatonic.* In this type, disturbances of motor behaviour are the most prominent feature.
4. *Paranoid.* The delusions are the predominant symptom in this type, while the rest of the personality tends to be well preserved.

Some authorities separate off the so-called 'paraphrenias' or late onset schizophrenias. These are mostly seen among spinsters or widows, who often have some degree of sensory impairment. They experience hallucinations, often with a strong sexual basis and express delusions of persecution. Their experiences are often limited to their own home and its immediate surroundings, and may stop, at least temporarily, when they enter hospital or move to new accommodation.

There are also states in which it is not possible to be certain whether the illness is schizophrenic or depressive, and in which the outcome tends to differ from that of the more typical illness.

Aetiology

The cause or causes of schizophrenia are not known, though a number of factors that may play a part have been suggested.

Hereditary. Twin studies and family studies have demonstrated the importance of genetic factors, though the exact mode of inheritance is still in dispute. Not all persons who have the appropriate genetic structure develop the clinical manifestations of the disease.

If one parent is schizophrenic the child is about twenty times as likely to develop the illness as a child who has no close relatives who have the disease.

Premorbid Personality. About 50 per cent of patients suffering from schizophrenia are described as being shy, withdrawn, and sensitive people, before the illness developed. This type of personality has been said to be more frequent in people of a particular body build: tall, narrow-chested, long extremities, and poor muscular development. However, only about a third of schizophrenic patients have this physique.

Endocrine Disturbances. A great number of investigations have been carried out to try to find some underlying endocrine or metabolic disorder in schizophrenics. At present it can only be said that no specific abnormalities have been demonstrated. There have been a number of reports of abnormal chemicals being found in the urine of schizophrenic patients, but the significance of those findings has not been finally established.

Prognosis. This may be considered as the likely outcome of the acute attack, the chance of further episodes, the likelihood of deterioration in personality, and their chance of returning to the community.

With treatment, the majority of acute patients lose their florid symptoms and are able to leave hospital within three to six months. Patients with a very acute onset of their illness, a previously outgoing personality, a tendency to be short and fat, tend to do better than those whose illness develops slowly, who are tall and thin, and of shy sensitive personality.

The disease was originally considered to lead, in almost every case, to a progressive deterioration in personality, intellect, and habits, but it is now realised that while some deterioration may be part and parcel of the illness, much of the dementia of the chronic schizophrenic was the result not of the disease but of the treatment the patient received.

Until fairly recently, the majority of people diagnosed as schizophrenic were doomed to spend the bulk of their lives in a psychiatric hospital, gradually gravitating to the back wards where they had the minimum of nursing and medical care, and spent most of the day sitting staring at each other or the standard yellow and brown paint work. From investigations of institutions where the inmates spend long periods having little contact with the outside world, exposed to long periods of boredom and with no social stimulus, it has been learnt that people who do *not* suffer from schizophrenia can end up showing many of the symptoms that were thought to be due to the disease. This condition has been called 'institutional neurosis'.

The social prognosis of the patient, that is his chances of leaving hospital and remaining in the outside world, depends on a number of factors not directly related to the severity of his illness. They can be considered under the following headings:

1. *Employment.* The majority of schizophrenic patients are slower, less accurate, and less productive than normal people in work tasks, so that if redundancy is prevalent they tend to be the first to be dismissed. Those who develop their illness in early adolescence may not have acquired training for any particular work and also may not have learned those general work habits of punctual and regular attendance, conformity to safety regulations, a keen eye for 'skiving', and a degree of enlightened self-interest that makes an employee acceptable to both employers and unions.

Those who have qualified for or held more highly-skilled jobs may present a different problem in that, while they can no longer cope with their previous employment, they are unwilling or unable to take less-skilled jobs. If the patient is to leave hospital and remain out, every effort must be made to help him find a suitable job, or to attempt to train him in both work habits and skills.

2. *Accommodation.* It has been found that some schizophrenic patients relapse more rapidly if they return to live with close relatives than if they are discharged to an environment in which there is not so great an emotional involvement. On the other hand, those who return to an isolated existence without the opportunity for making friends and taking part in social activities also tend to relapse. For many patients, hospital becomes their home and they are fearful and uncertain about looking after themselves; it is sometimes desirable to discharge them from hospital into small hostels with other ex-patients so that they can gradually adjust to life in the community.

While the community seems prepared to tolerate quite marked psychiatric symptoms, particularly if these have a religious or pseudoscientific flavour, certain forms of behaviour are not compatible with remaining out of hospital. Thus, aggressive acts resulting from hallucinations or delusions frequently lead to readmission; any form of abnormal sexual behaviour performed without a normal amount of discretion or gross neglect of conventional standards of hygiene and decency are not long tolerated.

Treatment

The methods of treatment, both physical and psychological, will be considered in detail in another chapter, but the aims of treatment, and the techniques employed may be summarised under the following headings:

1. *The Suppression of Symptoms.* It is not yet known for certain whether the present methods of treatment cure the illness or only suppress symptoms, but the rapid control of disturbed behaviour, which can usually be obtained by the use of tranquillising drugs alone or combined with ECT, enables psychological methods of treatment to be instituted much earlier and with greater hope of success.

2. *The Prevention of Deterioration.* This entails providing the patient with an environment that stimulates him and does not allow him to withdraw into a world of isolation and fantasy. The patient must be given the maximum degree of freedom and responsibility compatible with his own and other people's safety, which, in the majority of cases, means a degree of freedom little different from normal. He should spend at least part of each day working at some task that is rewarding both psychologically and financially, and he should return to normal employment as soon as possible, if necessary working from the hospital.

The patient should be encouraged to take part in social activities within the hospital, but the purpose of these functions should be kept in mind. The aim is to provide an opportunity for the patient to learn how to form personal relationships, and one schizophrenic patient dancing with another, each being oblivious of the other's presence, is not especially therapeutic.

3. *Rehabilitation.* This should start at the moment when the decision to admit the patient is first made. The aim of rehabilitation is twofold: firstly, to increase and develop the positive assets the patient possesses and, secondly, to reduce as far as possible the adverse factors in both the patient and his environment. The first aspect has been covered in the discussion of treatment, and the adverse environmental factors were mentioned in the section on prognosis. A further positive measure in rehabilitation is the organising of social agencies to provide sufficient support for the patient when he leaves hospital. These will be discussed under the social services in Chapter 20.

Nursing Care

The nursing care of schizophrenic patients can be considered, for convenience, as (*a*) the care of the acute episode, and (*b*) the management of the chronic state. It is hoped that by the correct treatment of the acute episode, the development of chronic features will be avoided or their extent limited.

Acute Episodes

The aims of observation of such patients are fourfold.

1. The confirmation or refutal of the diagnosis in patients having their first episode.
2. The recognition of signs suggesting improvement or worsening of their condition in response to treatment.
3. The recognition of evidence of drug side effects.
4. The noting of behaviour that precedes the onset of an acute episode in a patient who has been in hospital previously.

The diagnosis of schizophrenia, like most psychiatric conditions, depends on the presence or absence of certain symptoms that can be elicited only by careful and prolonged observation by a person who is aware of what to look for. Certain symptoms cannot be elicited directly, but only inferred from the observed behaviour of the patient. For example, patients may deny being hallucinated if asked, but that they are experiencing hallucinations may be suggested by their:

1. Shouting, talking, or laughing other than in response to people in their vicinity.
2. Apparent preoccupation or air of bewilderment.
3. Changing facial expressions, unrelated to events around them.
4. Tendency to unprovoked and impulsive acts of violence.

Hallucinations occur in a wide range of mental illnesses, but apart from in schizophrenia and severe depression, they are usually associated with alteration in the patient's level of consciousness.

Any behaviour suggesting that the patient is confused, not correctly orientated in space or time, or fluctuating in awareness should be noted and reported. Loss of consciousness, epileptiform attacks, transient paralyses, speech difficulties, must, of course, also be noted.

Delusional ideas may merge only by chance, when a related topic happens to be the subject of conversation, or when the patient has established a close enough relationship to be able to trust the nurse. When reporting ideas considered to be delusional the nurse should write down what the patient said, not merely comment that he is deluded. The nature of the delusion may be important, and the nurse must also remember that not all ideas which seem unlikely are, in fact, delusions!

Response to treatment should be recorded accurately and regularly under the following general headings:

1. Increase or diminution in florid symptoms.
2. Improvement or worsening in general behaviour.
3. Attitude to social activities.
4. Relationship to staff, patients, and relatives.
5. Performance at work.
6. Attitude to taking medication.

Avoid phrases such as 'patient is co-operative'. The phrase is meaningless unless co-operative in which way, with whom, and when, are stated. Drug side effects can present superficially as an increase in the symptoms of the disease and, therefore, it is important that the nurse should report accurately the changes in the patient's behaviour without recourse to jargon; thus 'the patient is more restless' may mean that he is pacing up and down, shouting, tense, and anxious, and potentially aggressive, or it may mean that the phenothiazine drugs he is having are making his legs feel uncomfortable in a way that he feels walking relieves. If asked, he may well describe this state of affairs, and as a consequence have his dosage decreased, whereas in the first instance the dosage would be increased.

The recognition of behaviour patterns that proceed an acute episode may mean that treatment can be instituted in time to abort an attack, with consequent benefit to both staff and patient.

In cases of catatonic stupor the nursing care is the same as that described under the care of the severely depressed patient. The care of the patient with acute schizophrenia corresponds to the care of the patient who is restless and aggressive, and is dealt with in Chapter 12.

However one regards the schizophrenic illnesses from the point of view of causation, it remains true that one result of the illness is a partial or complete breakdown of normal communication between the patient and the world around him. This creates difficulties in his interpersonal relationships, which can increase or perpetuate his symptoms and is of particular importance in the management of the chronic state.

In the acute phase it may be impossible to establish any real contact with the patient, but it is important to remember that even in the most disturbed phases the patient may be acutely aware of the attitudes of staff towards him and this may influence his subsequent relationship with them.

Nursing Aspects of the Chronic State

In nursing patients with chronic schizophrenia the aims can be summarised as, (1) the prevention of institutionalisation, and (2) resocialisation and rehabilitation. To achieve this, the nurse must form a therapeutic relationship with the patient, and the difficulties in doing this will be discussed.

The condition of 'institutional neurosis' has been clearly described by Russell Barton. The characteristic features are apathy, lack of initiative and interest, tendency to submit to authority and to surrender all responsibility for making plans or decisions. Such symptoms may arise in any person confined to an institution for prolonged periods and are not directly related to the disease that led to their admission. Many of the features described as part and parcel of chronic schizophrenia are probably the result of this confinement rather than the disease itself. Institutionalisation is treatable and preventable. It arises as the result of a number of factors that can be modified.

1. *Loss of Outside Contacts.* Many patients after being in hospital for some time are no longer visited by their friends or relatives, some of whom are well pleased to be rid of the burden. Others, however, will have stopped visiting because of the apparent lack of interest, or even hostility, exhibited by the patient. The nurse must try to explain to the relatives how important it is for the patient that a link with the world outside is maintained, however discouraging it may seem at times. Relatives may be traced and the patient encouraged to write to them, or failing that, the nurse can write on his behalf.

Every opportunity should be taken for encouraging the patient to go out into the community, and also for outsiders to come into the hospital. Holidays, day trips, visits to theatres, cinemas, shopping expeditions, and the like should form a regular part of ward routine.

The patient must be encouraged to take an interest in events in the outside world as reported in the newspapers, and on the radio or television. It is not sufficient to put the radio on loud, or sit the patient in front of a TV set—the reception of information must be supplemented by discussion in groups. The contribution of each patient must be encouraged.

2. *Loss of Personal Identity.* It has been pointed out by sociologists that everyone entering an institution is subjected to a 'stripping process' in which marks of individuality and personal identity are removed in order to make the individual more willing to conform to the rules of the institution. Clothes are replaced with a uniform, names replaced with numbers, photographs, wallets, handbags are taken away for 'safe-keeping'. Privacy is lost, and the person is expected to perform in public those acts that previously he was encouraged to keep private. Some patients react to this by becoming aggressive and obstructive, fiercely insisting on their right to be regarded as an individual, but others, particularly, those already unsure of themselves and predisposed to withdrawal, will surrender all personal responsibility.

3. *Loss of Personality.* In return for sacrificing their individuality the institution is prepared to take over all the responsibilities the patient previously had. This stems from the fact that this makes it easier to administrate such an institution, and it is justified on the false grounds that, because a patient experiences difficulties in dealing with certain responsibilities he is incapable of performing any.

To combat these factors it is necessary to: (*a*) increase personal identity, (*b*) modify staff attitudes, (*c*) increase the patients degree of responsibility, (*d*) establish a happy and permissive ward atmosphere, and (*e*) avoid long periods of idleness and boredom.

(*a*) Patients should not be deprived of those things that help to establish them as individuals. They should wear, and buy, their own clothes, which should be kept in individual lockers by their beds. They should be encouraged to decorate their rooms with photographs or pictures that have personal meaning for them.

(*b*) While the majority of staff in psychiatric hospitals are kind and well disposed towards their patients, the organisation of a traditional hospital tends to encourage an authoritarian attitude among the staff. This is revealed by the way in which patients, and junior staff, are *told* rather than *asked* to do things. If decision is questioned, the justification is often couched in terms of 'because I say so'. If patients are to develop initiative and increased self respect, this attitude must be modified by changing the system of ward organisation, and by helping staff to see and understand their attitude towards patients more clearly. Methods of achieving this are discussed under community therapy in Chapter 16.

(*c*) With a changed attitude, the staff can more readily allow and encourage the patients to assume responsibility for many of the functions of their daily life. The degree of responsibility the patient can cope with has to be judged in the light of knowledge about the particular patient, but in general it is better to err on the side of giving too much responsibility rather than too little.

(*d*) Tackling the above factors helps to establish a happy and permissive ward atmosphere, but this can occur only in a pleasant setting. Drab dirty wards with hideous furniture lower both staff and patient morale. The idea that 'they are too mad to care' is based on financial convenience rather than fact. Gay colours, light, and air probably have the same effects on psychotics as on the normal.

(*e*) To avoid long hours of boredom and loneliness it is necessary to have a detailed plan for each day of the week. However, the plan should be sufficiently flexible for unexpected events to be exploited and, also, sufficiently varied to prevent a dull routine developing.

A typical scheme is shown below:

PROGRAMME OF THE PATIENTS' DAY

MONDAY to FRIDAY

0700	Patients rise and wash.
0730	Breakfast.
0830–0930	Ward community meeting.
0930	Coffee break.
1000	Patients' activities in their respective groups, for example, sheltered workshops, industrial units, home group, gardening group, closed group.
1200	Lunch.
1245–1330	Ward community meeting.
1400	Patients' activities in their respective groups and group projects.
1600	Tea.

Evening activities vary each day—

1830–2100	(a) Dance in recreation hall.
	(b) Social in village hall; bingo session; fish and chips.
	(c) Cinema show in recreation hall.
	(d) Inter-ward socials.
	(e) Groups of patients go out to neighbouring hostels for psychiatric patients for the social evening.
2100	Night drinks, watching television.
2200	Bedtime.
Saturdays	Some patients go home for weekend leave, remaining patients follow sporting events during the afternoon. Social evenings are organised in the wards or units.
Sundays	Church services in the morning; community singing; piano recitals in the social centre. If the weather is fine, walks and organised outings and visits to various places of interest at an accessible distance from the hospital are arranged for the afternoon.

Relating to the Schizophrenic Patient

To establish a relationship with a patient suffering from schizo-phrenia, the nurse must to some extent be able to understand how different the external world appears to the patient, and how this creates the difficulties the patient has in responding in a normal way to other people.

There is considerable evidence that the processes of perception are disturbed in the schizophrenic. This applies to their perception of the world around them and their own inner world. When we look at a picture, listen to a talk, read an article, or just look out of the window we see or hear the event as a whole—individual items may claim our particular attention but we are able to fit them into the whole so that they make sense in relation to the rest. Occasionally, we have an experience in which some detail does not fit into the general picture; for example, if we hear a noise in the night and we can identify it as a door banging or a car starting up, it does not disturb us, but if it is a noise we cannot recognise or account for we feel anxious and apprehensive and either get up to investigate or pull the clothes over our heads and hope that it goes away.

It is possible that, for the schizophrenic, life is like this all the time: events do not relate to each other in the normal way; details stand out sharply against a blurred background, actions we take for granted break down into their component parts like watching an ultra-slow-motion film, so that to walk, smile, or talk requires an enormous conscious effort of organisation. Everyday life becomes extremely difficult and may well take on a terrifying air of menace. As a result, the patient may respond either by withdrawing as far as possible from it, or responding aggressively to it, on the principle of 'shoot first and ask questions afterwards'. In either event the patient attempts to limit his contact with other people and events occurring around him.

Establishing a relationship with such a patient is rather like establishing a relationship with a dog that has been ill-treated, and which either cowers away or bites the hand that feeds it. The first essential is endless patience; the relationship cannot be rushed, and initially the patient must be allowed to dictate the terms. For example, with a patient who is virtually mute it may be necessary to just sit with him for some time each day, either in silence or talking to him without expecting a reply, so that he learns that the nurse cares enough about him to spend time in this way and, also, that the nurse does not represent a threat to him. With the more accessible patients progress may be quicker, but the nurse must be prepared to 'learn the language' as many patients convey their needs or emotions by methods other than using words, or by using words in a way peculiar to themselves.

This is not to imply that everything a schizophrenic patient says is charged with symbolic meaning; some of it may just be disjointed words, but a great deal can be learnt if the nurse is prepared to try to understand what the patient is getting at. It is comparable to trying to communicate with a person who does not speak the same language: one becomes aware of gestures and expressions, one begins to recognise certain words and to exchange the equivalent word in one's own language. As the process continues, the degree of communication increases until you are both able to share common experiences in a meaningful way. This process requires toleration, patience, observation, and perserverance in high measure, for it may be slow and frustrating but the satisfaction of helping a patient, lost in a terrifying inner world, back to a more normal and less threatening existence is sufficient reward.

This type of relationship can be established only after close contact with the patient. Thus, the nurse will have to work closely with the patient throughout the day, not merely supervising his activities but playing an active part. She must be prepared to let the patient take his time, and while she may encourage the patient to greater effort, verbally and by example, she must resist the temptation to take over the task and do it herself. Like a child who never learns to dress himself, if his mother always insists on dressing him because it's quicker, so the patient who is not allowed to complete a task, however badly, never learns to act independently.

The nurse must treat the patient's symptoms seriously. It is no use telling a patient that his delusions are baseless, or that he is imagining his hallucinations. On the other hand, nor should the nurse join in these beliefs and act as if the delusions were true. The patient should be encouraged to talk of his ideas and experiences, and when mutual trust has been established he should be encouraged to discuss his ideas in terms of *why* he feels these things are happening to him. At this stage he can be helped to see that while his experiences are real to him, they represent a manifestation of his illness. When he is able to understand them better, his strange experiences become less terrifying and preoccupy him to a lesser extent, thus enabling him to take a greater interest in the external world. This increased interest and activity often diminishes still further the abnormal experiences, and the patient may reach a stage where he comes to terms with his illness and can lead a comparatively normal and satisfying life in spite of residual symptoms.

6 Organic Brain Syndromes—Acute

Unlike the rest of the organs of the body, the central nervous system does not produce new nerve cells to replace those lost as a result of ageing or damage.

This gradual loss of cells leads to a diminution in intellectual ability with age, which is shown in normal old people by their inability to learn new things, their tendency to remember events in their early life more clearly than recent happenings, and their reluctance to change their traditional way of life. In certain people, this cell loss is accelerated for an unknown reason so that they become prematurely aged and show, to an exaggerated degree, the changes mentioned. This condition is referred to as *senile dementia*. Similar changes sometimes occur in patients who are below the age of sixty-five, as a result of genetic factors or other unknown causes, and in these the condition is called *pre-senile dementia*. Various types of this illness are distinguished and will be described later.

At any age, the brain may be damaged as the result of disease or injury leading to intellectual deterioration, and loss of function of limbs, special senses, or such activities as speech. The end result depends on the area and extent of the damage, and the rate at which it occurs. It is possible to consider the symptoms and the care and treatment of the patients under two headings: (*a*) acute brain damage syndrome, and (*b*) chronic brain damage syndrome. The difference being not in rate of onset but in the fact that, in acute brain damage, there is the possibility of recovery if the disease process can be reversed or arrested, and in the chronic state, the changes cannot be reversed. It will be obvious that the acute illness can progress to a chronic state if not treated, and even with treatment a certain amount of irreparable damage may have occurred. Equally, acute episodes may arise in the course of chronic brain disease and may result in a worsening of the underlying condition or may clear up, leaving the patient neither worse nor better than prior to the acute episode.

Two Illustrative Stories

1. 'Hallo, fancy seeing you.' The patient stretched out his hand, his face breaking into a broad smile. 'I was only saying yesterday, that it was a long time since we last saw you.'

The doctor, who had never seen him in his life before, shook his hand with a slightly bewildered air, and muttered to the charge nurse: 'I don't know him do I?' 'Not as far as I'm aware', replied the charge nurse. 'He was admitted last night from the local police station. He was found wandering about and could give no account of himself. They have traced his wife from an address in his wallet and she is coming to the hospital this afternoon.'

The doctor tried to get a history from the patient, but it soon became obvious that he had no real recollection of events in the past few weeks, nor was he particularly reliable about more remote happenings. During the physical examination the doctor found that he had a fine tremor of the hands, and that he could no longer feel light touch or pin-prick over the lower part of his legs, and that these sensations were also impaired over his hands and forearms. He could not feel the vibration of a tuning fork when it was applied to his ankles or knees, and his muscles hurt when gently squeezed. In addition, the muscles of his legs and arms were weaker than normal and the reflexes were diminished (peripheral neuritis).

'It looks as if he has Korsakoff's syndrome', said the doctor. 'I bet he has been drinking heavily for some time.' This proved a correct guess, as his wife later stated that for months she had been worried about the way in which he had increased his drinking, neglecting everything in the process, including his diet. He had refused to see his doctor and had been abusive and violent towards his wife when she dared suggest this.

2. 'Wherever are you going Mrs Green?' asked the ward sister, as Mrs Green walked past her office, clad in nothing more substantial than a pair of slippers worn on the wrong feet.

In a rather dreamy voice she replied: 'I must go and cook the lunch. Bill will be home soon.'

'You cannot go anywhere dressed like that', said the sister leading her back to her bed. 'Put your nightie on before you catch cold.'

Mrs Green fumbled helplessly with the nightdress, eventually getting both arms through the opening designed for her head. The sister helped her into it, and then into bed. Seconds later she was out again and trying to get into the clothes cupboard. 'I want to ring up my husband', she explained.

While one of the nurses helped her back to bed, the sister rang for the house surgeon.

'Mrs Green is very restless and confused. Could you come and see her?'

She had been admitted four days before, following a car accident in which she had been knocked unconscious but had sustained no other injuries. For two days she had been deeply unconscious and then had become very restless and noisy; this had gradually been replaced by her present restlessness and confusion.

The house surgeon wrote her up for chlorpromazine (Largactil), and after her dose she slept for some hours. During the next few days she became quieter, and recognised that she was in hospital. She had no recollection of the past few days or of the accident. This loss of memory persisted, but she made an otherwise complete recovery.

Causes

The brain cells like all other living cells require that a number of environmental factors be kept relatively constant if they are to continue to live and carry out their normal functions. Their temperature must remain within a small range, and one of the commonest causes of acute brain disturbance is a rise in temperature due to an infection. Some people remain lucid at quite high temperature but others, and especially the very young and the very old, will show the clinical picture of *delirium* with a temperature only a few degrees above normal 37°C (98·6°F). A fall in body temperature such as may occur in myxoedema leads to stupor or coma, and in the early stages may produce a variety of mental disturbances. Such a fall in temperature may also occur in the elderly during very cold weather, and in all cases may be potentiated by *phenothiazine* drugs. The body temperature may be too low to be measured by a normal clinical thermometer, when a special low-reading rectal thermometer must be used.

The brain is well protected against physical injury by being enclosed in the bony skull and surrounded by a fluid cushion, but head injury as a result of traffic accidents is a feature of modern civilisation and is now a common cause of both acute and chronic brain damage. The clinical pictures resulting from head injury will be described later.

The cells require a constant supply of nutriments consisting of carbohydrates, fats, protein, and vitamins. The brain cells are particularly dependent on an adequate supply of vitamins, and while the fully developed picture of vitamin deficiency is comparatively rare in this country, milder states with predominantly mental symptoms are not uncommon, especially in the elderly or those who, due to other mental or physical illness, are not taking an adequate diet.

Glucose is the main source of energy for the brain cells, and inadequate amounts rapidly produce disturbances in brain function. Too little glucose in the blood is called *hypoglycaemia*, which produces confusion and behaviour disorders that rapidly pass into stupor or coma if untreated. This condition arises most commonly in diabetics who are having insulin and who take too big a dose or do not cover the insulin with a sufficient intake of carbohydrates in their diet. It can also occur in patients with an insulin-secreting tumour of the pancreas. Diabetics may also develop mental changes progressing to coma if they neglect to take their insulin. The blood sugar level is then higher than normal (n = 80–120 mg/100 of blood) but it is in a form the cells cannot utilise.

Brain cells require oxygen, and die if deprived of it for more than about 5 minutes. Oxygen is conveyed to the cells by the red blood cells, which contain haemoglobin. The blood takes up oxygen in the lungs and gives it up in the tissues, absorbing in return the carbon dioxide produced by the cells in the course of using the carbohydrates to produce energy. Lack of available oxygen can arise in a variety of ways. The mental changes resulting from lack of oxygen vary according to the degree of deprivation and its duration. Acute anoxia may arise as the result of sudden blood loss from injury, from interference with the exchange of oxygen in the lung due to obstruction of the airways, by replacement of oxygen with other gases such as carbon monoxide, or as a result of interruption in the pumping activity of the heart.

Chronic oxygen shortage can result from lack of haemoglobin (anaemias), chronic lung disease, chronic heart disease, and narrowing of the arteries by atheroma or their blockage by blood clot (thrombosis).

Not only must the cell receive adequate supplies of these substances, but, in addition, the waste products of metabolism, carbon dioxide and urea must be removed by the lungs and kidneys respectively.

One of the most common causes of acute brain syndrome is some form of poisoning, and the favourite poison used is alcohol (almost always self administered, without conscious suicidal intention!) closely followed by barbiturates (with conscious suicidal intent). The signs of acute alcoholic intoxication are well known and are similar to those of any other anaesthetic drug. Alcohol may also produce acute brain damage, either by its direct effects on cerebral vitamins or because the person who drinks excessively almost invariably eats inadequately. This type of damage produces the *dysmnesic syndrome* described below.

Although the causes of acute brain damage are legion, the clinical picture resulting tends to take the form of either a *delirium*, a *confusional state*, or a *dysmnesic syndrome*.

Symptoms

Delirium. A patient with delirium shows clouding of consciousness; that is, he seems less than normally aware of events occurring around him and less able to respond in the correct way. He may appear bewildered, restless, and confused. His thoughts may be dreamlike, or incoherent, and he may be experiencing illusions or hallucinations. This state is frequently associated with apprehension or extreme fear. The symptoms tend to be more marked at night.

While such conditions are usually transient and respond to treatment of the underlying illness, occasionally they persist for some weeks. Delirium may be produced by infective illnesses, with fever, toxic conditions, metabolic disturbances such as uraemia, deficiency diseases such as pellagra, heart failure, or head injury.

Confusional State. This term is not entirely satisfactory and the alterative name of *subacute delirious state* has been suggested. The condition consists of incoherence of speech, clouding of consciousness which fluctuates in severity, and a state of perplexity. The severity of symptoms is less than in delirium, but may persist for weeks or months, outlasting the underlying physical illness.

Dysmnesic Syndrome. This refers to those conditions in which the main feature is difficulty with memory. The recall of recent events is the most seriously impaired aspect, though memory for remote events may also be affected. The patient frequently shows increased suggestibility and can sometimes be persuaded to 'read' from a blank sheet of paper. The combination of increased suggestibility and recent memory loss leads to confabulation, That is, the patient covers up for the gaps in his memory by inventing the required information. Thus, a patient who has been confined to bed for several days may describe in detail how he had been to work that morning. The patient's mood is often euphoric and he is usually disoriented for time and place. Such conditions are comparatively common after head injuries.

A special form of this syndrome is that associated with deficiency of the vitamin B complex, in which the mental changes are accompanied by a polyneuritis. This condition may be produced by excessive alcohol intake and dietary deficiencies. It was first described by Sergei Korsakoff, in 1887, and is often referred to as Korsakoff's psychosis. A further variation is Wernike encephalopathy, both of which are described under alcoholism in Chapter 3.

Dysmnesic symptoms may arise from psychological causes, and there is a syndrome described by Ganser in which people confined in prisons develop a pseudo-dementia, as a means of avoiding their punishment. They tend to give approximate answers rather than failing to answer at all. For example, when asked how many days there are in a week they may say six or eight.

Treatment of Acute Brain Syndrome
The treatment is primarily directed at curing the underlying condition, but in addition it is often necessary to try to control the mental symptoms and improve the functioning of the brain cells. It has been demonstrated that in most cases of acute brain damage there is interference with the enzyme systems of the brain cells and that some of the most important enzymes and coenzymes involved are vitamins of the B complex. Under conditions of physical illness the demand for such vitamins is increased, and at the same time intake may be reduced by vomiting or loss of appetite. Therefore, in many cases of acute brain syndrome vitamin supplements are given by intramuscular or intravenous injection. This sometimes produces a striking improvement in the mental state.

The restlessness, agitation, and apprehension are best controlled by the use of major tranquillisers such as the phenothiazines. Hemi-neverin has been claimed to be particularly useful in such problems. The use of barbiturates should be avoided. Chloral is a useful hypnotic, but paraldehyde, which is always said to be a particularly safe drug, may lead to increased confusion and restlessness.

Apart from curing the underlying disease, the major factor in determining the outcome of such cases is the skilled nursing care. Many such patients could be managed in general hospital wards were it not for the anxiety they provoke in the nursing and medical staff.

Nursing Care

Skilled observation of such a patient is essential for correctly diagnosing both the nature of the mental disturbance and the under-lying illness.

Due to the fluctuating level of impaired awareness formal examina-tion by the doctor may coincide with a period of lucidity, so that correct diagnosis may depend on the nurse accurately observing and recording any episodes during which the patient demonstrates that he is not normally aware of his surroundings. The times at which the patient becomes confused should be carefully noted, and their relationship to other events such as meals, time of day, administra-tion of drugs, or the performance of other nursing procedures. These factors are important because the patient with a mild degree of disorientation, clouding of consciousness, and apprehension may be able to control his anxiety and restlessness until subjected to the extra stress of having an injection or other potentially painful treatment. The relationship to diet may be important in cases of spontaneous hypoglycaemia, while in patients in which the con-fusion is more marked after administration of drugs, it is probable that mental symptoms are being caused.

The nursing care of the acutely disturbed patient suffering from either organic or functional psychotic states is discussed separately under physical illness and special nursing problems in Chapter 11.

7 Organic Brain Syndromes—Chronic

Two Illustrative Stories

1. 'She is trying to poison me. She's after my money.' The benign-looking old man said, sitting up in bed, his dinner dripping slowly down the wall, the plate lying smashed on the floor. His daughter stood crying, upset by the apparent violence of his hatred of her. Her husband came rushing in having heard the crash and the shouting.

'Whatever is going on?' he asked, turning to his father-in-law. 'She has looked after you wonderfully. Ever since your stroke she has brought your meals up to you, cleaned you, and done everything for you, and this is all the thanks we get. Well I've had enough. It's the hospital for you, like it or not.'

His wife, however, was reluctant to let this happen, and said that she would look after him, if only he wasn't so aggressive and would eat the meals she cooked. Their family doctor prescribed some tablets, and in a few days the old man seemed to have lost the idea that his daughter was trying to kill him.

The weeks went by, until one night the family were awakened by shouts from the old man's room. They rushed in to find him trying to get out of bed, in spite of his paralysed leg, shouting that the room was on fire. They managed to get him back into bed and sent for the doctor.

'He's developed pneumonia, and in view of his restlessness I think we had better try to get him into hospital.' the doctor decided.

The general hospitals had no available beds, so he was admitted to the sick ward of the psychiatric hospital. He remained restless and confused, not seeming to know where he was, or recognising his relatives when they visited. At times he talked when no one was near. Gradually, the treatment with antibiotics cured the pneumonia and he became much more alert and less disturbed.

He could not say how old he was, nor could he perform simple tests of general knowledge. In addition, his right arm and leg were paralysed, and he had difficulty in finding the correct word when trying to ask for something. He had lost control of his bladder, but usually indicated when he wished to empty his bowels.

Once his temperature was down to normal he was sat out of bed, and each day he was encouraged to do a little more for himself. After a few weeks he was able to feed himself quite well with his left hand and could manage a few yards walking with the aid of a special support. By dint of taking him to the lavatory every few hours he regained some control over his bladder. He continued to make good progress until one day he suddenly slumped forward in his chair with a cry of pain, and almost before anyone could reach him, he died. Post mortem showed a clot of blood obstructing one of the main arteries supplying the heart. The artery itself was very thick-walled and the space in which the blood ran was much narrowed.

2. 'Granny is getting to be a real problem. I don't think she can go on living on her own much longer. The neighbours will start talking about us if we leave her there. She is going to kill herself if she isn't careful, the way she wanders out into the road; and the other day she went to boil the kettle, turned on the gas, but forgot to light it. Thank heavens I was there! She hadn't even eaten the meal the welfare had brought her—it was covered in mould—and I don't think she has had a bath in weeks. You'll have to do something.'

Bill sighed. What could he do? They had no spare room she could occupy.

'I'll see her doctor about her—perhaps they can get her into one of those old folk's homes or into hospital.'

'She'll not like that. You know how independent she is', said his wife.

'I wonder if you could come and assess an old lady for me?' said the GP. 'She isn't fit to live on her own any more, but I'm not sure whether she needs hospital treatment or just local authority hostel accommodation.'

The psychiatrist and the old lady's family doctor met outside her house, and were greeted by the old lady who said: 'Come in, Fred, and you George, it's a long time since I saw you.' She seemed very happy to see them, though, obviously mistaking them for relatives. They explained who they were and she said: 'Doctors! I don't need a doctor, I'm perfectly well.' She was adamant that she would not be physically examined and became quite angry at the suggestion. A few moments later, however, she was smiling again and was quite prepared to try to answer questions.

She said she was forty years old. Yes, she was married but her husband was at work and the children were at school. No, she didn't know what year it was, but she thought it was spring, and of course, it was Friday. She answered quite quickly, and her answers were relevant but incorrect. (It was Monday 15 August 1966. She was seventy-four years old, and her husband had died eight years previously.)

After discussing the problem, the psychiatrist said: 'She is obviously severely demented, and not capable of looking after herself at present, but without a physical examination and a more complete assessment of her I cannot say whether Part III accommodation would be suitable. She had better come into the psychogeriatic unit for a few weeks.'

They suggested this to the old lady, who refused to co-operate. The son was contacted and advised that if he would apply for her admission the two doctors would sign the recommendation for her compulsory admission under Section 25 of the Mental Health Act. In due course this was done, and after a period of assessment it was decided that she needed only a minimum of supervision and that her physical health was quite satisfactory. She was transferred to an old folks home, in exchange for another old lady who had become doubly incontinent and thus beyond the scope of the staff of the home.

In some conditions death of brain cells occurs with resulting impairment in mental functioning. The nature and degree of impairment will depend upon the extent of cell loss, the areas most affected, and the rate at which the loss occurs. The clinical picture presented by the patient will depend not only upon these factors, but to a considerable extent on previous personality, as certain traits become exaggerated, or others, which have previously been kept in check, emerge because of the patient's diminished ability to control or recognise them.

While the difficulties experienced by the patient are similar whatever the underlying cause, and their care and treatment present the same basic problems, it is usual to classify the dementing illnesses both on the basis of age of onset and the nature of the underlying cause. The possible causes have been outlined previously, and the more important subgroups of the dementing illnesses are described below.

Senile Dementia

Whether this condition should be regarded as a disease, or merely an extreme variation of a process common to all ageing human beings is debatable. The result of brain cell loss is a progressive deterioration in all aspects of the patient's personality, that is to say, intellectual performance, emotional response and control, and personal habits are all affected to a greater or lesser degree.

Intellectual Functions

The most striking feature is usually the patient's inability to remember events that have occurred recently. In some, this leads to *confabulation*. Failure of recent memory may prevent the patient dealing with any new information, so that although shown where his bed is, or where the lavatory is located, within minutes he has forgotten. This difficulty may be experienced not only for remembering places but also for time relationships, so that the patient no longer knows the hour, the day, the month, or the year, and is unable to say how old he is. Individuals may also be forgotten, so that the patient does not recognise his relatives. Such patients are said to be *disorientated* for time, place, or person.

Memory for distant events may, in comparison, be relatively good, and the patient tends to retreat more and more into his past, which seems clear, vivid, and immediate, compared to the cloudy, puzzling, chaotic, and threatening present.

Impaired recent memory may also lead to misinterpretation of events, and in some patients may lead to delusions, usually of persecution. A common example is of a patient who forgets where he has put something, becomes convinced it has been stolen, and accuses his relatives of robbing him.

The difficulty experienced in dealing with new tasks often results in the patient losing interest in everything that does not obviously and immediately affect him personally.

Emotional Response and Control

To some extent the emotional state may reflect the degree to which the patient is aware of his difficulties. When insight is retained, the patient commonly feels depressed or anxious. As the degree of dementia increases it may be replaced by a state of insightless euphoria. Typically, however, the associated emotional state is one of lability, so that the patient fluctuates between laughter and tears, sometimes without appropriate reason. Yet other patients become suspicious, hostile, and, at times, aggressive.

Personal Habits

As the patient becomes less aware of his surroundings, and of himself, and less able to deal with the problems of everyday living as a result of declining intellectual power and emotional control, his personal habits tend to deteriorate. Other patients remain aware of the social rules that govern their behaviour, but to their distress they can no longer carry out the necessary performances. Thus, the patient neglects to, or is unable to, tie knots, fasten zips and buttons, get arms and legs into the appropriate openings, and otherwise make sure that he is properly dressed. His clothes may also reflect, by the number and variety of stains and spots that cover them, his inability to manage cutlery. Personal cleanliness is neglected, and in many cases, control of bladder and bowel function is either lost or is performed without regard to the normal social conventions. Urinary and faecal incontinence is a very important factor in leading to admission of demented patients to hospital, and if it can be controlled it may enable the patient to return home.

The cause of senile dementia is not known, nor is there any effective treatment that halts or reverses the condition. Examination of the brain shows general shrinking with dilation of the ventricles. Microscopically, the brain shows loss of cells, the presence of plaques which stain darkly with silver, and alteration in the fibrils of the nerve cells.

The disease progresses until eventually the patient becomes helpless and virtually bedridden, death finally results from bronchopneumonia or one of the other complications of prolonged confinement to bed.

Arteriosclerotic Dementia

Either as a result of raised blood pressure from other causes, or due to some dietetic factor, blood vessels may become inelastic, irregular, thickened, and narrowed. Similar changes may arise as a result of ageing alone. An individual may have such changes in only some of his arteries, for instance those supplying his legs or his heart or his brain, while another may have all these affected. The result of these changes is that less blood reaches the tissues supplied by the affected arteries, which, in turn, may lead to impaired function or even death of the cells. The blood flow is slowed and the rough internal walls of the artery encourage clot formation so that the blood supply may fail completely, with inevitable death of the cells in the area supplied. Conversely, if the blood pressure is high the smaller blood vessels may rupture and the escaping blood will destroy the brain tissue. Such events are referred to as 'cerebral vascular accidents'.

The effects of this alteration in the blood vessels supplying the brain may either be a general dementia similar to senile dementia, or the loss of specific brain functions, such as speech, voluntary movement of a limb or limbs, or the appreciation of sensation. In many cases both dementia and focal signs develop. The brain damage that occurs may lead to the development of epileptic fits of various kinds.

There is no specific treatment, and management of such patients is the same as for other forms of chronic brain syndrome.

Dementia Secondary to Infection

The most important of these conditions is that produced by the treponema pallidum. This spirochaete is the causative organism of syphilis, a disease acquired by having intercourse with an infected person. The organism gets into the blood stream and may pass to any part of the body. In about 4 per cent of people who catch the disease the central nervous system is affected, the condition then being known as neurosyphilis. This may take one of four forms.

1. Cerebral or Meningo-vascular Syphilis
In this type, damage is limited to the tissues covering the brain (meninges) and to the blood vessels supplying it. The membranes become thickened, and the blood vessels become narrowed. The mental symptoms tend to resemble those of arteriosclerotic dementia.

2. Tabes Dorsalis
In this form, damage is limited to the posterior tracts of the spinal cord, causing impairment of the patient's ability to recognise where

his limbs are in space. Thus, he has difficulty in walking, particularly in the dark or with his eyes closed. For full details of the neurological signs a textbook of neurology should be consulted.

3. General Paralysis of the Insane (General Paresis)

This is the form of most concern to psychiatrists as it is in this variety that the mental faculties are most affected. The condition usually develops many years after the original infection, and may start with mental changes or physical signs.

Physical Signs

1. *Speech disorders.* The patient can no longer get his tongue round words, so his speech becomes slurred in a way that suggests he may be drunk.
2. *Pupils.* In about 50 per cent of patients the pupils no longer constrict or dilate in response to changes in the light, but continue to respond to accommodation. These changes were described by Argyll Robertson in 1869 and are known by his name.

Mental Changes

The condition, in its early stages, may mimic almost any mental disorder. The commonest form probably is one of increasing dementia without special features, and the next most common is that of dementia associated with euphoria. The so-called 'expansive form' tends to be the type most people think of when asked to describe the symptoms of GPI, but it is probably no commoner than the type in which depressive features are dominant. Other patients present a clinical picture indistinguishable from schizophrenia.

The diagnosis of GPI can be made in such cases only by the presence of physical signs and by special investigations. It is for this reason that all patients admitted to mental hospitals, irrespective of their diagnosis, have their blood tested for the Wassermann reaction, and other tests designed to demonstrate the presence of a syphilitic infection.

Wassermann test. When spirochaetes invade the body they stimulate the formation of an antibody. This antibody can be detected in the blood and/or cerebrospinal fluid by a special test named after its discoverer, Wassermann. Positive results occur occasionally in conditions other than syphilis, such as glandular fever, leprosy, malaria, and yaws. The test is of value, not only for diagnosis, but also as a measure of the patients response to treatment.

Kahn. This is a more sensitive test, and is thus more likely be affected by other conditions apart from syphilis, leading to 'false positive' results.

Various other serological tests are used when doubt about the diagnosis cannot be resolved by the results of the WR and Kahn tests.

MENTAL CHANGES FOLLOWING HEAD INJURY

In these days of fast vehicles severe head injuries are becoming increasingly common. As neurosurgeons improve their techniques, more and more victims avoid death but survive with severe brain damage in the long-stay wards of mental hospitals. The effects on mental function of trauma can be divided into three groups. The first two groups have already been described in general terms in this chapter and Chapter 8, Epilepsy.

1. Acute
   (*a*) Concussion
   (*b*) Coma
   (*c*) Korsakoff's syndrome

2. Chronic—Organic
   (*a*) Post-traumatic personality disorders
   (*b*) Dementia with or without focal damage
   (*c*) Post-traumatic epilepsy

3. Chronic—Neurotic

Post-traumatic anxiety. This state may develop after even comparatively trivial head injuries. There is often an element of 'compensation neurosis' present. That is, the patient anticipates compensation from insurance, employer, or state, and consciously or unconsciously feels that if his symptoms persist, he is likely to get more money. Such cases often undergo a miraculous improvement when the cash is paid out.

The symptoms complained of usually resemble those experienced immediately after recovering consciousness, i.e. headache, dizziness, impaired memory, and fatigue. Development of this condition may be encouraged by over-cautious handling of the patient in the early days after he has regained consciousness. It may be avoided by early mobilisation, short hospitalisation, and rapid return to work. The quicker any financial claims can be settled the better are the patient's chances of returning to full function.

Cerebral Neoplasms

Neoplasms (new growths) may be benign or malignant. Those that grow inside the skull may arise from the coverings of the brain, from brain cells, or from cells concerned with the supporting structures and blood vessels of the brain. Both benign and malignant growths produce symptoms in one or more of the following ways:

1. By destruction of surrounding brain cells.
2. By irritation of brain cells through pressure on them.
3. By obstructing the free flow of the cerebrospinal fluid through the ventricles and around the brain.

The signs that suggest the presence of an intracranial neoplasm are a combination of some of the following:

1. Headache.
2. Giddiness.
3. Vomiting.
4. Slow pulse.
5. Papilloedema: obstruction to venous return from the retina by raised intracranial pressure causes swelling of the optic discs.
6. Fits.
7. Progressive dementia.
8. Focal neurological signs.

Tumours arising in the frontal lobes of the brain are particularly likely to produce personality changes and progressive dementia. Those arising on the temporal lobe frequently cause some form of temporal lobe fits, as described in Chapter 8.

Primary Presenile Dementias

Alzheimer's Disease

The changes occurring in the brain in this disease are identical to those described under senile dementia, but the disease may start at a much younger age. Clinically, the patient appears prematurely aged, with personality changes and impaired memory. Speech difficulties are almost always a feature, and this becomes gradually worse until the patient is mute or incoherent. The muscles become stiff, and walking is difficult, though the patient may be hyperactive. Terminally, the patient is confined to bed, severely demented, totally aphasic, and incontinent. There is no treatment that ameliorates the condition, and death, when it comes, usually occurs from broncho-pneumonia.

Pick's Disease

The brain cell loss in this condition, unlike Alzheimer's disease, is restricted to the frontal and temporal lobes. It is commoner in women, but the disease is much rarer than Alzheimer's disease. Clinically it is virtually impossible to distinguish the two conditions, so that the final diagnosis depends on post-mortem examination. It is possible that these conditions fall into the category of auto-immune reactions.

Huntington's Chorea

This is a rare condition characterised by a combination of dementia and involuntary movements, due to degeneration of cells in the cortex, and extra pyramidal nuclei. It is an inherited disease, due to a dominant gene. This means that if one parent has the condition there is a 50 per cent chance that an offspring may also have the disease.

The symptoms usually start between the ages of thirty and forty-five, though it may be possible to detect evidence of brain damage by psychological tests at a much earlier age. The first signs are often a change in temperament, progressing to a disintegration of the personality. Attention, judgement, and memory failure develop at the same time.

The choreiform movements of the limbs, are jerky, irregular, and clumsy and in the early stages the patient may try to turn them into apparently voluntary movements, such as brushing back the hair, or crossing the legs.

As the disease advances, walking becomes impossible, the patient is confined to bed, swallowing becomes impaired, and death occurs generally, within about fifteen years from onset of symptoms. There is no fundamental treatment, but some relief from the symptoms can be obtained by the use of anti-parkinsonian agents, and tranquillisers.

Nursing Aspects

The nursing aspects of patients with chronic brain syndrome include:

1. Care of the physically ill.
2. Special nursing problems of the restless and confused patients.
3. Habit training.
4. Prevention of institutionalisation.

These aspects are dealt with in detail in the respective chapters.

8 Epilepsy

Illustrative Story

It was a lovely warm day, and John was thinking about the gardening he was going to do when he got home. The bus, as always, was late. Suddenly, John felt a curious sinking feeling in his stomach; the thought 'I'm going to have a fit' had hardly formed itself in his mind when the world exploded into blackness.

He's had a fit! He's bitten his tongue! Wasn't it awful? Good job he was on the pavement. Should we get an ambulance? Give him air! Make room please! John could hear the voices coming and going. They are talking about me, he thought. I must tell them I am all right, and I must get up. But the right words would not come out and his legs and arms would not obey him. He felt like a puppet with no one to pull the strings. Yet, strangely, he was on his feet and a voice—surely not his—was saying: 'I'm OK now. No, no, I don't need an ambulance.' His head ached with the effort as he began to push his way through the crowd which reluctantly parted to allow him to pass. He continued on his way, turning left at the crossroads, then right and right again. He had walked for about ten minutes, when suddenly he stopped and looked round him with a bewildered expression. 'What am I doing here?' he asked himself. 'I should be catching the bus home. Where on earth am I?' Gradually he realised what must have happened: 'Another of my damn turns', he said aloud, startling an old lady who happened to be passing.

Introduction and Classification

Like all living cells the neurones in the brain use glucose and oxygen to produce energy. In brain cells, however, some of this energy is in the form of electricity. The changes in electrical activity of the brain can be recorded by using a machine called an electro-encephalogram (EEG). When a recording is made with the subject relaxing, with closed eyes in a darkened room, the changes in activity follow a regular pattern, occurring at a rate of approximately ten cycles a second. This rhythm is called *alpha rhythm*, and it is replaced by irregular, rapid, low-amplitude activity if the subject opens his eyes or indulges in any form of mental effort. The rhythm also changes as the subject passes into sleep.

As a result of a wide range of causes, abnormal electrical activity may occur in the brain from time to time. These abnormal discharges are of greater voltage than normal and may occur at rates either slower or faster than ten a second.

The condition in which these abnormal discharges occur is called epilepsy, and it can be divided into different sub-groups either on the basis of the clinical picture produced, or on the basis of the underlying cause. The classifications tend to overlap because, to some extent, the clinical picture produced by the abnormal discharge depends upon:

(*a*) The area of brain in which the discharge arises.
(*b*) The extent to which the discharge spreads to other parts of the brain.
(*c*) The length of time for which the discharge persists.
(*d*) The state of function of the brain as a whole.

The following is a common way of dividing up the epilepsies:

(1) petit mal; (2) grand mal; (3) 'focal' fits; (4) temporal lobe epilepsy; (5) status epilepticus.

1. Petit Mal

This term used to be used to describe any attack in which the patient had only a short loss of consciousness without a generalised convulsion. It should now be restricted to cases in which there is a characteristic EEG finding of three per second spike and wave discharges. The clinical picture is one of brief frequent attacks of impaired consciousness, during which the patient may blink rhythmically, nod his head, stare, jerk his arms, or fall to the floor. Attacks usually appear before or at puberty, tend to disappear as the patient gets older, and are comparatively rare in adults. No cause can be demonstrated in the majority of cases.

2. Grand Mal

This term is applied to attacks in which a generalised convulsion occurs, probably as a result of the abnormal discharge involving both those areas of the brain that control consciousness, and muscle tone. Clinically, the attack can be divided into three parts.

A. *The aura.* In about three-fifths of all cases, the patient experiences some form of warning of an attack. The particular form this takes depends on the part of the brain in which the discharge arises. It may consist of a complex mental state, such as a feeling that the event has been experienced before (*deja vu*), or that everything has become unreal. The aura may involve one of the special senses so that the patient experiences hallucinations of taste, smell, sight, or hearing. Giddiness is a common aura. General sensations may occur, especially involving the stomach. An involuntary movement of a limb or of the head may occur.

B. *The convulsion.* The patient loses consciousness and falls to the ground. The muscles go into a state of *tonic* contraction, that is, they contract as hard as they can. The body takes up a position that reflects the relative strength of the different muscle group. The neck is extended, the head may be rotated to one side. The upper arms are drawn in towards the trunk and are flexed at the elbow and wrist. The fingers are straight but bent at the knuckles. The thumb is drawn over towards the little finger. The back may be arched, and the lower limbs are extended, the feet tending to turn inwards.

The respiratory muscles are also in spasm and the respiration ceases so that the patient becomes progressively cyanosed. The *tonic phase* lasts for up to half a minute and then gives way to the *clonic phase* in which the sustained muscular contraction gives way to short sharp jerks. During this phase the tongue may be bitten, and the patient may be incontinent of urine, or less often, of faeces. The intervals between the muscular contractions become longer, and they finally cease.

C. *Post-convulsive phase.* After the clonic phase the patient remains unconscious either for a few minutes or up to half an hour. After recovering consciousness some patients sleep for several hours. Most patients are mentally normal as soon as they recover consciousness, but in some, abnormal mental states persist for some time. These will be described later.

3. 'Focal' fits

This group includes cases in which the discharge remains localised in the area in which it arises, or spreads only to relatively close parts. At times a patient who has localised fits may have a grand mal seizure because the discharge has spread further afield. The symptoms produced by a focal discharge depend on the area of the brain affected. If the motor cortex is affected the attack may start with the spasm of the thumb, big toe, or the angle of the mouth, gradually spreading to involve other muscle groups. If the sensory cortex is the site of the focus, tingling or painful sensations may be felt in part of, or in the whole of, one side of the body.

The commonest and most important of the focal epilepsies are those in which the abnormal discharge arises in the anterior temporal lobe.

4. Temporal Lobe Epilepsy

This condition is often called psychomotor epilepsy. If the abnormal discharge remains localised to the anterior temporal lobe, there are no clinical signs, but when it spreads outside this area the patient may behave in a variety of ways. He may become confused, vague, or negativistic and may perform quite complicated activities in an automatic way, being unaware of his actions. He may run, jump, fight, dance, shout, or cry, the attack lasting from a few seconds to several minutes. During an attack the patient may experience hallucinations or illusions. He may have a disturbed sense of reality of the world or of his own body. In some patients the attack consists of brief periods resembling mania or schizophrenia. Other patients have outbursts of uncontrollable rage and may be extremely violent.

In addition to the acute, short-lasting attacks, about half the patients with a temporal lobe focus show evidence of a continuing psychiatric disorder. Some show a personality disorder, while others have a psychotic illness. This aspect of their illness does not usually respond to treatment with anti-convulsant drugs and often proves more of a handicap than the fits themselves.

5. Status Epilepticus

This condition consists of repeated seizures without the patient regaining consciousness in the intervals between convulsions. If the cycle is not interrupted it may lead to death, or severe residual brain damage. It is now usually treated by giving intravenous or intramuscular valium. Intramuscular sodium amytal may also be used.

Causes of Epilepsy

An epileptic fit can be produced in anyone if sufficient stimulus, i.e. an electrical current, is applied to the brain. Some people require only a minimal stimulus to produce a fit, while others are extremely resistant. The degree to which one's brain is resistant probably depends on inherited factors. Some people develop fits without any apparent precipitating cause—a condition referred to as idiopathic epilepsy. In other cases it is possible to demonstrate the precipitating factor. A wide range of conditions can produce fits, and they can be divided into *local* (within the skull) and *general*.

LOCAL

1. *Trauma.* Brain injury is especially liable to occur when a baby is being delivered. In later life, penetrating injuries of the brain are very likely to produce epilepsy.
2. *Space-occupying Lesions.* Tumours or blood clots in the brain substance or within the skull.
3. *Inflammatory Conditions.* Meningitis, encephalitis, cerebral abscess, neurosyphilis, etc.
4. *Congenital Abnormalities.* Congenital diplegia, etc.
5. *Degenerative Conditions.* Presenile dementias, etc.
6. *Circulatory Disorders.* Arteriosclerosis, haemorrhage, thrombosis, embolism, hypertensive encephalopathy, and cerebral ischaemia.

GENERAL

1. *Toxic Agents.* A wide range of drugs may produce fits. Convulsions may also be caused by withdrawing drugs, such as alcohol or barbiturates, from patients who are addicted to them.
2. *Oxygen Lack.* Due to asphyxia, gas poisoning, etc.
3. *Metabolic Disorders.* Uraemia, hepatic coma, hypoglycaemia, alkalosis.
4. *Endocrine Disorders.* Hypoparathyroidism.
5. *Acute Infections.* Especially in children.

Psychological Factors

In patients who suffer from epileptic attacks, emotional stress may precipitate an attack or lead to a greater frequency of fits.

Psychiatric Aspects of Epilepsy

About one in ten of the population show some abnormality in their EEG, but only one in two hundred have any form of fits. Of these, the vast majority with or without treatment live otherwise perfectly normal lives in the community. A small minority have to be cared for either in special epileptic communities or in the wards of mental hospitals. Those in the psychiatric hospital fall into one of the following categories:

1. Those in whom the fit is of the psychomotor type, and during which the patient behaves in a violent and dangerous manner.
2. Those who in addition to having psychomotor attacks also have coexistent psychotic or personality disorders.
3. Those in whom recurrent fits have led to organic brain damage.
4. Patients with severe neurotic difficulties arising as a result of their own or society's attitude towards epilepsy.
5. Patients with organic brain damage in whom fits occur as a secondary and relatively unimportant complication.
6. Short-term admissions of patients with mental changes occurring in the post-convulsive phase of a fit.

Treatment of Epilepsy

The aim of drug treatment in epilepsy is to raise the resistance of the brain cells so that the abnormal discharges are limited to the area in which they arise, and do not produce clinical symptoms. The choice of drugs depends to some extent on the type of fit, and it is often necessary to combine different drugs before control is obtained. There are a great many anticonvulsant drugs, of which the following are commonly used (the trade names are given in parentheses):

PHENOBARBITONE
A long-acting barbiturate which is effective in controlling epilepsy but has the disadvantage of tending to make the patient drowsy.
　　Daily dose: 120 to 480 mg.

PRIMIDONE (*Mysoline*)
Similar in effect to phenobarbitone, with similar side effects. Used in grand mal.
　　Daily dose: 250 to 2,000 mg.

HYDANTOIN (*Epineutin*)

Often given in combination with phenobarbitone. Does not cause drowsiness but may produce dizziness, nausea, and unsteadiness. In some cases skin rashes, or overgrowth of the gums may occur. Not used for petit mal.

Daily dose: 200 to 600 mg.

SULTHIAME (*Ospolot*)

Especially used in temporal lobe epilepsy. May make the patient overbreathe, feel drowsy, or suffer gastro-intestinal upsets.

Daily dose: 400 to 800 mg daily.

TROXIDONE (*Triolione*)

Particularly effective in petit mal seizures, but may lead to more frequent or more severe attacks of grand mal. The eyes of some patients become very sensitive to bright light on this drug.

Nursing Care

In some hospitals, the care of the epileptic patient is directed to eliminating, as far as is humanly possible, all risk that the patient may harm himself during a fit. Most people would agree that the restrictions this imposes are so great as to deprive the patient of leading any kind of meaningful life. It is necessary to accept that life for everyone entails some degree of risk and eventually proves fatal; the epileptic should therefore be encouraged to lead as full a life as possible, restricted only by simple precautions against obvious dangers. Thus, they should be able to work, but not at jobs which involve unguarded machinery, climbing heights, working close to open water or fires, or driving vehicles.

The avoidance of fits depends on regular medication, and the nurse must help the patient to understand the need for taking the tablets as prescribed. If the patient refuses to take his drugs, the doctor should be notified.

Observation of a patient may reveal changes in mood or behaviour before a fit occurs. The recognition of these signs may mean that the fit can be avoided by taking appropriate action.

During a fit, the patient should be prevented from injuring himself against articles of furniture. There is little purpose in attempting to insert something between the patient's teeth, as this may produce more damage than it prevents. As soon as the convulsion has terminated the care of the patient is as that of someone who is unconscious—the most important aspect being to keep a clear airway. The mouth must be opened, and any obstruction such as dentures or food removed. If the patient's tongue has fallen back it should be hooked forward; the head is then turned to the side to prevent a recurrence. Following a fit, the patient should be kept under close observation, as he may, although apparently normal, be still in a state of post-epileptic confusion.

The details of the fit should be recorded as soon as possible; the time of onset and recovery, warning signs, if any, the various stages of the fit, and any evidence that one part of the body was more involved than the rest. Incontinence of urine and/or faeces should be noted. The patient should be examined for any evidence of injury sustained during the convulsion. An accurate description may help to distinguish the fit due to an abnormal discharge in the brain from the hysterical fit which is emotionally determined.

It may be extremely difficult to relate to epileptic patients who have psychotic conditions, in addition to their epilepsy, or those whose personality has been altered by chronic brain damage. Many epileptics, even without these features, present a problem of management as they tend to reject the attempts of the nursing staff to help them. This attitude is understandable when the patient's own experience of life is considered. It is probable that the epileptic in a mental hospital has learnt that his illness leads to his rejection by many people in the community: he may have lost his job when it was discovered that he had fits; his marriage may have broken up if his wife could not tolerate his fits; and his children may have been terrified by his convulsions. He tends to regard himself as a failure and an outcast, and responds to other people by withdrawal or by aggression.

The nurse must remain tolerant and friendly, 'swift to praise and slow to chide.' She must make sure that the patient is treated with scrupulous fairness; such patients are often on the lookout for anything which could be construed as a slight or as a sign of rejection.

A nurse may be asked by relatives about the advisability of a patient who suffers from epilepsy getting married, and what risk there is of the children developing the disorder. No general rules can be laid down as the term epilepsy covers a wide range of conditions with different causes, and advice can be given only on the basis of detailed knowledge of the individual patient.

Severe epilepsy may prove a great social handicap, even in the absence of any secondary psychiatric problems, and neither the sufferer nor his prospective partner should underestimate the difficulties they are likely to have. The epileptic patient should never hide his condition from his prospective marriage partner, and both should be encouraged to discuss their plans with their family doctor.

As for the chance of children of an epileptic patient developing fits, the overall figure is one in forty (five times that of the non-epileptic parent having an epileptic child). Such general figures are of little use in specific cases when factors such as the family history of both partners, the type of epilepsy, and the possible underlying cause must all be taken into consideration.

9 Child Psychiatry and Mental Subnormality

Child psychiatry and mental subnormality are both topics requiring a separate book to cover adequately.

Nurses training to work in the field of adult mental disorders need to know and understand something of child development and its disorders, if they are to have full awareness of the nature and cause of adult disorders. Many subnormal children develop additional psychiatric disorders in later life and may need mental hospital care. This chapter provides a bare outline of the subject. It aims to provide only an introduction to some of the problems involved and the range of provisions provided for the care and treatment of such patients.

Child Psychiatry

The psychiatry of childhood is largely the psychiatry of the family, for the child is greatly influenced by his immediate environment, which is usually provided by his parents and his siblings. A child requires love, a stable home, and consistent handling. In the absence of these he is likely to develop some degree of disturbance. As a rule young children do not express their difficulties in words but reveal them in their behaviour. Psychiatric disorders in children can be divided roughly into four types: (1) behaviour disorders, (2) neurotic illness, (3) psychosomatic conditions, and (4) psychoses.

1. Behaviour Disorders
Perfectly normal children behave in the following ways for short periods as they grow up, and the condition is only abnormal when it persists for a long time, or when it recurs after a long period of absence. Thumbsucking, nailbiting, and temper tantrums occur frequently in normal children, but may represent feelings of tension and anxiety. Treatment is directed at reducing the causes of anxiety,

113

and the situation is made worse by attempts to stop the habit by punishments.

Bed Wetting (*nocturnal enuresis*). This is a common problem. Most children are dry at night by the age of three, though occasional 'accidents' may occur for the next year or two. Thus, bed wetting is only abnormal when it occurs after the age of five.

In a small number of cases there is a physical cause for the problem, but in the vast majority it is a psychological condition. There are a number of possible causes.

(*a*) The child sleeps too deeply to be roused by the sensation of a full bladder. Such cases may respond to treatment with small doses of amphetanine, which lightens the level of their sleep.

(*b*) Lack of proper training. In families of low intelligence, or those living in poor housing conditions, the child may not receive adequate training in using the pot or lavatory. The use of a special undersheet which sets off a buzzer when wet, may help to establish the habit of waking before the bladder is emptied.

(*c*) Regression to earlier habits. A child who is anxious, jealous, or depressed may return to bed wetting after a period of being dry. Common precipitating causes of such behaviour are: the arrival of a new baby, separation from parents, or physical illness. The situation may be made worse by the response of the parents to the bed wetting. Excessive fussing, or strict discipline, may both make the child continue the habit. Treatment with tofranil in small doses at bedtime has been claimed to help in such cases.

2. Neurotic Symptoms and Disorders

Anxiety. The anxious child may develop specific fears (phobias) or may express his anxiety in more general ways. This may take the form of restlessness and overactivity. He is often described as fidgety, and may be punished for behaving in this way. Punishment makes the situation even worse. The child may develop other signs of tension, such as nailbiting and stammering. His sleep may be disturbed, and he may have nightmares or even start sleep-walking. Physical signs of anxiety such as nausea and vomiting, diarrhoea, headaches, and even fainting may occur. He may become panic-stricken if separated from his parents, and consequently may refuse to go to school.

Hysteria. This form of behaviour closely resembles hysteria in the adult. The range of symptoms includes loss of function of various parts of the body and disturbed function of automatic actions such as breathing, swallowing, and bowel and bladder actions. Mental symptoms may include fugue states and amnesia. Anxiety may be expressed in the form of single symptoms.

Phobias. These are specific, exaggerated fears and may concern such things as heights, darkness, animals, and closed spaces. School phobia is an important type. While the child expresses a fear of the school or the teachers, it is often found that the real source of anxiety is the separation from the mother that is involved in attending school. The child may be rather immature and dependent, and the mother is often herself an anxious over-protective kind of person. School phobia can, however, be the presenting symptom of a wide range of underlying disturbances.

3. Motor Disturbances

These may take the form of habit spasms (tics) or of stammering. *Tics* are sudden involuntary movements involving groups of muscles. They occur in spasms and may affect any part of the body, though most commonly they are seen in the facial muscles, and in the head and neck muscles. *Stammering* is a common disorder. The child may repeat the first letter of a word in an explosive kind of way, or may be unable to get certain words out at all.

4. Psychoses in Children

Psychotic illness, apart from organic states, is rare in children. It may take the form of manic depressive illness of a schizophrenic-like condition.

Manic-Depressive Episodes. Manic episodes are very rare, but depression, in which the child may have almost delusional beliefs that he is not wanted or is about to die, are common. Sometimes a child in such a state attempts suicide.

Schizophrenic-like Conditions. The relationship of these conditions to adult schizophrenia is not clear, but there is some evidence that such states have an organic basis. There are several subdivisions, but the most commonly used name is 'childhood autism' (autism means self-absorbed, shut off in a world of fantasy).

The story is usually that the child who has developed normally for some years, begins to withdraw from the world around him. He no longer forms normal relationships with his parents or siblings. His use of language changes, and he may become totally mute or use words in peculiar ways. He seems to be unable to adjust to any kind of change and may become very disturbed when quite trivial alterations are made, such as rearranging furniture in a room. He may develop marked obsessional features and may have episodes of increased activity. His movements may be awkward and uncoordinated, and he may develop a range of mannerisms. A number of other abnormal symptoms may also be found, including temper tantrums, destructive behaviour, bed wetting, and other behaviour disturbances.

Child Psychiatric Services

Child guidance clinics were first established in the UK in 1928. The clinics are usually staffed by a team, consisting of a psychiatrist, a clinical psychologist, and a social worker. There are two types of clinic: those run by the local authority, usually called Child Guidance Centres, and those run by the hospital service, called Child Psychiatric Clinics.

The guidance centres are generally run by an educational psychologist, and the children tend to be referred by the schools. The psychiatric clinic, on the other hand, is run by a psychiatrist and referals mostly come from general practitioners and hospital doctors. Children are usually referred to such clinics up to school-leaving age, but in some centres, they may continue in the care of the clinic up to the age of eighteen.

The aim of the clinic is to establish a diagnosis and provide outpatient treatment. At present there are very few in-patient units for children and adolescents, apart from the provisions made for the subnormal.

The psychiatric social worker plays a very important part in the treatment of children with mental disorders. The family situation is of vital importance and the social worker acts as the link between the home and the clinic. She may act as psychotherapist as well as providing practical help in resolving the social problems the family may have.

The clinical psychologist is not medically qualified, but has taken a degree in psychology followed by a special training in clinical psychology. They have special skill in the use of objective tests that assess the patient's intelligence, personality, and symptomatology, which help the psychiatrist to establish the diagnosis and which may be able to forecast the patient's likely response to treatment. Psychotherapy and various forms of behaviour therapy may also be undertaken by the clinical psychologist, and they often provide advice on rehabilitation and suitable employment. Finally, because of their knowledge of experimental methods and statistics, they assist in the planning and carrying out of research projects.

Mental Subnormality

Two illustrative Stories

1. 'I'm very worried about Tim. He's so different from my other children.' 'How do you mean?' the health visitor asked Mrs. Roberts.

'Well, he is so much slower at learning to do things. He is over two, and he is hardly talking at all. His walking is still very unsteady, and he tries to walk straight through things, instead of going round them.'

'I expect he is just a late developer', said the health visitor, 'but to set your mind at rest I'll arrange for him to be seen at a special assessment clinic.'

2. 'Thank you for coming to see me' the headmaster said.' I wanted to talk to you both about your son. Since he was away from school last term with measles, there seems to have been a marked falling off in his school work. I'm not sure if this is due to some emotional trouble that he is having, or if it is the result of his illness. In any case, I think we should ask for an expert opinion, and with your permission I will ask the school medical officer to see him.'

Definition

Intelligence is difficult to define, yet, like an elephant, it is something we all recognise when we see it. A person's intelligence is demonstrated by his ability to solve problems. These problems may be real or abstract, but their solution requires: (*a*) an ability to concentrate on the problem without being distracted; (*b*) an ability to see relationships between different objects, facts, or circumstances; and (*c*) a capacity to criticise one's solution if it does not completely solve the problem.

The combination of these three factors makes up the person's general intellectual ability. In addition, the person may have special skills in relation to certain tasks, such as mathematics or music. Although these are usually related to one's general level of intelligence, this is not always so.

General intelligence can be measured by devising special tests. These consist of a variety of different types of problems the person is asked to solve. The tests are made by trying out a series of problems, on a large number of people of the same age, and then selecting a range of problems, starting with some that everybody in the tested population could answer, and ending with problems that no one in the tested group could solve. When the final test is given to a fresh group of people, if it has been properly designed, it will be found that most people can answer about half the questions, a few can answer almost all the problems, and a few can answer hardly any.

When such tests are performed on large numbers of people, it is found that the scores follow a normal distribution, that is, when plotted as a graph, most scores cluster around the average score, giving a bell-shaped graph as shown.

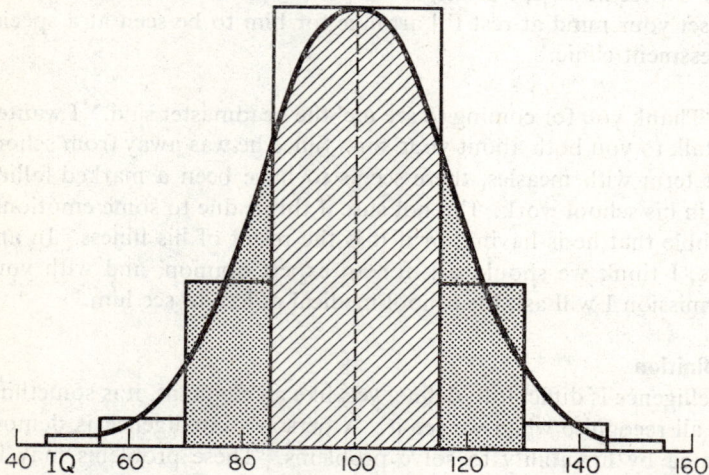

FIG. 1. Curve indicates the normal distribution of intelligence among the population as a whole.

The scores are often expressed as an IQ (intelligence quotient). It can be seen that very few people in the population have very high levels of intelligence (IQ over 140), and very few have extremely low levels (IQ 30 to 60). A similar kind of curve would be obtained if one plotted people's height or weight.

People with an IQ of below 60 fall into the severely subnormal group, while those with an IQ of between 60 and 90 form the subnormal group. The degree of handicap they suffer reflects the level of intelligence, thus at the lowest level of IQ the person is incapable of independent existence, having to be nursed like a baby, while at the highest levels the degree of handicap is mainly demonstrated by a failure to benefit from schooling. For legal purposes, people of below normal intelligence are divided into two groups, the severely subnormal and the subnormal.

Mental subnormality is defined in the Mental Health Act as, 'a state of arrested or incomplete development of mind, which includes subnormality of intelligence, and is of a nature or degree which requires, or is susceptible to medical treatment or other special care or training.'

Severe subnormality, means a state of arrested or incomplete development of mind, which includes subnormality of intelligence, and is of such a nature or degree that the patient is incapable of living an independent life or of guarding himself against serious exploitation, or will be so incapable when of an age to do so.

While this definition recognises that 'mind' comprises more than 'intelligence', it makes clear that defects of character and personality are not enough on their own to make a person subnormal. The definition of severe subnormality, takes into account social considerations as well as the assessment of level of intelligence as shown by special tests. By including 'arrested' as well as 'incomplete' development of mind, the definition covers people in whom normal development is stopped as a result of disease or injury.

Many degrees of subnormality cannot be diagnosed with certainty until the child starts to attend school, and even then the lesser degrees of subnormality may be missed. Subnormality can be suspected if a child fails to achieve the normal milestones of development. From an extensive study of children during the early years of life it has been possible to draw up a time-table for developing skills. While individual children differ in the rate at which they acquire these skills, a child who is markedly behind others of his own age in *all* performances should be suspected of being subnormal.

Diagnosis is usually made at a special assessment clinic run by the regional hospital board and local health authority. Some conditions causing mental subnormality can be diagnosed by the facial and physical appearance of the child at or shortly after birth. (Mongolism is an example.) Other disorders that give rise to mental subnormality can be diagnosed by the presence of certain chemicals taken in a blood test taken routinely before a baby is 14 days old (e.g. phenylketonuria).

Causes of Subnormality

The causes can be divided into those which have genetic basis, and those acquired while the child is still in the womb, during birth, or in the first fifteen years of life. Brain damage after the age of fifteen is regarded as causing dementia, as by this age intelligence is normally fully developed.

Genetically Determined. In these conditions, either a gene for the disease is passed on from the parent(s) or there is a failure in normal division of the chromosomes (e.g. mongolism). Some genetic disorders take the form of an absence of certain essential enzymes which, in turn, leads to brain damage (e.g. phenylketonuria).

Acquired Conditions. Some 'infections' of the mother during pregnancy can cause brain damage in the foetus. Syphilis and rubella (German measles) are well known examples.

The baby's brain may be damaged during the process of being born, either as a result of injury or of being deprived of oxygen (birth trauma). Prolonged levels of low blood sugar in the early days of life may also cause death of brain cells.

When a mother who has Rhesus-negative blood has a child by a Rhesus-positive father, and the foetus is Rhesus positive, an antibody reaction occurs between the foetus and the mother (rhesus incompatibility), which in some cases produces brain damage.

Prolonged absence of normal intellectual stimulation can lead to permanent failure of normal mental development. Such lack of stimulation may arise when a parent is severely mentally disturbed.

Nursing Care

The most severe degrees of subnormality condemn the sufferer to a totally dependent existence. He has to be nursed in a cot, fed, and cleaned like a baby. The life span is usually not very long, death resulting from some intercurrent infection.

The severely subnormal, by definition, is not capable of protecting himself against everyday dangers, or against exploitation. Some can be managed at home if the parents are given enough help, but where there are other children to be looked after, and when the child is defective in his habits, destructive, or aggressive, it may be necessary for him to be admitted to a hospital for the subnormal. Here the child receives medical care designed to minimise any physical handicaps, and also receives special training—at first in such motor skills as walking and bladder and bowel control; later he will attend the hospital school where the emphasis is on practical rather than academic subjects. Even simple skills may take much time and effort before the child masters them.

At about the age of fifteen the child leaves school and moves on to some form of work training. The type of work chosen depends on the ability of the patient. Some will be able to take up residential jobs as maids or farm labourers, while the more handicapped may be unable to work except in some form of sheltered workshop.

People with subnormal intelligence should not be admitted to an ordinary mental hospital unless they have some additional psychiatric illness. In the past, such patients drifted into a back ward where they received no training. The mentally subnormal person may develop any form of mental illness.

The nurse must recognise the difficulties that life presents for such people, and the degree of frustration this engenders. This is particularly true for those with the less severe handicap, for they are often not recognised as being less capable and may be expected to cope with the full demands of independent life in a highly technical and fast-moving world.

One major problem in looking after such patients is that of impulsive behaviour of a destructive or aggressive kind. In some instances this may occur without any real reason, and, if such episodes are frequent, may make it necessary to put the patient on a phenothiazine drug. Often, however, there is some precipitating cause, and the nurse should try to discover what it is. One common reason is disappointment. A member of the staff or a relative promises the patient something and then fails to provide it. Like a child, the subnormal patient should be treated with complete honesty, and if a promise is made it must be kept.

10 Physical Illness and Psychiatry

Mind and body have long been considered as separate entities, capable of existing without each other, yet able to influence each other's working. Yet, in practical terms, it is not possible to isolate the two: everything that affects the body must have some effect on the mind, and vice versa, though the extent of this effect may vary from very slight to very great. The ways in which this interrelationship can work are as follows:

1. Physical illness affecting the brain directly may disturb mental functioning. This is discussed in the chapters on acute and chronic brain syndrome (*see* Chapters 6 and 7).

2. Physical conditions may interfere with the functioning of the brain indirectly by causing impairment of oxygen supply, inadequate nutrition, failure of the removal of waste products, or alteration in hormone levels. These conditions are discussed below and under acute and chronic brain syndromes (*see* Chapters 6 and 7).

3. Physical illness, through pain and discomfort, and through disability and dependence, will influence the mental state of the patient. This is discussed below.

4. Mental state may cause physical changes and may present with complaints of pain, or altered function of parts of the body.

5. In some cases these changes in function, caused by emotional factors, produce actual changes in the body, which do not return to normal even when the emotional factors no longer operate. These conditions are usually labelled 'psychosomatic illness'.

6. Finally, the presence of a mental illness may prevent the patient seeking help, or being able to draw attention to a physical illness. It may also lead people looking after the patient to assume that any new symptom is 'only in his mind' so that the presence of a physical illness is missed or ignored.

Physical Illness Which May Produce Mental Changes

Almost any disease may, in some instances, produce organic mental disorder, but the more important are described below.

Thyroid Disorders

The thyroid gland is one of the endocrine glands; that is, it produces a secretion which passes directly from the cells into the blood stream, and not by way of a system of ducts. The secretion consists of a hormone, that is, a chemical substance which acts on chemical processes in other cells without being changed itself in the process. The hormone produced by the thyroid is called thyroxine, and it contains iodine. Its action is to increase the rate at which cells in the body carry out oxidation. Thus, it increases the metabolic rate. The thyroid gland may produce too much or too little of its hormone, leading to conditions called hyperthyroidism, and hypothyroidism respectively.

HYPERTHYROIDISM (*Thyrotoxicosis*)

This is due to excess production of thyroxine. The patient may present with symptoms and signs suggesting an anxiety state. They feel tense and anxious and may be restless and overactive; the appetite may be increased, but in spite of eating more they tend to lose weight; they may perspire, and when the arms are held out there may be a fine tremor of the hands; and the pulse rate is increased and may be irregular. The blood pressure is raised, typically having a large difference between the systolic and diastolic pressures (that is a high 'pulse pressure') which may lead to heart failure.

Sometimes the eyes may be affected, the lids tend to be drawn back and the eyeballs may protrude (exophthalmos), giving the patient a staring expression. The thyroid gland may be enlarged and the increased blood flow through it may cause a murmuring sound when heard through a stethoscope (thyroid bruit). In cases of extreme enlargement, particularly if the gland extends down behind the breast bone, the patient may have difficulty in breathing or in swallowing.

Rarely, patients with hyperthyroidism develop mental symptoms resembling a confusional state or a schizophrenic illness, but usually the problem is to decide between hyperthyroidism and an anxiety state. The diagnosis is based on the results of certain tests:

1. *Sleeping Pulse Rate.* The pulse rate in both conditions tends to be raised, but if due to anxiety the rate tends to return to a normal level when the patient is asleep.

In hyperthyroidism, although the rate falls during sleep, it rarely returns to a normal level.

2. *Basal Metabolic Rate* (BMR). This is a measure of the amount of oxygen a patient uses during a given time, while at rest. It is not used very often now because of the technical difficulties involved. In hyperthyroidism the BMR is raised and lowered in hypothyroidism.

3. *Radioactive Iodine Uptake.* This test depends on one fact, that almost all the iodine in the body is concentrated in the thyroid. This concentration is increased if the thyroid is overactive, decreased if it is underactive. In order to measure the concentration a known amount of iodine is given in a radioactive form that can then be measured over the thyroid gland and the concentration worked out. Radioactive iodine is also used, in much larger doses, to treat hyperthyroidism by destroying thyroid tissue with radiation.

4. *Serum Protein-Bound Iodine.* In this test the amount of iodine bound to protein circulating in the blood is measured chemically. Normal levels are between 3 to 7 mg: it is more valuable in detecting mild underactivity than overactivity.

5. *T3 and T4.* A more direct measurement of thyroid function is provided by resin uptake tests. A sample of the patient's serum is treated with radioactive T3 or T4. A resin is then added to the mixture to extract all free hormone and this is estimated by measuring the radioactivity.

Hyperthyroidism may be treated by:

1. Surgical removal of part of the gland.
2. Radioactive iodine.
3. Antithyroid drugs. Carbimazole is the most commonly used drug for this purpose. It is given in doses of 10 mg t.d.s. initially, reducing to 5 mg t.d.s. after four to six weeks.

HYPOTHYROIDISM

This failure of production of thyroxine may occur in the foetus, in which case it produces a condition called 'cretinism', that is, one form of mental subnormality. Treatment, to be effective, must be started as soon as possible after birth, and it is important to recognise the condition in its early stage if severe subnormality is to be avoided.

In the adult, the disease is often called *myxoedema* because of the jelly-like substance that is sometimes deposited in the tissues. The patient is most commonly a middle-aged woman, or someone who has had hyperthyroidism which has been over-treated. The onset is slow, and in the early stages, before the physical changes are very striking, the patient is often thought to be depressed. There is a loss of interest, a slowing down of movements, and the patient complains of inability to think quickly, or to concentrate. Everything seems a great effort, and patients may complain that they are 'old before their time'. Memory impairment may be marked and lead to a diagnosis of presenile or senile dementia.

Physical changes reflect the slowing down process. Weight increases, and the patient finds difficulty in keeping warm even in hot weather. Her hair becomes dry and brittle, and may start to fall out. Her eyebrows become thin and sparse, particularly the outer margins. Her face becomes rounded, and her features become coarse and bloated. There is often marked puffiness of the eyelids. The pulse rate falls, as does the temperature. In severe conditions the patient may pass into coma and die from hypothermia (low temperature) or from cardiac arrest. Such patients are very liable to a severe fall in temperature if given phenothiazine drugs. To record such temperatures it is necessary to use a special rectal thermometer.

The mental changes most commonly suggest either a depressive illness or a dementing condition, but sometimes a schizophrenic-like illness is seen, particularly of the paranoid type. This sometimes responds to treatment of the hypothyroidism. This condition has been called *myxoedema madness*.

The tests for thyroid under activity are the same as those described above, but in addition, the serum cholesterol level is measured as it is almost always abnormally high, and it can be used to measure the patient's response to treatment.

Treatment consists of giving either some form of thyroid extract or, preferably, the actual synthesised hormone L. thyroxine. The dose depends on clinical response, but is in the order of 0·1 mg a day to 0·1 mg tds.

Other disorders of the endocrine glands can cause mental symptoms. For descriptions of the various conditions a textbook of medicine should be consulted.

Anaemia
Anaemia is a condition in which there is not enough haemoglobin to carry sufficient oxygen to meet the body's requirements. This leads to the sufferer feeling tired and apathetic, and becoming breathless on exercise. In severe degrees it may lead to heart failure with the consequent development of oedema, usually showing as swelling of the ankles. The early symptoms of anaemia may be thought to be due to depression or anxiety. In more severe conditions the relative shortage of oxygen reaching the brain may produce symptoms of confusion, particularly in elderly patients. The type of anaemia that is due to vitamin B12 deficiency is sometimes associated with actual damage to nerve cells, most often involving the spinal cord (subacute combined degeneration), but sometimes also affecting the cells of the brain.

Anaemia may arise from:

1. *Chronic Blood Loss.* Common causes being frequent heavy menstruation (menorrhoea) in women, or from bleeding piles in either sex. Carcinoma of the gastro-intestinal tract may also lead to chronic blood loss.

2. *Lack of Iron, Folic Acid and Vitamin B12 in the Diet.* This may arise through (*a*) food fads, which, in turn, may reflect some underlying mental disorder, (*b*) as a result of poverty or ignorance, or (*c*) because the demands of the body are increased without an increased intake. This last cause operates in pregnancy.

3. *Interference with Absorption of Iron, Folic Acid or B12.* This can result from a large number of diseases of the gut, in which the area for absorption is reduced, or in which the passage of food through the gut becomes too rapid for absorption to take place.

Vitamin Deficiency Diseases
An inadequate diet may lead to the development of diseases due to lack of specific vitamins. These disorders are described separately, but frequently combinations of these diseases occur together as the diet is lacking in more than one vitamin.

Vitamin A. Present in milk products, fish, liver oils, and green vegetables. Deficiency may cause poor night vision, but no mental symptoms have been described.

*Vitamin B*1 (*Thiamine Aneurine*). Present in meat, yeast, and whole grain. Deficiency may lead to symptoms of Korsakoff's disease or Wernikes' encephalopathy, and may arise because of chronic gastro-intestinal disorders. Thiamine deficiency, also responsible for beri-beri, is a disease in which peripheral nerves lose their myelin coat, and become unable to function, and in which the heart may be affected, leading to congestive cardiac failure.

*Vitamin B*2 (*Nicotinamide*). Found in milk, liver, eggs, and cereals. Deficiency produces a disease called pellagra, the symptoms of which are a combination of gastro-intestinal upset, skin rashes, neurological involvement, and mental symptoms of depression leading into a final dementia, and death if untreated. The disease is endemic in Southern Europe, Africa, and the southern states of USA.

*Vitamin B*12. Addison described a form of anaemia which was inevitably fatal, and which in some cases was associated with damage to the spinal cord. A small number of such patients also developed a mental state closely resembling paranoid schizophrenia. The disease is due to a failure to absorb sufficient vitamin B12. In some cases this is due to dietary deficiency, but in others it is due to the failure of the stomach to secrete a special substance called 'intrinsic factor'. It was discovered that patients could be kept alive by feeding them large amounts of raw liver. Later, the active factor, vitamin B12 was extracted, and it can now be synthesised. Its chemical name is cyanocobalamin (trade name Cytamin). Treatment is by injection, but recently a preparation that can be taken by mouth, as maintenance therapy, has been developed. Treatment has to be continued for the rest of the patient's life.

Vitamin C. Present in citrus fruits, green vegetables, and potatoes, and is easily destroyed in cooking: the body needs about 30 mg a day. Deficiency causes *scurvy*, a disease in which there is bleeding into the skin, ulceration and bleeding from the gums, anaemia, and general debility. There are no specific mental symptoms.

Vitamin D. Occurs in milk products and fish liver oils; it can also be manufactured by the skin in the presence of sunlight. Deficiency in children causes rickets, in which the bones fail to develop normally. Although deficiency diseases are rare in an affluent society, they still occur in the relatively underprivileged, such as pensioners. They also occur more frequently in the mentally disordered who, because of their mental condition, cannot, or will not, take an adequate diet.

Psychosomatic Conditions

There is a group of diseases in which emotional factors appear to be important in producing a change in physical function which may later lead to irreversible damage to the organ involved. These disorders are called psychosomatic (mind-body) diseases, though, as has been stated, all diseases involve physical and emotional aspects. The conditions generally discussed under this heading are, bronchial asthma, peptic ulceration, and ulcerative colitis.

Bronchial Asthma

In this condition the small tubes, bronchioles, carrying the air into the lung tissue become constricted. The patient finds it difficult to breathe out, so that the air spaces (alveoli) become distended with partly de-oxygenated air and may rupture to form large balloon-like pockets called bullae. The relative lack of oxygen reaching the blood, and the increase in carbon dioxide, stimulate the respiratory centre so that the patient breathes even harder, distending the lungs further. Each time he breathes out, the air passing through the constricted tubes makes a typical wheezing sound, followed by a panting intake as the patient tries to get more oxygen.

In some cases, allergic factors seem to be of major importance in triggering off an attack, while in others there are definite emotional causes. In the latter, it may be possible to resolve these difficulties and the disease clears up, but frequently physical changes have occurred which leave the lungs and bronchioles permanently damaged. It has been claimed that a specific type of personality and a particular form of stress are seen in asthmatics, but this has not been confirmed by research.

Peptic Ulceration

Ulcers may develop in the stomach or in the first part of the duodenum. While the exact mechanism of their development is not known, it is in part due to excess secretion of hydrochloric acid. It is further known that emotional stress leads to increased acid secretion. The condition is not associated exclusively with one personality type or with a particular form of stress, but it tends to occur relatively more often in people employed in the more demanding and responsible occupations.

Ulcerative Colitis

In this disorder the patient has episodes of diarrhoea during which blood and mucus are passed in the motions, which are soft or liquid. The mucosa of the colon becomes hyperaemic and there may be extensive areas of ulceration. The patient may die through blood loss, fluid or electrolyte loss, or through perforation of the gut, with consequent peritonitis. Treatment of the acute attack is with steroids, both by mouth and in retention enemas, and with non-absorbable sulphonamides. Some patients have to have the colon removed and are left with an ileostomy.

Mental Disorders Presenting with Physical Symptoms

Many people feel frightened or ashamed by the thought that they might be suffering from some form of emotional or mental disorder. This attitude towards mental illness is shared by some doctors, who tend to regard such states as being due to wickedness, weakness, or a combination of the two. It is not surprising, therefore, that many patients find it easier to convince themselves and their doctors that their trouble is physical. The particular choice of symptom may reflect the patient's personality: it may have a symbolic relationship to the underlying problem, it may be one of the physical symptoms caused by the mental state, or it may just be a complaint the patient knows or thinks will be of special interest to the doctor involved. Probably the commonest complaint is pain, and the commonest pain—a headache.

Another frequent complaint is of some disturbance of the digestive system. Most Britons are fascinated by their bowels; for some, anything less than two motions a day is taken as a sign of intestinal obstruction. Any disturbance in their regularity may well be, for them, the most important aspect of their disorder. The anxious patient may complain of diarrhoea; the depressed, of constipation.

The recent emphasis on avoiding obesity for health and aesthetic reasons has made most people very aware of their weight. Loss in weight may be a presenting complaint in cases of anxiety, depression, or schizophrenia, while gain in weight may be complained of by patients who overeat in an attempt to reverse their feelings of depression.

Nursing Care

A detailed consideration of this topic lies outside the scope of this book, but it is very important for the psychiatric nurse to know the general principles involved. The patient with a pre-existing mental illness who develops a physical disorder may be unable or unwilling to call attention to it in the normal way. Even worse, if he does complain, the staff may assume that it is due to his mental state and ignore the possibility of physical disease. Good observation is essential if this trap is to be avoided. The nurse must recognise the signs of common physical illnesses even in the absence of specific complaints by the patient.

One of the commonest conditions is a pyrexia, that is, a rise in temperature. There are many causes of pyrexia, but the signs and symptoms are similar whatever the cause. The patient may appear flushed and may be sweating or shivering. He may complain of generalised aches and pains and of feeling nauseated. His temperature when taken with a clinical thermometer is above the normal level of 36·9°C (98·4°F). His pulse is faster than normal, usually by ten beats a minute for every degree rise in temperature. Having established the presence of pyrexia the next step is to discover what system of the body is the most likely site of the trouble.

Respiratory System

Probably commonest of all causes of a pyrexia is an infection of the upper respiratory tract—a common cold or, more serious, influenza. While in the fit person these are of little consequence, in the old and infirm they may lead on to infection of the lungs, such as bronchitis or pneumonia. One sign of a chest infection is a cough, which may be dry or productive of sputum; the sputum may be colourless and frothy or purulent, in which case it is green or yellow; the patient has difficulty in breathing and may complain of pain in the chest; the respiratory rate is increased; and the breathing may be noisy, either wheezing or bubbly.

Gastro-intestinal Tract

Infection of the gut is usually accompanied by diarrhoea. Soft, or liquid faeces, often foul smelling, are passed at frequent intervals.

Common symptoms of systemic disorders are those due to disturbed functioning of the gastro-intestinal tract. Acute diarrhoea is usually caused by infection, but in elderly patients a common cause is chronic constipation. This paradoxical result is due to hard rock-like faeces becoming impacted in the rectum. The faeces above become liquified and leak past the obstruction. Alternating periods of diarrhoea and constipation may indicate the presence of a cancerous growth in the rectum or sigmoid colon.

Constipation

This may arise through lack of bulk in the diet. Many people dose themselves regularly and unnecessarily with 'opening medicines'. When these are discontinued the patient becomes constipated. In itself, constipation is of no importance; it is only when the faeces become impacted that symptoms develop. There is no justification for routine purgatives, especially for patients taking a diet with sufficient roughage.

Vomiting

The reflex emptying of the stomach contents back through the mouth is controlled by a centre in the brain, located in the floor of the fourth ventricle. Stimuli to this centre may arise in the stomach from the other viscera, from general toxic causes, or from the organ of balance in the middle ear. Thus, vomiting may be a feature of gastritis, peptic ulceration, obstruction of the pylorus, or carcinoma of the stomach. It occurs in appendicitis, intestinal obstruction, peritonis, and gall-bladder disease: the commonest cause in young women is pregnancy.

It may also be brought on by certain drugs, and by some foods. Nervous causes include emotional upsets. Organic diseases such as cerebral tumours, migraine, travel sickness, Meniere's disease, and many others may also cause vomiting.

Urinary Tract

The bladder is a common site of infection, especially in women, and in men with enlargement of the prostate gland and consequent retention of urine. The local signs and symptoms are:
1. Frequency—an increase in the number of times urine is passed.
2. Urgency—the patient feels unable to delay passing urine.

3. Dysuria—the urine stings or 'burns' the urethra as it passes through.

4. Haematuria—In severe cases there may be blood in the urine and in all cases there is pus in the urine to a greater or lesser extent. The urine may be foul-smelling.

Skin

The skin may be affected in some generalised infective process, and some form of rash may develop. Common examples are measles, chicken-pox, and scarlet fever. Local infections of the skin may take the form of a cellulitis in which the affected area is red, swollen, hot, and painful, or the infection may arise in a hair follicle, forming a boil.

Weight Loss

Generalised weight loss may reflect poor food intake, itself a feature of a number of psychiatric illnesses. It may occur in spite of adequate diet in such conditions as hyperthyroidism and diabetes mellitus.

Weight Gain

This may occur as a result of compulsive overeating. It is a not uncommon effect of chlorpromazine, and may also occur in myxoedema. It may also occur in patients on amitriptyline.

Two important aspects of the observation of the physically ill are the recording of blood pressure values, pulse and respiratory rates, temperature and fluid intake and output. All these measures may be of vital importance in the assessment of the patient's condition and response to treatment. The collection and examination of certain specimens also plays an important part in the diagnosis of physical disorders.

Temperature

Normal temperature ranges from 36·1°C (97°F) to 37·2°C (99°F) with an average of 36·9°C (98·4°F). Readings are taken at set times in the day and are recorded on the appropriate chart. In order to obtain a correct value, it is necessary to leave the thermometer in position for at least the time marked on it. Temperatures may be measured by placing the clinical thermometer in the patient's mouth, or in the axilla. In some instances, it is necessary to measure rectal temperatures with a special thermometer.

Pulse

The pulse is usually felt at the wrist by lightly compressing the radial artery against the underlying bone. When taking the pulse the nurse should record the rate, the rhythm, and volume. The value of recording the sleeping pulse in hyperthyroidism has been mentioned.

Respiration

The normal adult rate is between fifteen and twenty times a minute. It is faster after exercise and when the patient is emotionally disturbed, as well as in diseases of the respiratory tract. It is also affected by a variety of metabolic disorders and by damage to the vital centres in the medulla.

Blood Pressure

This pressure depends on the pumping action of the heart and the resistance to expansion exerted by the walls of the blood vessels. Two pressures are measured: that exerted when the heart contracts, the *systolic value*, and that exerted during the time the heart is filling, the *diastolic value*. The systolic is, of course, higher than the diastolic. The actual values vary with age but a fit young adult has a value of about 120/70 mm of mercury.

A wide range of conditions may lead to a change in blood pressure. Exercise and excitement increase the systolic pressure. Chronic renal damage may lead to permanent increase in both systolic and diastolic values. Arteriosclerosis may also cause high blood pressures. Fall in blood pressure may arise as a result of acute damage to the heart muscle, as in coronary artery thrombosis. It may be due to interference with the nervous control of the degree of contraction of the blood vessels, leading to relaxation of the artery walls. This is probably the mechanism by which certain drugs such as chlorpromazine and imipramine produce a fall in blood pressure. This fall is more pronounced when the patient stands up (postural hypotension) and it is important, therefore, to record the patient's blood pressure both lying and standing. Acute loss of blood also causes hypotension.

Fluid Balance

One essential for the continued life and activity of a cell is a supply of fluid and certain inorganic salts. The cell itself is largely composed of water, and most cells are in addition, surrounded by fluids. The fluid inside the cell is called intracellular, that outside the cell extracellular. There is a constant exchange between the cell and its exterior of fluid and substances dissolved in it.

In an adult human, about 70 per cent of the body weight consists of water. This is divided up into:

50 per cent bodyweight—intracellular.
15 per cent bodyweight—extracellular.
5 per cent bodyweight—water in the bloodstream.

The normal adult requires to take in about 2·5 to 3 litres of water every twenty-four hours, and to maintain normal salt balance he must take in 5 g of sodium chloride and 3 g of potassium chloride. To remain in fluid balance he must, therefore, excrete the same amount. This is done as follows:

1. Evaporation through skin and lungs 1 to 1·5 litres in twenty-four hours.
2. Excretion of urine by kidneys 1 to 1·5 litres in twenty-four hours. Thus, the normal individual takes in and puts out the same amount of fluid and salts in twenty-four hours.

In a wide range of conditions this process may be interfered with, and the patient is no longer in fluid and electrolyte (salts) balance. It is then essential to restore this balance, and to do so, it is necessary to measure and record fluid intake and output.

CONDITIONS IN WHICH THE PATIENT BECOMES SHORT OF FLUID—DEHYDRATION

1. *Diminished Intake*
   (a) Failure of nursing care of very weak or ill patients.
   (b) Painful condition of mouth, throat, and oesophagus.
   (c) Coma.
   (d) Mental state, in which patient refuses or is unable to drink.

2. *Excessive Output*
   (a) Vomiting.
   (b) Diarrhoea.
   (c) Drainage from ileostomy, colostomy, etc.
   (d) Obstruction of the intestines.
   (e) Renal disease with failure to concentrate or reabsorb.
   (f) Fluid loss from severe burns.
   (g) Haemorrhage.

CONDITIONS IN WHICH EXCESSIVE FLUID IS RETAINED OR GIVEN
1. Over-enthusiastic transfusion in cases of dehydration.
2. Congestive cardiac failure.
3. Renal damage.
4. Compulsive water drinking.

RECORDING FLUID INTAKE AND OUTPUT
All fluids given in twenty-four hours, whatever route they are given by, must be recorded.

Intake
1. Oral drinks and fluid food.
2. Intragastric—tube feeding.
3. Intravenous—transfusion of blood or electrolytes.
4. Rectal drip.
5. Subcutaneous.
The volume should be measured in millilitres, and the nature of the fluid recorded.

Output
Route, type, and volume are recorded.
1. Gut—vomit, gastric suction, liquid faeces, etc.
2. Bladder—urinary volume and specific gravity.
3. Blood loss—measured and estimated.

Collection of Specimens
One important task of the nurse is the collection and observation of a variety of specimens. These may be required for laboratory examination, or the nurse may test them herself on the ward. The following are commonly investigated.

SPUTUM
This is collected in a special container and should be routinely observed for amount, colour, and consistency. Special specimens for bacteriological examination are usually collected first thing in the morning, the patient being instructed to spit into a sterile sputum jar, labelled with his name and ward, which is then sent to the laboratory.

Green or yellow sputum indicates the presence of pus. Bright red, frothy blood signifies bleeding from the lung, while rusty specimens indicate the resolution of a pneumonic process.

VOMIT

This should be saved in a covered bowl for inspection by the doctor. The contents, and their colour and odour, should be noted and the presence of bright red blood or altered dark blood, that looks like coffee grounds, should be particularly looked for.

FAECES

These should be routinely kept for laboratory examination in cases of diarrhoea, and may be specially requested when the patient is suspected of bleeding into the gut, so that the stool may be tested for occult blood. In cases of diarrhoea, the colour, consistency, and any abnormal contents such as mucus or blood should be noted. Stools may also be examined for the presence of a variety of different parasitic worms.

URINE

All new admissions have a routine examination of their urine. This is collected in a clean specimen jar. It is tested for the presence of glucose, acetone, and protein, and is examined microscopically for the presence of bacteria and white cells. The urine in some cases may be subjected to special tests, which require particular types of specimen. For bacteriological investigation in which the urine is to be cultured, either a midstream or a catheter specimen is collected in a sterile jar.

For some biochemical investigations, a twenty-four hour specimen. is required. This is collected in a winchester bottle, containing an appropriate preservative The patient empties his bladder at 8 a.m. and this specimen is thrown away. All subsequent urine passed is collected up to and including 8 a.m. the following day. Details of ward urine testing can be found in most practical nursing textbooks.

11 Special Nursing Problems—1
The Old, the Frail, and the Physically Ill

Old people in mental hospitals are there for one of three reasons:

1. They have some mental illness unrelated to old age (e.g. depression, schizophrenia).
2. They have grown old in hospital, having originally been admitted with schizophrenia and never been discharged.
3. They have some form of organic brain disease that, temporarily or permanently, makes it impossible for them to be cared for at home.

In fact, while these are the reasons for admission, many remain in hospital even when well enough to leave, because there is nowhere suitable for them to go. Old age rarely comes alone; many old people, whatever their mental state, have a number of physical complaints of varying seriousness. Thus, the nursing care of old people involves physical and psychological problems. Many such patients die in hospital, and one of the most vital aspects of nursing the aged is the provision of terminal care—an unpleasant name for a nursing task that calls for the highest levels of skill and humanity.

Old People Who are not Seriously Physically Ill

There is no more depressing sight than a ward full of old people sitting slumped in chairs arranged around the walls of a large bare room, with the smell of stale urine and disinfectant adding its special contribution to an atmosphere of despair. This is not only depressing but unnecessary, as can be seen when visiting an old folks' ward that is integrated, has an active programme involving work, entertainment, and patient participation in the running of the ward.

The normal old person does not spend all day dozing in front of the fire. Physical effort is, of course, reduced, and the range of interests more limited, but old people benefit from continuing to do such tasks as they are capable of. Occupational therapy helps to reduce behaviour disturbances among geriatric patients. Exercise is an important requirement, helping to avoid the dangers of prolonged immobility and inducing mild physical tiredness that helps to eliminate the need for night sedation. Exercise can take the form of walking in the hospital grounds, if the weather is suitable, or indoor activities, such as 'musical movement' in which the patients play various simple instruments, clap in time, or even dance.

Entertainment is vitally important in combating lethargy, hopelessness, and boredom. Turning a radio or TV set full on, does *not* constitute entertainment. Community singing, visiting concert parties, and film shows, help relieve the tedium of ward life, but best of all are outings to places of interest in the district. The fitter patients can be taken individually, or in small groups to the local shopping centre, and encouraged to buy things for themselves. The more severely demented, or physically frail will be less able to look after themselves, but should be encouraged to do so to the limit of their ability, even if it is more time-consuming than the nurse doing it for them.

Disoriented patients require constant help in remembering who they are, where they are, and what time it is. For this reason, patients should always be called by their own name, and not some non-specific title such as Gran or Pop. They should be told what day it is, and, preferably, there should always be a large calendar in the ward. The various rooms in the ward should be clearly labelled in print large enough for patients with poor vision to read, and supplemented where applicable with visual signs.

The nurse's relationship to her patients can be summarised in the phrase, 'do unto others as you would be done by'. If the nurse treats each patient as she would wish her parents to be treated if they were in hospital, she will not go far wrong.

Many people entering a geriatric ward are surprised and alarmed to find the majority of the old people up and about. Even those who seem very frail or even physically ill are encouraged to spend as little time as possible in bed, and to do as much for themselves as possible. This is not due to callousness on the part of the staff, but because putting an old person to bed can produce harmful effects, and may, in fact, lead to the death of the patient.

The Risks of Bed-rest

1. *The Development of Bedsores.* This is discussed in detail later.

2. *Pneumonia.* A patient in bed, in a semi-prone position finds it difficult to expand his chest fully, with the result that breathing becomes shallow, and the lower parts of the lung do not become filled with air. In addition, the normal secretions of the lung and bronchi tend to run downwards and pool in the bases of the lung. This nonaerated, waterlogged tissue provides an excellent breeding ground for bacteria, and the patient develops a basal pneumonia. This is sometimes called hypostatic pneumonia.

Broncho-pneumonia is an infection involving scattered areas of the lungs. It is common in old people and frequently the cause of death in people with other forms of serious illnesses.

Lobar pneumonia tends to be a disease of young and middle-age adults. One or more lobes are affected, the onset is rapid, and the patient becomes seriously ill. In the days before antibiotics, there was a high death-rate in this condition, but now it is rarely allowed to progress to this stage.

3. *Deep Vein Thrombosis.* The flow of blood from the legs through the deep veins back to the right atrium of the heart, depends in part on the squeezing effect produced by moving the muscles of the legs. A patient in bed is unable to move his legs, so that the blood tends to pool in the veins: slow-moving blood is liable to clot and, therefore, the vein becomes obstructed by a thrombus. This itself may not be too serious as the blood usually finds alternative veins to flow through, although the leg may become swollen, painful, warm, and blue in colour.

4. *Pulmonary Embolus.* The danger aspect of a deep vein thrombosis lies in the fact that part of the clot may break off, forming an embolus, pass up the veins to the right atrium, through the tricuspid valve into the right ventricle, and then along the pulmonary artery to the lungs. Here, it will block off the blood vessels and cause an area of the lung supplied by that particular artery to die as a result of ischaemia (lack of blood). This condition is called pulmonary infarction, and if the area affected is large, the patient may collapse and die.

5. *Muscle-wasting and Joint Deformity.* Muscles that are not used tend to waste away, so that the patient finds increasing weakness of movement of the limbs. The limbs may then remain fixed in one

position for long periods, and the joints themselves then become changed, and movement of them becomes restricted and painful.

6. *Bone Changes*. Not only do the muscles waste if not used, the bones to which they are attached are no longer under the same degree of stress. This leads to alteration in the structure of the bone, which becomes weaker and more liable to fracture under strain. The combination of weakness and lack of practice may make walking very difficult for the patient when he is finally allowed out of bed. The patient tends to fall, and in so doing may fracture the weakened bone.

7. *Renal Complications*. The changes in the bones may lead to an increased amount of calcium in the blood. This is excreted by the kidneys, and in certain circumstances a high level of calcium being excreted into the urine may cause stones to form. These renal calculi, as they are called, sometimes obstruct the ureter and prevent urine passing into the bladder. The back pressure eventually damages the kidney. Other stones pass down the ureter into the bladder. The passing of such a stone may give rise to severe abdominal pain— so-called 'renal colic'. It may also cause bleeding from ureter or bladder, the blood being passed in the urine (haematuria).

The nursing care of a patient confined to bed must include measures to avoid the development of these complications. The key to this is movement. This may be *active*, in which the patient performs certain exercises himself, or *passive*, in which the limbs are moved by the nurse.

Few hospitals have enough physiotherapists to look after all the patients requiring this care, so the nurse may have to carry out the supervision of these activities. Attention is directed particularly towards, (*a*) breathing exercises, (*b*) active movements of upper and lower limbs, and (*c*) active exercise of small joints or wrist and hand. These exercises may be involved in performing various types of occupational therapy.

Pressure Sores

One of the most common problems in the nursing care of patients confined to bed, particularly elderly patients, is the prevention and treatment of pressure sores. Prolonged pressure on one part of the body prevents blood reaching the tissues, which then die. Pressure occurs most frequently in parts of the body where the force is concentrated on a bony prominence such as the heels, buttocks, or sacrum.

In the normal person, the first symptom of excessive or prolonged pressure on some area is pain and discomfort, which causes the person to change position. In those who are ill, however, sensory impairment, paralysis, general weakness, confusion, altered consciousness, or mental apathy may prevent the patient from feeling or responding to the pain. In people with hardened blood vessels, anaemia, or dietary deficiencies, the tissues are more prone to break down. Pressure concentrated over a bony prominence usually causes death of the deeper tissues first; thus, even when the skin appears only red, extensive damage may have already occurred beneath. In other patients the skin breaks down first, this is usually the result of a 'shearing' force. These forces arise as the result of a dragging movement of the skin against the bedclothes and may be caused by incorrectly moving the patient, or by his own tendency to slip down the bed when placed in a sitting or semi-prone position. The sores are more likely to occur if the tissues are wet, as with incontinent patients, or if the bed clothes are rough or wrinkled.

PREVENTION OF BED SORES

1. The best method is to keep the patient as active and mobile as possible so that prolonged pressure on any area of tissue is avoided. Very few patients actually need to be kept in bed all day, and should be sat out whenever possible.
2. If the patient is in bed and not actively moving, he or she must be turned at least every two hours and sometimes hourly.
3. Patients when lifted must *not* be dragged up the bed.
4. Extra pressure from heavy bedclothes should be avoided by using cradles.
5. Beds must be kept clean and dry and unwrinkled. Incontinent patients may be kept dry by being 'potted' at regular and frequent intervals. It is sometimes necessary to use an indwelling catheter, although this carries the risk of inducing a urinary infection.
6. The skin must be kept clean and dry. No ointments, cream, or lotions have been shown to be especially effective. Careful drying of the skin and the application of a bland powder help.
7. The use of mechanical devices, such as a ripple mattress, to prevent prolonged pressure on one area should be looked upon as

additional to the nursing care described, and not as a substitute for it.

The main aim must be the prevention of further pressure to the area by intensive use of the measures described.

Local treatment consists of the removal of all dead and infected tissue. This can be encouraged by the use of Eusol, hypertonic saline, or other preparations. The actual technique used depends largely on the preferences and prejudices of the medical and nursing staff concerned. Infected sores may require the use of local or systemic antibiotics.

Urinary Incontinence

One of the most difficult problems of management in elderly patients is presented by those who are unable to control their bladders so that they wet themselves or pass their urine at times or in places that are not socially acceptable. In those who are also unable to control their bowels, the nursing care becomes so heavy as to be virtually impossible at home. Incontinence of urine, faeces, or both, is a frequent reason for the admission of a patient to hospital. Among old people in hospital about a fifth are incontinent at some time. Incontinence may also be a feature of the behaviour of severely disturbed psychotics, in whom it may represent a regression to early behaviour pattern.

CAUSES OF URINARY INCONTINENCE

1. Nerve damage causing the destruction of the areas of the brain involved in the voluntary control of the bladder muscles. This may be due to general brain damage, as in senile or arteriosclertotic dementia, or to localised lesions such as a frontal lobe tumour.
2. Damage to the spinal nerves supplying the bladder as a result of spinal injury, malignant tumours, or other diseases of the spinal cord and nerves.
3. Confusion due to disturbed brain function may render the patient unaware of his need to empty his bladder, unable to find the appropriate place to do so, or unable to indicate his needs to other people.
4. Unconsciousness makes a patient unable to control the emptying of his bladder.

LOCAL CAUSES

1. Obstruction at the bladder neck or in the urethra may make it impossible to empty the bladder completely; the bladder may become overfilled, with consequent leaking of urine (retention with overflow). The most common cause for such obstruction in men is an enlarged prostate. Certain drugs cause spasm of the muscles closing off the bladder, and this may also produce retention with overflow. Impacted faeces can also indirectly interfere with bladder function.

2. Increased irritability of the bladder, causes the bladder to empty more frequently. The most common cause is an acute urinary infection. Women, because of their much shorter urethra, which opens relatively close to the anus, are much more frequent sufferers from urinary infection than men.

3. Bladder muscles may be too weak to continue functioning in the very frail.

GENERAL

1. Confining the patient to bed may of itself often seem to precipitate incontinence in patients, who just manage to keep dry while up and about. It may relate to the difficulty most people have in using bottles or bedpans.

2. Patients who are unable to express themselves clearly may be thought to be wandering or restless and are led back to their bed or chair, when they are, in fact, indicating their need to empty their bladders. Also, patients who have difficulty in finding their way about, or who are unable to remember directions or instructions, may not be able to find the lavatory in time. It is rare to find a geriatric ward in which the lavatory is clearly indicated, both in words and symbols, so that even for the mentally unimpaired, finding it in time becomes a major task.

Habit Training

Many patients with chronic brain syndromes show deterioration in their toilet and feeding habits. This falling off can be arrested or reversed by 'habit training', by taking small groups of patients and establishing a regular pattern of behaviour. Each day at the same time, the same tasks are performed, and the patients are instructed in simple terms, and encouraged to act on their own initiative. Such a group requires tact and patience on the part of the nurse, but the rewards in terms of improved behaviour, and the general pleasantness of the ward can be considerable.

Habit training is the first elementary step in the rehabilitiation programme of long-stay patients. As a result of this intensive training, many patients have improved and shown signs of being 'remotivated' to take a more active interest in the hospital life and participate in the outside community. As a result of the more varied rehabilitation facilities that followed habit training, many patients have reached a level of improvement where discharge home, or to a hostel, has become possible.

The nurses may sometimes think that habit training is the nursing of the past, and occasionally may associate the term 'habit training' with institutionalisation because of the regularity and time-tables to which the patients are encouraged to conform. However, there is a need for habit training even today, and this elementary but important step in rehabilitation can be beneficial to a variety of patients whose habits of personal hygiene and level of functioning have reached a very low level.

AIMS OF HABIT TRAINING

1. To prevent further deterioration.

2. To improve a patient's personal appearance and hygiene, with the patient himself showing interest, ability, and some initiative to maintain it.

3. To restore the self-respect and the feeling of the patient himself that he is respected as an individual, with his own rights, thoughts, feelings, and his own range of interests. This may be extremely difficult or impossible to achieve in patients who suffer from a rapidly progressive organic degeneration of the brain, but it is not beyond hope with patients who display deteriorated habits when suffering from any other forms of mental illnesses or who are regressed in their behaviour because of their prolonged stay in a mental hospital.

4. To achieve a general improvement in the patient's mental state, and his own control of acceptable behaviour, so that he can benefit from a wider rehabilitation programme and can lead a fuller and more independent form of life, either within the hospital or in the community.

ESSENTIAL PRINCIPLES IN HABIT TRAINING

1. Belief and determination on the part of nurses, that improvement, no matter how small and no matter how long it will take to achieve, will be seen in patients as a result of habit training.

2. Habits are acquired by repeated practice regularly performed; for example, going regularly to the lavatory, washing hands afterwards, washing or shaving, and brushing teeth.

3. Example of other people and the influence of stimulating environment is the important factor in acquisition of habits. The attractive, neat, and clean appearance of the nurses themselves, properly set tables at meal times, clean and attractive wards and furnishings, beds, dormitories, lavatories, and washrooms, are examples that may influence the patient's habits.

4. Supply of information and repeated explanations in a friendly manner by the nurse to the patient regarding the desirability and benefits of recommended habits, is also essential.

5. Notice should be taken of any reactions or negative objections shown by the patients because these would provide ideal opportunities to obtain some indication of what the patient thinks about the recommended habits, how he understands them, and why he may object either to the way you request him to do certain things or to the suggested habit as such. Reactions may be passive, the patient not showing any initiative at all, and the nurse will have to do everything for the patient herself. Don't get disheartened! Try again, time and time again; for example, giving the patient a face flannel, soap, even having to wash his face. One day the patient may show an indication that he is ready to try it himself: this is the beginning. Any initiative shown by the patient should be allowed to continue; avoid returning to the previous step.

6. Reward is another essential factor in habit formation. Personal and social approval is the best reward for adult people. Complimentary remarks should be made in the presence of other patients, 'Mrs Jones looks very smart this morning, her hair looks tidy. Don't you think so, Mrs Martin?' There is a lot of truth in the saying: 'If you regard me as a cabbage, I will behave like one'. Criticising remarks by the nurse on the faulty habits of the patients, are less likely to succeed than compliments and approval.

TECHNIQUE AND PRACTICE

1. Small groups of patients, six to eight in number.

2. The same nurse, preferably, working with one group. This is now difficult when most of the nurses in psychiatric hospitals work on a shift system of duties. Nurses on opposite shifts should have opportunities for discussions to achieve a similar approach in the group's habit training programme and share the information about the patient's peculiarities and progress.

3. Each patient should have his own personal toilet requisites, face flannel, towel, soap, tooth brush, and bedside locker. Personal or individual variety of clothing should be used, marked by the name of the patient or recognisable by a different material or colour.

4. Simple and regular routine is followed; for example, patients rise, go to the lavatory, make their own beds with the help of the nurse, attend to morning toilet.

During breakfast time, the nurse should stay with the patients, supervise and encourage proper table manners and eating habits. Some patients may require assistance with eating; more able patients could be encouraged to help the others. Throughout the day the patients are encouraged to go to the lavatory, especially to empty the bladder to prevent incontinence of urine. The time interval may be every four hours, but always following each meal or drink. Each visit to the lavatory is followed by hand washing and arranging clothing to maintain a respectable appearance.

Bowel action is encouraged every morning after breakfast to develop a regular daily habit. Peristaltic action of the bowel is usually stimulated by the food and drink intake during breakfast, and this is regarded as the most opportune time for the bowel action from the physiological point of view.

5. The patient's day is spent in a group with the same nurse, and the programme is very similar to the one outlined in Chapter 5, on schizophrenias, under the heading of *Nursing Aspects of the Chronic State*. In this group, there is an excellent opportunity to promote nurse-patient understanding, acceptance and therapeutic relationship. With her knowledge and understanding of each individual patient, the nurse can encourage fuller development of the particular interests and capabilities the patient may still possess.

Some aspects of the patient's personality are not completely eroded by mental illness, and those aspects should be utilised and expanded in the hope of a general improvement.

The Unconscious Patient

Patients may lose consciousness for a wide variety of reasons. The unconscious patient requires prompt first aid, and the cause has to be established. Common causes of unconsciousness in a mental hospital are:

1. ECT
2. Epilepsy
3. Overdoses—including alcohol
4. Strokes (cerebral vascular accidents)
5. Faints (syncope)
6. Hypoglycaemia (low blood sugar, usually after insulin)
7. Heart attacks (coronary thrombosis)

Less common causes include, uraemia, liver failure, diabetic coma, meningitis, encephalitis, and cerebral tumours. Hysterical patients may present with apparent loss of consciousness.

The care of the patient who is unconscious can be considered under three headings; (a) first-aid measures, (b) nursing care of cases of prolonged unconsciousness, and (c) diagnosis of the cause of unconsciousness.

1. First Aid

When someone is found unconscious, the first thing that has to be established is whether it is safe to attend to him. If he is in contact with a live source of electricity, he must either be dragged clear, using some non-conducting object to move him, or the electric supply must be switched off. If he is in a gas-filled room, he must be dragged into the open air, or a gas-free place.

When this has been done, or when there is no danger to the person giving first aid, the essential thing to do before anything else is to *make sure that the patient has a clear airway,* i.e., see that there is nothing obstructing the passage of air down the trachea. The most common cause of obstruction is the patient's own tongue, which falls backwards and obstructs the larynx. This should be pulled forward, and the patient's head turned to one side to stop it falling back again. False teeth and food materials may also get stuck in the throat, and must be removed. Having made sure that the airway is clear, see if the patient breathes of his own accord. If he does not, the next thing to check is whether his heart is beating. If the patient's heart is beating but he is not breathing, it is necessary to apply some form of *artificial respiration*. If the heart has stopped, then, in addition, *external cardiac massage* must be performed.

When loss of consciousness is associated with external bleeding, an attempt must be made to control the blood loss by the application of pressure, either at the site of bleeding, or over the appropriate pressure point.

2. Prolonged Unconsciousness

Patients who remain unconscious for more than a few hours require special nursing care.

Position. Nurse in the lateral position, turning the patient at least every two hours, and paying special attention to pressure areas.

Respiratory tract. Regular cleaning of mouth and pharynx and sucking out of excessive secretions is essential. When the respiration is depressed, a tracheotomy may be performed, the patient usually being transferred to a specialised unit for intensive care. Patients are usually given an antibiotic to prevent chest infections developing.

Feeding. This will have to be carried out by means of an oesophageal tube. A diet of fortified milk, with additional vitamins and iron is usually satisfactory; a volume of 1·5 litres providing sufficient fluid and calories.

Bowel and bladder. The unconscious patient may be incontinent or may develop retention of urine. This is dealt with by inserting a self-retaining catheter, which is changed every three days.

3. Diagnosis of the Cause of Unconsciousness

Although this is the responsibility of the doctor, the nurse will be expected to assist by observation and the collection of specimens. The nurse should note the circumstances in which the patient lost consciousness, or was found. She should, where appropriate, search for evidence of an overdose—empty pill bottles, and the like. She should also look for signs of drinking—empty gin bottles, etc.

The specimens that may be required for investigation are:

1. Vomit, or results of a stomach wash out; for testing for drugs,
2. Urine; presence of glucose, acetone, drugs,
3. Blood; bloodsugar level, urea, electrolytes,
4. CSF; for protein, cells, bacteria, etc., and measurement of its pressure during lumbar puncture.

Care of the Dying

Death is a problem that has to be faced by everyone, not only their own death, but that of their loved ones. For some people, death is seen as merely a necessary prelude to everlasting life, for others it is an end—to be feared or longed for. In every case it is a venture into the unknown. Those who are privileged to care for someone who is dying have the same responsibilities to the patient as they would have when seeing a friend off on a long journey to a new land. They must provide hope, comfort, encouragement—and love. They must not give the impression that they are impatient for the invalid to be gone, nor must they imply that they have done all that can be expected and their task is accomplished. The patient must be allowed to leave his life with as much dignity as he would wish. No attempt should be spared to make him comfortable. This involves attention to all aspects of his care, especially: (*a*) pain and discomfort, (*b*) thirst, (*c*) emotional needs, and (*d*) spiritual needs.

No one need die in hospital suffering from pain. Adequate doses of analgesic drugs should be given if the patient is experiencing pain. The choice of drug, and dosage, is the responsibility of the doctor, but the timing of doses is usually left to the nurse. She should remember that the patient knows how he feels better than she does! Analgesics are often supplemented by tranquillising drugs, and patients may complain that they feel too drowsy—again they should be allowed to dictate the degree to which they are tranquillised. Less obvious, but just as distressing for the patient as frank pain, are various degrees of physical discomfort. Every effort should be made to reduce sources of discomfort to the minimum, the dying patient rarely likes to be flat in the bed, and should be propped up.

Thirst is a torture, and care should be taken that the patient is given frequent sips of iced water or any other fluid that he likes. Alcohol is an excellent sedative and a great comfort to those who have been accustomed to drinking it. Regular attention to bowel and bladder actions also helps to reduce potential sources of discomfort.

Many of the patients who die in mental hospitals have lost the ability to express their emotional needs, as a result of brain damage, but to assume that because they cannot communicate, they no longer have any is not justifiable. The greatest need of any patient approaching death, is time—the nurse must find time to sit with the patient, particularly if there are no friends or relatives to perform this service. Given time, the patient may wish to talk of his fears, anxieties, hopes, or expectations, but even those who do not or cannot speak, seem to derive comfort from the presence of someone who cares.

Patients who have some form of religious belief may wish to see a priest before they die, and it is important that they are enabled to do so. Other patients may accept the offer of seeing a cleric if it is made. The nurse should not try to impose her own belief, or lack of it, on the patient.

The nurse must remember that death is never a tragedy for the person who is dead—he has either started on a great adventure or has entered a state of unknowing. The tragedy is for those who are left; left with problems of love and hate, guilt, and sorrow, with which they have to come to terms. By being calm but sympathetic and allowing the relatives to talk, even at length, of their memories, anxieties, and regrets, the nurse can help them to adjust to this sometimes devastating experience.

12 Special Nursing Problems—2 Aggressive, Confused and Restless Patients

Aggressive Patients

Aggression is a normal biological response to certain situations and is essential for the survival of the individual, and the species. However, even in the individual it has to be controlled or inhibited at times. An animal facing danger can either fight or run away, and it must learn the correct response, or die. In man, not only does this apply but, in addition, society can only survive if the individual and the group controls aggression.

The small child expresses aggression when frustrated or anxious, and its parents respond in a way that they feel appropriate. Sometimes they respond so aggressively themselves that the child becomes terrified of his own feelings, attempts to repress and deny them, develops extreme guilt when this fails and, thus, never comes to terms with his aggressive drives. Such children may develop into adults with obsessional personalities that may turn their aggressive drives on to themselves, in the form of depressive illnesses or obsessional states in which they become preoccupied with thoughts of violence. When the parents, for some reason, do not help the child to control his aggressive drive, the child may develop into an excessively violent adolescent or adult. In the course of normal development the child learns to divert his aggressive drives into socially acceptable channels, only rarely expressing them in the form of overt violence. Various forms of sport provide an excellent outlet for aggressive drives.

Overt violence may occur among adults for a variety of reasons, that can be listed as follows:

1. Failure of conditioning during childhood, that may be seen in the so-called aggressive psychopath.
2. Removal of social restrictions on violence, usually experienced

151

during times of war, but which can also develop in a ward in which the staff are aggressive to the patients or to each other— violence begets violence.

3. Aggression is the normal response to frustration. Each individual has a different level of tolerance for frustration, and if this level is exceeded, aggression may result. The types of frustration and their causes will be considered later.

4. Anxiety and fear, i.e. a threat to the individual's safety either physical or mental, may produce an aggressive response.

5. Failure of the individual's normal control mechanism. In the presence of impaired brain function due to any cause, the individual may be less able to appreciate the nature of his behaviour or exercise control over it.

Aggression is experienced as a powerful urge to release energy in such a way that the frustrating circumstance is altered, or the threat eliminated. It may be sublimated into constructive efforts to deal with the problem or it may explode as either verbal threats, or actual physical violence. The physical violence may be directed at objects, other people, or at the patient himself—taking the form of suicide or self-mutilation.

Dealing with Aggression

Prevention is always better than cure. To limit the likelihood of violence it is necessary to:

1. Limit the amount of frustration patients experience. Frustration arises when basic human needs are denied or thwarted.

2. Avoid situations that are threatening for the patients.

3. Provide suitable outlets for aggressive drives.

4. Help patients to control their need to use overt violence.

5. Learn to recognise and control one's own aggressive drives.

The need to modify one's immediate environment and to carry out some form of useful and rewarding work appears to be almost universal in humans. If this need cannot be satisfied, boredom and frustration result. Wards that have an active programme of occupation and entertainment have a much lower incidence of overt aggression than wards where the patients spend hours merely sitting, or performing routine and uninteresting tasks.

Freedom is recognised as one of the basic rights of a human being, and most people resent restriction of their freedom. Freedom not only implies freedom of movement but also freedom of choice. Patients should be allowed the absolute maximum of both. It is always easier and safer to say 'no' to patients' requests than it is to say 'yes', and thus take the responsibility for any undesirable consequences, but in so doing the nurse is likely to exchange one problem for another. The need to restrict patients' freedom of movement is very limited: it is almost always possible to arrange that the patient remains under some form of supervision even if he is not prepared to remain on the ward. As was clearly demonstrated in prisoner of war camps, and is daily demonstrated in prisons, the more effort one puts into keeping someone *in*, the more effort they will put into trying to get *out*. At times, of course, it is essential that a patient be confined to a limited area, and this is discussed later.

Everyone experiences some degree of sexual need that, under normal circumstances, is either satisfied in socially acceptable ways or sublimated into some other activity. It is well known that when normal outlets are not available and methods of sublimation are limited, sexual needs begin to assume greater than normal importance. Under these circumstances there is either a tendency to resort to homosexual activity or to divert some of the energy into violence. While normal sexual outlets are not usually provided in the setting of a mental hospital, two things can be done. First, patients can be allowed weekend leave whenever possible, and secondly, there should be as much integration of the sexes within the hospital as possible. In this way, some of the sexual energy is released in the same conventional way that it is in the community outside the hospital, by means of social activities, such as dances, socials, and other entertainments, and through sharing the everyday tasks.

All human beings, even though they may not admit it to themselves or other people, have a need for affection, respect, and love. Deprived of these, the individual may respond with aggression. The nurse must try to give each patient the feeling that she is genuinely interested in him as an individual, respects him, and wishes him well. Nurses sometimes regard the patients as an unnecessary evil, to be treated with scant regard and less affection. Such nurses are the ones who usually have the most problems with violence.

Reducing the Patient's Anxiety and Fear
Anxiety and fear arise as a result of factors the patient considers to be threatening. These can be divided into external and internal threats.

External. Actual physical threats are likely to provoke aggressive behaviour on the part of some patients. Such threats may be made by nurses on the ground that if a patient is warned in time he is less likely to be aggressive himself. In general, the patient who responds in this way would probably not have been violent anyway. The potentially violent patient is more likely to respond with even greater violence than he would otherwise have done. Violent behaviour by one patient may start off a kind of chain reaction in the ward, some patients acting violently because of fear, while others take the opportunity of reduced restriction. For this reason, it is often advisable to try to limit the number of patients involved in a violent incident to a minimum, although, in a ward where there is a fairly high level of tolerance of disturbed behaviour, such incidents can provide a useful subject for group discussion leading to a greater understanding of the causes of violent feelings and behaviour in both those involved and the spectators.

Physical threats should not, of course, be made to the patient, but it is important to remember that some acts the nurse regards as forming part of 'treatment' may be regarded by the patient as physically threatening. Medication may be regarded as some form of poisoning, or it may remind the patient of incidents in childhood when he was forced to take some evil-tasting substance by a parent or other authoritative figure. In either case, it is likely that the patient's refusal will be much stronger than rational reasons would explain. In such cases the nurse should try any appropriate method of persuasion, but should never try to force the patient to take the drug. If she fails to persuade him, she should report the incident to the medical officer, who can decide on the appropriate action. When it is considered vital that the patient should have the drug, it will probably be ordered in an injectable form. Giving injections to resistive patients is discussed later.

Injections are often regarded by patients with an irrational degree of fear (everyone knows of soldiers fainting when having an inoculation) and it has been suggested that for some people injections have an unconscious sexual significance.

ECT, as the lay name 'shock' treatment suggests, is regarded by many people with great terror; usually their anxieties can be dealt with by adequate explanation and reassurance. However, some patients will need additional sedation on the days on which they are to have ECT.

Patients may feel threatened, or actually be threatened by other patients, and staff should try to be aware of such incidents, as the patient concerned may be afraid to mention it. Many of these incidents can be resolved by discussion between those involved, but sometimes it is necessary to transfer one of the patients to another ward.

Internal factors. The patient may feel that because he is in hospital, his job, marriage, social position, and the like, may be in some danger. This may be a real fear, or it may represent a symptom of his illness. Every effort should be made to help the patient to discuss his problems and help him to find a solution to them.

Other internal factors are those concerning the patient's earlier life experiences. Being in hospital may bring to the surface difficulties the patient has had in relating to people in authority, or it may aggravate fears about going mad, losing control, or being shut away. Such fears, if not expressed verbally may give rise to violent acting-out behaviour. Again, this may be avoided if the nurse is able to get the patient to talk about his fears. In patients who are experiencing hallucinations or who have delusional beliefs, violence may arise without apparent reason, because they are responding to the world as they see it, and not to the 'real' world as seen by the nurse.

Providing Outlets for Aggressive Feelings

The importance of occupational and recreational opportunities has been mentioned but, in addition, some provision for a more direct expression of aggressive feeling is required. In everyday life, few people express their aggression in physical terms, but the vast majority do express them verbally. Every winter Saturday, thousands of men who are angry with their wives, their bosses, or themselves, go off and shout at a football referee—and feel much better as a result. Patients must also be given adequate opportunity to 'shout at the ref'. The 'ref', in turn, must learn to tolerate this abuse and come to terms with it. Some form of regular community meeting provides such an opportunity.

Few hospitals make any provision for patients to act in a physically violent way, without causing any real damage. The best that most hospitals do is to be fairly tolerant of aggression directed at objects, on the principle that a broken window is better than a broken head. There may well be scope for providing such things as punch bags (painted to look like the matron or medical superintendent!), or piles of old dishes that can be smashed against a wall.

Raising the Patient's Ability to Control His Aggression

This can be done in three ways:

1. by the use of drugs that help to damp down aggression or mental activity in general; for example, the major tranquillisers and the sedative drugs;
2. by helping the patient to gain insight into the reasons for his acts;
3. by encouraging him to talk about his difficulties, rather than acting them out in the form of violence. This implies that the nurse must be prepared to listen to the patient when he feels the need, however time-consuming or inconvenient this might be.

Recognising and Controlling One's own Aggression

After an incident of violence the injured party tends to put all the blame on the aggressor, but often a bystander will comment: 'It is no more than she deserved'. Many incidents are, in fact, provoked deliberately or unconsciously by the aggressive needs of the 'innocent' victim. If such events are to be avoided, the nurse must learn to recognise her own drives and the kind of situation that provokes them. As many of these are unconsciously determined. there is a limit to the amount of insight the nurse can acquire on her own. This is why some form of staff meeting in which there is free discussion, and even criticism, of members' treatment of patients can be of great value. Such groups must, however, be run by an experienced person, if they are not to degenerate into mere destructive back-biting sessions.

When Prevention Fails

In spite of every care, incidents of violence do occur from time to time and have to be dealt with in a practical way. The aim is to prevent the patient from harming himself or others, using the minimum degree of force and restraint to achieve this end. While the exact techniques employed vary from place to place, and differ in different situations, some general guidance can be given.

Assess the Situation Before Acting. The nurse who knows her patients well will not only be more likely to avoid situations that provoke aggression, but will deal more efficiently with those that do occur. If the nurse considers that the patient requires physically restraining, she should never attempt to do this on her own. Either she or the patient will get hurt. The aim of restraint may be:

1. to prevent the patient harming himself or others while appropriate steps are taken;
2. to remove the patient to a side room from which potentially dangerous articles of furniture have been removed;
3. to hold the patient while an injection is given.

To give an injection to a resistive patient efficiently, and with the minimum risk to all involved, at least four skilled nurses are required. One to hold each arm, one to hold the patient's legs, and the fourth to give the injection. The patient often becomes less violent when faced with such a show of strength. Each nurse must know exactly what her particular task is, and must carry it out at exactly the same time as the others. It is no use hanging on to one arm while being punched with the other. In grasping the patient, an attempt should be made to grip the arms near the shoulders, rather than at the wrists, as in this way more effective restraint is obtained with the expenditure of less force. Restraint should be applied only for the shortest possible time. In those rare instances when it is necessary to seclude a patient in a side room, the medical officer must at once be informed.

Following any violent episode an attempt should be made to try to discover the causes and to find a way in which further episodes can be avoided. It is important that in reporting such incidents the nurse should refrain from over-dramatising the event, otherwise the patient may be regarded with far greater fear than he deserves and the resulting staff anxiety can prevent his having the treatment he requires. The patient must also be helped to rehabilitate himself in his own eyes and in the eyes of the other people involved. Many incidents can be avoided or limited if the patient is given the chance to 'climb down' without too much loss of face.

Confused and Restless Patients

Much of the restlessness and occasional violence of patients suffering from conditions in which their awareness of their surrounding is impaired, arises from fear. Their world is full of menace, no longer familiar and safe, but changing and unremembered. Shapes and shadows loom and threaten, and the patient's terror is like that of a small child waking in a dimly lit room, full of bogy men and hobgoblins. Other confused patients are more anxious than fearful. They may be preoccupied by the need to perform tasks that have been part of their everyday life, but that are no longer appropriate—old ladies wish to prepare lunch for their long dead husbands, or whimper in terror at the thought of being late for school.

The primary need in nursing such patients is to provide some anchor of stability to which they can cling. Time and time again, the nurse must be prepared to provide explanations and reassurance. The more stable the surroundings the better, and in the more acute phase, the same nurse should stay with the patient as far as it is practical. There are some advantages in nursing the patient in a side room, where disturbing factors can be limited. Such a room should be softly lit, thus avoiding dark shadows that might form the basis for illusional misinterpretation by the patient.

While the more severe cases will require adequate sedation, drugs should be avoided if possible, as many tend to cause confusion themselves. Full attention should be paid to factors that may be contributing to the patient's restlessness, common examples are thirst, a full bladder, and a loaded rectum.

When the patient has to be nursed in bed, cot sides should be avoided, if possible, as they tend to increase the patient's fear and provoke even more vigorous attempts to escape.

The nurse must note anything that seems to increase the patient's confusion. She should record the times when the patient is worse, as this may give a clue to the underlying cause. An increase in symptoms shortly after a drug is given may suggest that the confusion is a side effect of the medication. A patient who is worse shortly before the next meal is due may be showing signs of hypoglycaemia. Attention must be directed at ensuring that the patient has an adequate intake of food and fluids, and it is often necessary to give extra vitamins.

Adequate opportunity for exercise should be provided. Patients who refuse to remain seated for more than a few minutes often settle if they are first taken for a walk around the hospital or its grounds. An attempt should always be made to understand the motives under-lying the patient's restlessness as, occasionally, these are perfectly rational and can be satisfied. Not infrequently, the patient is trying to find the lavatory, and if he fails, will reward the nurse by being incontinent.

Patients who are restless but not confused, i.e. in hypomania and catatonic schizophrenia, present similar problems. In the most severe states, death may result from exhaustion or through failure to take food and fluid. In part, they do not eat and drink because they cannot spare the time. To overcome this, they must be allowed to eat and drink at any time they wish, however inconvenient. During the acute phase, their diet may have to be in liquid form.

Part Two

The Nature of Mental Disorder,
   its Recognition and its Treatment

13 The Nature of Mental Disorders

In Part One, various disorders have been presented and described under the general heading of illnesses. For most people, illness conjures up a picture of someone in bed, looking pale and interesting, being ministered to by quiet-voiced angels in nurse's uniform, and occasionally taking medicines prescribed by an infinitely wise and devastatingly handsome doctor. The problems described earlier seem to have little in common with this picture, and in an attempt to sort out this confusion a mental illness must be defined, and this, in turn, forces one to define mental health. Health and illness are considered to be the province of medicine, and so the definition usually given is based on the same kind of thinking as that used to define a disease such as tuberculosis, or cancer of the lung. However, this type of definition is not really applicable to 'mental health' because it can apply only to a very restricted range of the problems that are considered to be the province of psychiatry. This approach to the problem also encourages the idea that there is some absolute standard of mental health against which one's own level can be measured. In practice it is not possible to define this standard.

If this 'medical' approach is not entirely satisfactory, it may help if we use a different model around which to organise an approach to the problem. A possible model to use is fitness. Everyone recognises that fitness is not the same as health or illness— it is possible to be unfit, yet free from any disease process: at the same time, illness can render one unfit. Fitness is also relative; it is not an absolute state, but is always judged relative to the demands made upon the individual—thus, a man might be fit enough to run for a bus, but not fit enough to run a mile. The degree of fitness that is satisfactory for an individual is that which enables him to cope easily with the demands normally made upon him and still have a little extra resistence in reserve. Using 'fitness' in place of 'health' or 'ill health' leads to thinking in terms of games, and this model can prove very useful in sorting out our ideas about mental health and the ways in which it can fail, and also in understanding what factors can lead to its failure.

Living things differ in one fundamental respect from the non-living—they are capable of organised activity. At its lowest level, this organised activity is restricted to a molecule—the viruses organise their molecules in such a way that they are able to make more of themselves. In simple unicellular creatures, various constituents of the cell carry out specific organised activities that enable the cell to survive and reproduce. In the evolutionary process, multicellular organisms developed, then groups of cells within the organism undertook special activities and, finally, the individual organism began to co-operate with other individuals in increasingly complex activities, producing man, with his almost infinite capacity for complex organised behaviour. The very complexity of human behaviour makes it difficult to describe and to recognise underlying principles, and it is for this reason that it is helpful to use a 'model' rather than the 'real thing'. Now one form of organised activity that is familiar to almost everyone is a game. As man is a social animal, and his activities mostly involve other people, it is obviously better to use the model of a team game such as football.

To play a game successfully and derive satisfaction from it, the player must have the necessary physical attributes; he must master the basic skills involved; he must know the rules and understand, emotionally as well as intellectually, the need to observe them. He must be able to relate to his team mates and to modify his own behaviour to fit in with their needs. To enjoy the game he must have reasonable facilities to play; the standard of the match in which he plays must not be too high for his talents, nor yet too low to place any demands on him. Given these factors he will be fit to play and enjoy the game. So it is in life. A human being needs to have some aim and purpose in life that, with effort, he can achieve. He may be unable to do so because adverse factors render him unfit. Illness, in the medical sense is one such factor.

Thus, when we consider the field of mental health or ill health, we can do so by looking at the way in which the person is temporarily or permanently 'unfit' to cope with his life situation.

1. Lack of Physical Attributes
For a variety of reasons the embryo may fail to develop a normal brain, or the baby may sustain damage to the brain while in the

uterus, or during the process of being born. (This may be associated with physical handicaps as well.) In such cases, the brain is unable to reach a normal level of functioning and the child is of subnormal intelligence. The degree of subnormality depends on the site and extent of the damage, and can be assessed by the child's performance in a variety of test situations. Even those who are only slightly subnormal find life much more difficult than people of normal intelligence and, thus, are liable to develop forms of neurotic breakdown.

2. Lack of Basic Skills

Apart from having a normal brain, to develop the vast range of skills demanded in a complex society the individual requires normally functioning sense organs. If blind or deaf, the child will require a special training, and if the condition is partial and unrecognised the child may be considered to be of subnormal intelligence. Lack of proper training in the early years of life may prevent a child from mastering such important tasks as reading and writing. Even a poor command of the spoken word can prove very limiting in terms of earnings and career prospects.

3. Learning and Obeying the Rules

Life in a community, demands, to a greater or lesser degree, that all members conform to a code of rules that may limit the individual's freedom but benefit the majority. These rules have to be learnt, but even more important, the individual must want to obey them. He learns to do so by being rewarded when he observes them and punished when he does not. Gradually he develops a sense of guilt, so that when he transgresses, although he may not be found out, he feels unhappy and anxious within himself. This usually becomes more effective than the punishment imposed if he is discovered. The development of this emotion of guilt is a complex process, but it seems to occur only if the child has the opportunity of learning right from wrong by the example given him by people he loves during the first years of his life. These are usually his parents, or parent substitutes when the real parents are absent. If this relationship is not formed, because of absence of a parent, or because of the parents' own abnormal behaviour, the child is very likely to fail in learning, both how to love and how important it is to consider the needs and wishes of other people. This failure leads to the development of a type of personality we call psychopathic.

4. The Standards of 'Play'

The ability of a person to perform in life is determined in part by inherited factors, and in part by the training and experience he has had. Thus, for all of us there is a limit to the amount of stress we can cope with. When exposed to a higher level, or when the stress continues for too long, we have to find some way of dealing with it. One method of escape is to give up playing—in life that would mean killing oneself. A less drastic method is to become ill—this is often easier than recognising that one is unable to meet the demands placed upon one. The person in this situation experiences anxiety which, in turn, leads to the development of a variety of symptoms for which the sufferer then seeks help. This pattern of behaviour is called 'neurotic'.

5. Unfit Through Illness

Finally, there are those who may have been coping adequately but then develop some form of illness that alters their mental state so that they can no longer manage. These illnesses fall into two broad groups. Those in which the underlying cause, or at least the nature of the brain damage, is known, and those in which a physical change is suspected but has not been proved. The former are grouped under the title, organic brain syndromes (organic psychoses) and the latter are called 'functional psychoses'. Thus, the types of problem that are the concern of psychiatry can be classified under the following headings. It must be remembered, however, that an individual can have a mixture of these conditions, and it is not always possible to slot a person into one neat pigeon hole.

Classification

1. Mental Handicap

This implies a failure to develop to a normal degree of intelligence. As intelligence is a measure of the person's ability, both to solve intellectual problems and acquire special skills, this failure implies that the patient will experience more difficulties in dealing with life than some of those more fortunately endowed. Thus, the milder degrees of subnormality of intelligence are sometimes associated with other forms of mental disorder.

2. Psychopathic Personality

A person who is unable to learn from his mistakes, who finds it difficult to tolerate even mild degrees of frustration, and who has difficulty in appreciating other people's emotional needs, is most likely to come into conflict with society, and here treatment is requested by society rather than by the patient. However, many people with these difficulties have insight into their behaviour and become depressed or anxious when they realise the mess they are making of their own and other peoples' lives. Such people may ask for treatment of their depression or anxiety.

3. Neurotic Illnesses

These are usually subdivided into, (*a*) anxiety states, (*b*) obsessional states, and (*c*) hysteria. In practice, the boundaries between these subdivisions tend to be blurred. The basic nature of the condition is a feeling of anxiety, which the patient attempts to reduce unconsciously by developing some form of symptom. The symptom may lead to the patient's escaping from the stressful situation; it may represent the problems in a symbolic form, or it may be a somatic consequence of anxiety. The type of symptom developed will depend on the patient's underlying personality and the nature of the stress he is experiencing.

4. Sexual Disorders

These conditions do not really form a separate group. Sexual deviations may result from neurotic conditions or as a part of a general psychopathic problem. The sexual relationship is the most intense and, thus, the most difficult of all human relationships. As such, it is a potent source of stress. This is increased because of the moralistic aspects that equate sex and sin.

5. Functional Psychoses

These are illnesses in which it is suspected, but not proven, that there is an underlying malfunction of the brain, probably at a biochemical level. This malfunction may be the cause of the illness, or it may lead to the persistence of symptoms when the situation that precipitated the illness, no longer exists. The functional psychoses are subdivided into:

(*a*) Affective disorders: depression (endogenous); hypomania; and mania. In these illnesses, the primary feature is a change in the patient's mood, and all his symptoms are understandable in terms of his changed mood.

(*b*) The schizophrenias: a diffuse and ill-defined group of conditions that can be subdivided in a number of ways, the most common being the division into simple hebephrenic, catatonic, and paranoid. As our knowledge and understanding of these conditions increases, more satisfactory classifications may be devised.

6. Organic Psychoses

These are due to interference, temporary or permanent, with the function of brain cells. They are subdivided on the basis of the length of time for which the failure of function persists into acute and chronic. Both may be due to one or more of the following causes:

1. Trauma
2. Infection
3. Neoplasm
4. Degeneration
5. Vascular disorders
6. Toxins
7. Metabolic disorders
8. Endocrine disorders
9. Heat or cold
10. Auto-immunity

The practice of classifying and of making a diagnosis in such terms has often been criticised. It is claimed that it enables one to 'hang a label on a patient' and, thus, to dismiss his problems and his needs. Such action is not, however, the fault of classification but demonstrates the need of the person who uses it in this way to intellectualise his own difficulties in dealing with the patient. Classification provides a framework on which our increasing knowledge can be organised. This framework must be modified as necessary—it is not God-given and immutable. We must always be prepared to modify our classification to fit our patients, and not expect them to slip neatly into pigeon holes of our devising.

The words neurosis and psychosis require some further explanation, though neither can be defined in a completely satisfactory way. Roughly speaking, the neuroses are those milder forms of disorder that lay people refer to as 'nervous breakdowns', while the psychoses are the more serious disorders that in lay terms would be referred to as 'madness'. However, in some severe neurotic states the patient may be far more incapacitated than someone with a mild form of a psychotic illness.

Another point of differentiation sometimes used is that of 'insight'. The neurotic is aware that he is in some way unwell, and usually seeks medical help, whereas the psychotic may deny that he is ill, and either seeks no help or the help of agencies such as the police. Again, this does not apply in a number of cases. The most important difference is that in psychotic states the patient experiences either some change in the world around him, or a difference within himself. Thus, the person with an anxiety state may feel afraid of crowds, or traffic or open spaces, but he still recognises the world as being the same as it was when he was not anxious; the schizophrenic patient, however, may say that he is afraid because the world has changed in some subtle way that he cannot understand and that it is full of menace. Even this difference is not universal, as many patients with psychotic illnesses do not experience this, while some with marked neurotic symptoms describe alterations in their perception of the world around them, or in their own identity.

The Recognition of Mental Disorder

The fact that a person is experiencing some difficulty in coping with life, the nature of his difficulty, and his attempts to deal with it, can be recognised from the way in which he behaves. Thus, the diagnosis of mental disorder of any kind is based on the observation of the person's behaviour, including, of course, his own description of his problem. There are very few forms of behaviour that occur only when the patient's mental state is abnormal; hence each item has to be weighed in relation to other aspects of the patient's behaviour, previous personality, and present situation before deciding that it indicates mental disorder. In order to observe effectively, the nurse must learn to organise her observations in a systematic way. A typical scheme of observation and recording is as follows:

1. General Appearance and Activity

Under normal circumstances, people expose very little of themselves to the public gaze, most of their body, especially men, being covered by clothes, hence the description of a person's appearance is based mainly on their facial expression and their dress.

The face is the mirror of the emotions, so that in general, the patient's face shows how he feels. Thus, the depressed patient may appear sad, worried, careworn, or tearful, or the schizophrenic patient may show in his facial expression a different emotion from the one he claims when asked how he feels in his spirits. The anxious patient may demonstrate his feelings by the sweat beading his pale face, his dry lips that he licks nervously, and his rather apprehensive expression, as clearly as by his description of how he feels.

The presence of physical disorders may be shown by the typical facial changes: the puffy, coarse-featured face of myxoedema; the large-jawed, heavy face of acromegaly; the moon face of Cushing's disease; the pop-eyed look of hyperthyroidism, and the mask-like features of Parkinsonism are common examples.

Clothes may also reflect the mood of the patient, and also indicate how aware and concerned he is with himself and other people. The nurse should note whether the state of dress is appropriate to the patient's age and social position. Are they clean and correctly fastened? Dirty, stained clothing, with undone buttons may indicate some degree of dementia, or some difficulty in coping with the intricate tasks involved in dressing. Some bizarre forms of dress may indicate the presence of delusions—if they do not merely reflect the latest products of Paris or Carnaby Street!

Activity may be increased or decreased in a variety of mental disorders. Abnormal forms of activity may be present as mannerisms or stereotypes. These may represent some form of behaviour that was once meaningful but is now merely habitual. In hypomania, mania, agitated depression, or catatonic excitement, the patient may be extremely restless and aggressive if restrained. A similar picture is seen in some cases of organic brain syndrome.

In severe depression, and in catatonic schizophrenia, the patient's movements may be much reduced, even to the state of stupor. Slowness and difficulty in moving may be a sign of organic nerve damage, such as occurs in Parkinsonism. The way in which the patient walks (gait) may also reveal the presence of organic disease, or mental disorder. The shuffling walk of Parkinsonism; the high stepping, feet slapping walk of tabes dorsalis; and the stiff-legged, broad-based, tentative step of some dementias are examples of organic disorders. Abnormal gaits of various forms may also be seen in schizophrenia and in hysteria.

Speech is probably the most revealing activity of all, both in what is said and the way in which it is said. The patient may describe certain mental experiences that do not often occur in normal people. Some of the more common are:

(a) *Hallucinations* are sensory impressions occurring in the absence of external stimuli. Thus, the patient sees, hears, feels, smells, or tastes something, when there is nothing in his environment to give rise to these sensations. The patient may recognise that these experiences are abnormal, or may accept them as being real. Hallucinations may occur in any form of mental disorder, and also sometimes occur in normal people, particularly during the time of going off to sleep, or when waking up. In the absence of organic brain disease, they most often occur in schizophrenia, when they are usually auditory or olfactory (smell).

(b) *Deja vu* is the feeling that 'this has all happened before'. This experience is quite common among 'normal' people, but it may occur as part of an epileptic fit, especially of the temporal lobe type.

(c) *Depersonalisation* is an experience that also occurs in normal people from time to time, as well as in physical disease, or after taking drugs. It has been described in most mental disorders, but is particularly common in phobic anxiety states. The patient describes it as 'like being outside oneself—floating above one's own head—feeling detached and distant from one's own body'.

(d) *Derealisation*, makes the patient feel that the world around him has changed in some way, while he himself has remained the same. This state is described by some schizophrenics, more rarely by depressed patients, and also by patients with anxiety states.

(e) A *delusion* is defined as a false belief that the patient maintains, in spite of proof to the contrary and that it is not in keeping with his educational, religious, and social background.

The form of a patient's speech is as important as its content. He may be extremely talkative, as in hypomania, or he may say almost nothing, as in depression or schizophrenia. His speech may indicate the difficulty he is having in organising his thoughts into logical sequence, or it may reveal an absence of ideas, or an inability to change from one idea to another. In some cases of organic brain damage, the patient has specific difficulties with speech. He may be unable to understand spoken or written words. He may understand them, but be unable to find the correct words to express what he wants to say himself. Difficulties of this kind are referred to as 'dysphasia'.

2. Memory and Orientation

In the organic brain syndromes, alteration in the patient's memory and his knowledge of who he is, where he is, and when it is, may all be affected. Memory is divided roughly into recent and remote. The former is tested by asking the patient about events that have taken place in the last few minutes, hours, or days, and immediate memory is tested by asking him to remember some simple information, and by asking him to repeat a series of numbers, immediately after being told them. Remote memory is tested by inquiring about events in the patient's childhood, or adult life, that everyone of his education might be expected to know. Orientation is divided into time, place and person. It is assessed by asking the patient to say where he is, i.e. in hospital, what day it is, of what month and in what year, and by asking him to name relatives or friends. Disorders of orientation usually indicate some form of organic brain damage, though it may occur in hysteria. The observation of a patient usually includes some assessment of his attention and concentration, of his intellectual level, of his judgement, and his insight into his illness.

14 Causes of Mental Disorders

As was pointed out in the previous chapter, mental disorder covers a wide range of human behaviour. It includes failure of development of normal mental functioning, certain personality deviations, particular kinds of reaction to stress, and also structural or biochemical disorders of the brain. It is obvious that when talking about *causes* of mental disorder, we can talk only in terms of the various factors that seem to be playing a part in producing the particular disorder in a particular individual at that time.

There is rarely one cause, rather it is the interplay of several separate factors combining to produce the condition. These factors can be considered under personal and environmental. Personal factors consist of (*a*) the patient's inherited characteristics, and (*b*) his development and experiences during childhood.* These combine to determine what kind of person he is, what his needs, attitudes and capabilities are, and how he tends to deal with difficulties and frustrations.

The environmental factors are those features in his physical and emotional surroundings that may be a source of frustration and anxiety for him and, also, any changes in the internal environment of his brain cells that may be causing impaired function.

While it is convenient to discuss these factors separately, it must be remembered that usually it is the interplay of a number of them that produces the disorder.

Personal Factors

The type of person we are, with respect to personality, physique, our ability to resist stress, and the type of illness we are liable to develop, is determined by the interplay of two factors. First, our inherited

* In the following pages, the development of a child is described in a way that is based on the work of psychoanalysts. This is not the only way of describing this process, nor even the most satisfactory way, but it is helpful to have an outline knowledge of this theory.

characteristics and, secondly, the range and nature of the intellectual and emotional experiences we undergo during our early life. We are like a plant—the *kind* of plant that grows depends on the seed sown, but the *quality* of the plant will depend on the soil it grows in, the weather it is exposed to, and the care and attention it receives.

Inheritance

Each human being is the result of the fusion of two cells, one from the father, one from the mother. The nuclei of these cells each contain rod-like structures called chromosomes, made up of a number of small particles called genes. These carry the 'blue print' for the baby's future development; determining its physical characteristics, mental abilities and, in some cases, the diseases that will emerge as the individual matures. To some extent the type of individual that will develop, both in physique and personality, is determined at the moment of fusion of the two cells. However, many characteristics are not fixed absolutely, and whether or not they develop, or to what extent they do so, depends on the presence or absence of certain environmental factors during the individual's life.

Few mental disorders are entirely genetically determined. One example of such a disorder is Huntington's Chorea, which is due to a dominant gene. Some forms of mental subnormality, such as mongolism, are due to chromosomal abnormalities. Mental disorders such as schizophrenia and manic depressive psychosis have some genetical basis, though the exact mode of inheritance has not been fully established. One problem in determining the part contributed by genetic structure is that in most cases the parents not only provide the genes but also the early environment in which patterns of future behaviour may be established.

Childhood

The baby in the womb is in an almost ideal environment. It is warm and safe, and supplied with all the essential substances for the maintenance of life. The first stress it experiences, in normal circumstances, is the process of birth. The baby is pushed and squeezed along a narrow passage from which it emerges into a cold and apparently hostile world. The emotional consequences of this event can only be speculated upon, and as it is a universal experience it can hardly explain why only some individuals develop emotional problems later. On the physical side, however, it is a period of considerable risk, for during this period the brain may be exposed to periods of relative oxygen shortage, and the blood vessels in the brain may be torn, as may be the brain tissue itself. Brain damage occurring at this time may lead to a wide range of intellectual or physical handicaps that determine the baby's future abilities and limitations.

For those that escape this danger, the world at first consists only of self. The tiny baby is aware of pain and discomfort associated with hunger, and is aware of pleasure and satisfaction when it is fed. It expresses the former by crying and the latter by sleeping. Gradually, it learns to associate the feeling of pleasure with the act of sucking, and becomes dimly aware of the breast or bottle with which it is fed. As the various parts of its brain and nervous system become active the baby's awareness of the world increases. It begins to focus its eyes, it becomes actively aware of objects placed in its hands, it learns to respond to certain sounds in a more complex way than by a mere 'startle' reflex. Then it begins to put these separate experiences together, learning to grasp with its hands the object it sees with its eyes, learning to turn its head and eyes to see where the noise came from. Emotionally, he remains totally self-centred. His needs for warmth, air, and food dominate his existence and must be immediately satisfied. Failure to do so leads to the expression of rage and anxiety by crying. His increasing awareness of the physical world enables him to associate relief of unpleasant sensations with the presence of his mother, who thus comes to have enormous emotional significance for him. His experience of this other person will to some extent determine his reaction to other people who make up his immediate world. The child whose needs are satisfied begins to learn the complex emotional response of faith, trust, happiness, and need that is conveniently called love. At this stage of development the child derives satisfaction and experiences the emotion of love as a result of feeding; thus the mouth is the area of his body that assumes greatest importance for him. This stage of development has been called the oral phase.

At some stage the child is taken off the bottle or breast and begins to feed from a spoon. The act of sucking is pleasurable in itself, apart from satisfying hunger, and the child may be very angry at losing this pleasure. Weaning tends to coincide with the eruption of the first teeth, often a painful experience, and the child finds that it can not only use its mouth to express anger, by shouting, but by biting as well.

At about one year old the child starts to learn to walk, and becomes much less dependent. By eighteen months to two years, the child is developing some control over the emptying of his bladder and bowels. Retaining urine and faeces tends to be pleasurable until a certain degree of distention is reached, when it becomes a pleasure to pass them. Thus, the child now has a second source of pleasurable experience.

Parents are usually anxious for the child to become clean and dry— rewarding him for using his pot—punishing him for using his pants. Thus, the child learns that he can derive secondary pleasures from performing his functions at the proper time. On the other hand, he learns that he can punish his parents by refusing to do so. When the parents are too concerned with pot training, as a result of their own fears about dirt, or guilt about their sexual organs, the child may become very anxious about these activities. He may respond by refusing to be trained, or he may develop a fear of dirt, and excessive shame about his body and its functions. It is thought that this may lead to the development of an obsessional type of personality. The stage at which the child uses these activities to punish his parents is referred to as the 'anal phase'.

At about the age of three the child becomes more aware of the physical differences between his body and other people, and he may begin to question why his genitalia differ from his sister's. At this time, also, the child tends to become very possessive towards the parent of the opposite sex. Little boys become clinging and demand that their mother does everything for them. If father tries to help, he is pushed away with shouts of 'I don't want you'. Little girls, on the other hand, tend to turn to their fathers, announcing that 'when I grow up, I'm going to marry my daddy'. These positive feelings may be accompanied by aggressive rivalry feelings for the other parent. This stage of development, Freud called the Oedipus complex, after a Greek story of a boy who unknowingly killed his father and married his mother, subsequently being punished by the Gods for so doing. This stage of development is considered to be of particular importance in shaping the child's future attitudes to his relationship with members of the opposite sex, as well as those of his own sex.

The little boy, in competing with his father for his mother's affection, may feel very anxious about the way in which his father will respond. He may fear that he will be severely punished for his temerity. If, however, his parents handle the situation with tolerance, the little boy begins to imitate his father's behaviour, and develops masculine interests and attitudes—a process known as Identification.

When his father is absent, or has himself a poorly developed masculinity, the little boy may not have a suitable model to copy. This may result in his failing to achieve a satisfactory male role in later life, and prevent him from forming normal relationships with other men or with women. A mother may either over-encourage the child's advances, allowing him to replace her husband in her affections, or she may actively reject his love. In both cases, the boy may subsequently have difficulty in relating to women. On the one hand, he may feel guilty at being 'unfaithful' to his loving mother, while, on the other, he may fear further rejection and ridicule.

The little girl at this stage, goes through a similar process of rivalry with her mother, but if she realises that her father loves her mother, she will try to copy her ways of behaving. If her mother is a well-adjusted and feminine woman, the little girl stands a good chance of developing into a stable and mature woman, but if her mother has faulty attitudes to her own femininity, the child's personality may be warped. The little girl's relationship to her father is also vitally important. An excessively loving response, particularly if overtly sexual, by the father, may arouse considerable guilt in the child. Rejection, on the other hand, can make the little girl give up the feminine role and try to become a male.

The ways in which unresolved difficulties at this stage of development can predispose to later psychiatric problems, can be summarised as follows:

1. The relationship between members of the opposite sex, especially at a sexual level, may be regarded as an aggressive act, linked with ideas of inflicting punishment, or being punished oneself.

2. Sexual feelings may be linked with the idea of wickedness and have to be suppressed or satisfied only in 'forbidden' ways.

3. Faulty attitudes towards parents may lead the person to doubt his own masculinity. This may result either in a withdrawal from heterosexual activities, or an excessive indulgence in them.

4. Over-identification with the parent of the opposite sex may result in a reversal of sexual role. This may take the form of

homosexual behaviour, or it may be expressed by excessively aggressive, competitive behaviour in women, or by excessively dependent behaviour in men.

Any of these developments will tend to prevent the establishment of stable, satisfying, and adult relationships with other people. This, in turn, tends to create secondary stress, which may result in some form of psychiatric illness.

Probably no one passes through childhood entirely unscathed, but most people reach a reasonable level of maturity and independence, and when exposed to stress, respond by dealing with the situation in a realistic way; that is, taking positive steps to alter those things that are giving rise to the stress, e.g. if a man is worried because he is in debt, he will work overtime until his debt is paid off. However, there are many situations in life that cannot be resolved at a realistic level, e.g. a dead parent cannot be brought back to life. When faced with such a problem, the normal person resorts to some form of unconscious mental behaviour, referred to as a 'mental mechanism', in order to reduce his feelings of anxiety and depression to a tolerable level. If these mechanisms fail to alleviate his feelings he may use them to such a degree that they begin to interfere with his normal life, and at this stage he may show symptoms of a psychiatric illness.

The types of mental mechanisms commonly employed are:

1. *Rationalisation.* This is a means of finding some logical and acceptable explanation for our behaviour, which helps to avoid awareness of the underlying motives. For example, a young man who wants a sports car because he feels it will make him more attractive to young women, offers as the reason for buying one the idea that it enables him to get some fresh air while he drives.

2. *Projection.* This technique consists of shifting blame, or guilt on to other people, rather than recognising our own responsibilities and shortcomings. Thus, a man who is not promoted because he is not very good at his job, may convince himself that the reason for his failure is that his superiors have a grudge against him. In extreme forms, this technique leads to the development of delusional ideas, and even hallucinations.

3. *Reaction-formation.* This is a method of concealing from ourselves some strong desire that we are ashamed of, by strongly advocating the complete opposite. Thus, a man with strong homosexual desires may react by denouncing homosexuality and become

an active member of organisations devoted to stamping out such practices.

4. *Dissociation.* This is another method of dealing with threatening memories or emotions by splitting them off from the conscious part of the mind. Dissociation is particularly used by people of hysterical personality.

5. *Sublimation.* Mental energy that under different circumstances might be directed in sexual or aggressive activity can be channeled into more socially acceptable activities. In this method an outlet is found for some of the drives that would otherwise be frustrated; it is one of the most satisfactory forms of defence mechanism. The youth dealing with his aggressive drives by playing rugby, and the spinster, denied the satisfaction of children of her own, teaching other people's, are examples of the value of this technique, both for themselves and society.

6. *Regression.* This is the return to techniques that were of value at an earlier time in the person's life. At times everyone reverts to earlier forms of behaviour. 'You are behaving like a child', 'don't be such a baby' are the comments provoked by such behaviour. It is commonly evoked by rivalry between brothers and sisters, and the little boy who is suddenly faced with a new baby on whom his mother seems to lavish all her affections may try to regain her love and attention by reverting to the time when he was not pot-trained. In extreme forms, this type of behaviour in an adult indicates a serious mental disturbance. Some schizophrenics exhibit this type of behaviour.

Adolescence

Between the ages of ten to twelve years, most children begin to change physically, in response to altered hormone levels. The so-called secondary sexual characteristics begin to develop, the boy's voice breaks, facial and pubic hair begins to grow, and spontaneous ejaculation of seminal fluid may occur. Girls' breasts begin to develop, pubic hair grows, and after some time the onset of menstruation occurs. Both are then physically sexually mature, in that they are now capable of reproducing. Emotional maturity, however, is not usually achieved at the same time. This period of life is full of stress, mostly related to the conflict between physical maturity and emotional immaturity. A conflict is reflected in most adults' attitude towards the adolescent—at one moment demanding that the child acts as an adult; the next moment insisting that the young adult is only a child and must be treated as such.

The adolescent himself fluctuates between wanting independence and responsibility and wishing to continue in the protected child-parent relationship. On top of this comes the demands of increasing sexual awareness. The physical urge to indulge in sexual activities comes into conflict with the moral restrictions placed on such activities by society. This awareness of the opposite sex as objects of desire, and also of status, forces the adolescent into a greater awareness of himself as an individual, and the way he compares to his peers. Doubts about his or her physical or emotional attractiveness to the opposite sex, based on real or imaginary defects, can prevent the establishments of normal relationships, a failure that may distort his or her life for ever.

Apart from the stress created by the onset of sexual maturity, society imposes a number of other tasks that may cause problems for the adolescent. During this period come most of the educational hurdles by way of examinations. Failure in these not only leads to diminished self respect, but may also determine the type of education the individual receives, and hence, the kind of occupation open to him.

Marriage
For many people, marriage is seen as a method of resolving some of the conflicts associated with their sexual needs, and is entered into because the partners find each other sexually attractive. Some have to marry because the girl becomes pregnant, while others use marriage as a means of escape from loneliness, an unhappy home, or insecurity. It is only after the ceremony that they begin to realise the difficulties involved in living in a close interdependent relationship with another person.

During the early part of marriage sexual difficulties may prove a major problem. This may be the result of ignorance, or due to the one partner being forced to recognise unconscious fears or guilt that have previously been avoided by using moral grounds as a reason for limiting sexual activities. Some of these difficulties are more fully discussed in the chapter on neurotic illnesses. Many people experience a sense of disappointment; having been led to expect some ecstatic emotional state, they feel let down by the actual performance. This may make them despise their partner, or themselves, as failures, or may result in their avoiding further intercourse and subsequent disappointment. There is much more to a marriage than going to bed, but failure in the sexual aspects tends to exacerbate any other difficulties in the relationships, and diminishes the chances of eventual adjustment.

Childbirth

Pregnancy and childbirth are potential sources of stress both physical and mental, for husband as well as wife. For the women there is the problem of physical discomfort, morning sickness in the early months, increasing girth and weight later. This is easily tolerated by the well-adjusted woman who wants a child, but may lead to neurotic breakdown in a person with low tolerance, or in someone who consciously or unconsciously does not want the baby. Emotionally there may be a considerable degree of fear, arising as a result of faulty education or abnormal parental attitudes towards childbirth. Much can be accomplished in dealing with this problem by good antenatal care and training for childbirth.

Following delivery, the physical changes that occur may precipitate a psychotic illness of a depressive or schizophrenic type—sometimes referred to as pueperal psychosis. In other women, the birth of a stillborn or deformed baby may precipitate a reactive depression or an anxiety state. Many women find that they are much more emotionally labile in the months following childbirth than at other periods of their life.

A husband during the pregnancy of his wife often develops neurotic or psychosomatic conditions, perhaps reflecting his anxiety about his wife, or sometimes because of the threat the child represents as a rival. This may become more marked when the baby arrives and the mother devotes all her time, love and attention to it. The husband feels excluded and jealous, and may revert to the kind of behaviour that he utilised as a child to compete with his brother and sisters for his parent's attention.

Both parents may be exposed to the strain of a constantly crying child and sleepless nights. This is often aggravated if they are living with in-laws, or in shared accommodation, where they feel that other people are being disturbed by the noise. For people of obsessional personalities the arrival of a child means dirt and mess and the disruption of their set way of life. This may trigger off a depressive illness, often characterised by obsessional fears of harming the child.

Work

To achieve status and independence it is necessary for most men to have some form of regular employment. Failure to hold a job may reflect faulty personality development, or the presence of some psychiatric disorder. Prolonged unemployment can lead to deterioration in a person's morale that may make employment at a later date difficult or even impossible.

Work not only confers benefits, but also imposes a variety of stresses and strains. The obsessional person may find the level of responsibility demanded too high, or conversely may feel that his efforts are not appreciated sufficiently. This may lead to his becoming depressed, either blaming himself for his shortcomings, or projecting the blame on to his work mates. People of schizoid personality may find the major stress at work is that of relating to a large number of people. They may find that their interest and tastes differ from the majority and that they tend to be excluded from discussions and other activities. This exclusion may increase their sense of isolation.

The notion that overwork causes mental breakdown is incorrect. A history of increased work preceding the development of a mental disorder usually represents an early symptom of the complaint rather than its cause. Thus, in hypomania the patient may take on extra tasks because of his false sense of confidence and limitless energy. The depressed patient, on the other hand, may be much slower and less efficient in coping with his work, and feels obliged to work longer, or to take work home with him in order to maintain his previous level.

The most common occupation for women remains housework, and being a housewife may present a number of problems. For many it means giving up another job that gave financial independence and provided interest and social contacts. Instead, the housewife is financially dependent, and isolated in her home. The work involved may take relatively little time, but tends to be boring and repetitive. If she takes an excessive pride in it she may feel upset when the family disturb her ordered environment with their muddy boots and untidy habits. The housewife's horizons tend to be limited to her children and the four walls of her home. Many families now live on new housing estates far from their parents and childhood friends. The community around them consists of similar families and thus lacks the range of interests and experience provided by a population in which all age groups are represented. Consequently, the housewife becomes bored, lonely, and perhaps anxious. She envies her husband his freedom and outside interests. Some women as a result unconsciously develop symptoms that, in part, are designed to make their husband pay more attention to them, while also involving other people in helping them find some solution to their problem. Thus, the house-bound housewife syndrome may reflect not only anxiety or depression on the wife's part, but also her attempt to prevent her husband continuing to work. This leads to her both having company during the day and also forces the husband to seek help because of the financial loss entailed in missing work.

Middle-age

For woman middle-age is the time when their ability to have children comes to an end. Not only is this time associated with some uncomfortable physical symptoms such as 'hot flushes', but it also has profound psychological effects. For the childless woman it means the end of any faint hope of having her own child, while for the woman with a family it may mean the end of fearing a further pregnancy. In either case, the change in attitude and the alteration in hormone levels may alter the woman's desire for, or satisfaction from, sexual intercourse. This, in turn, may create new problems for the husband.

This time of life coincides with children reaching an age at which they leave home and establish families of their own. For a woman who has devoted most of her time and energy to looking after her children this separation may convince her that she is of no further use to anyone. The combination of loss of loved ones, feelings of uselessness, and physical change frequently precipitates a depressive illness, particularly in people of obsessional personality. The depression is commonly associated with agitation and restlessness, a combination of symptoms that is sometimes referred to as 'involutional melancholia'.

In men, middle-age has less-marked physical features, but it is a time when they, too, are forced to see that their ambitions may not be fully achieved. In middle-age, death takes on a more personal threat. For children and young adults death is unreal, they feel immortal; for the aged, death may be welcome, but in middle life it becomes a harsh reality, heightened by the loss of friends and relatives of one's own generation. Depressive illnesses in men reach a peak frequency between the ages of 60 and 70.

Retirement

Retirement represents a considerable stress, both for the person retiring, and their immediate relatives. Loss of regular employment entails a loss of status as well as a fall in income. There is a tendency to feel that one is now 'on the shelf', no longer needed or respected. For those who have invested most of their time and interest in work, retirement may be a period of boredom. Few people prepare realistically for their retirement. Far too many dream of a little cottage by the sea, where they will potter about pruning the roses, and playing with their visiting grandchildren. The reality of an isolated bungalow up an unmade road, with a rubble-filled garden where they see no one they know for months on end, not infrequently precipitates acute depression.

The wife who has developed a comfortable routine of housework, coffee with her friends, and a trip to the shops in the afternoon may not relish having an ash-dropping, paper-reading, carpet-slippered nuisance sitting about, getting in her way, and pestering her for his lunch. Little habits that had gradually become unnoticed may, with the increased contact, suddenly start to grate again. Illness may seem to be the only way of escape. As the time passes the problems of retirement merge with those of old age.

Old Age

Increasing physical and mental deterioration afflicts many people as they become older, as has been described previously, but even those who retain their physical health and mental faculties may have considerable emotional stress to cope with. Bereavement is a situation everyone has to cope with at some time in their life, but probably the most severe deprivation is experienced by the old person when husband or wife dies. For children death is unreal, for young adults, the loss of a loved one can be dealt with by time and by new hopes and experiences, but for the old, death of a spouse may seem the end.

Loneliness and a feeling of uselessness are a feature of many old people's lives in modern urban societies. This combination of rejection and social isolation may make the old person feel there is little point in continuing to live, and they may court death either by neglecting themselves, or by attempting suicide.

Poverty, in a relative sense, is also the lot of many old people, in spite of the Welfare State, and for these the combination of poor diet, lack of warmth, and the depressing experience of trying to live on too little while surrounded by affluence may lead to depression, or even to deficiency disorders.

Physical illnesses of a degenerative kind become increasingly common with advancing age, and either through a direct effect on the brain, or because of the emotional effects of chronic physical handicaps, may profoundly effect the mental state of the old person.

15 The Role of a Nurse

Asked to define the role of a nurse, most people would say 'looking after sick people', 'caring for the ill' or something similar. While such definitions are basically correct, they tend to stress the passive role of the patient. The patient is seen as someone who is treated, cared for, looked after, without any effort on his own part, except to follow instructions and not argue. *The changing emphasis in psychiatric nursing is towards the idea that the patient plays an active part in his own recovery, and that recovery may, in fact, be delayed, if the nurse increases the patient's degree of dependence.*

While no individual possesses all the qualities required in equal measure, it is possible to outline those activities in which the nurse must be proficient. None can be completely neglected, however skilled the nurse may become in other aspects of her work, and all must be based on a sound theoretical knowledge if they are to be developed and used to full advantage.

The work of the nurse can still be considered under the following headings:

1. Observation
2. Nursing procedures
3. Psychotherapy
4. Care and protection of the patient.

Observation

One reason that patients are admitted to psychiatric hospitals is for 'observation'. The nurse being in closest contact for the longest period with the patient is best able to perform this task. To carry it out properly, the nurse must understand the reason for observation, must know what to look for, recognise it when she sees it, and must then be able to record and pass on her observations accurately and intelligibly.

The reasons for observing a patient can be summarised as:

1. To ascertain the signs and symptoms on which a diagnosis can be made.
2. To note improvement or deterioration in the patient's condition in response to treatment, including drug side effects, or to changes in his environment.
3. To be aware of any new physical or mental illness developing.
4. To recognise signs that suggest the patient is likely to behave in such a way as to harm himself or others.
5. To assess those factors in the patient's personality that can be exploited in aiding his recovery.

The value of the nurse as observer derives as much from her training as her innate ability; for it is through her training that she comes to know and to recognise the subtle changes in behaviour that reflect particular mental states. It must be pointed out, however, that in respect of observation there are two aphorisms that at first glance appear mutually contradictory. These are: (*a*) one only recognises that which one knows; and (*b*) one only sees that which one wants to see.

The nurse will make more accurate and valuable observations if she possesses a sound theoretical knowledge, but only if she keeps an open mind in respect to the patient's diagnosis. Otherwise, she will tend unconsciously to stress those signs that fit into her preconceived idea while conveniently blocking out those signs that do not fit. The skilled observer is one who can extract the relevant and significant facets of behaviour, whether they support or contradict the presumptive diagnosis.

Observation is of value only if the results can be conveyed to everyone else concerned in the treatment of the patient. In recording or reporting observations the nurse must be careful to distinguish between the observation made and conclusions drawn from it. All too often, a nurse will write in the report book, 'Mr X is very hallucinated'. She has, in fact, noticed that on a number of occasions, Mr X has laughed without apparent cause. While her deduction may be correct, there are other possible explanations and the conclusion should be drawn only in the light of other facets of behaviour. The nurse should always record the *actual behaviour*, and not just her explanation of it.

Another frequent error in reporting is the use of jargon. Certain words and phrases used in psychiatry have either an accurately defined meaning, and no other, or a special meaning in psychiatry that is different from their meaning in everyday life. Such words should be used only if the nurse is certain of their definition. It is greatly preferable to describe observations in straightforward everyday language, than to use words incorrectly. Not only does the latter demonstrate ignorance, but it may also create confusion. To make the situation even worse, the jargon word is all too often spelt incorrectly.

To summarise, the nurse must know what to look for, she must not shut her mind to observations that do not fit in, and she must record her observation in simple, clear language.

In this book, an attempt is made to point out the type of behaviour that must be looked for and recorded in each of the major psychiatric illnesses. In no sense is this comprehensive, it is intended to act as an outline the nurse must fill in as a result of her experience.

Nursing Procedures

In the course of her duties the nurse is expected to assist with, or perform, a number of technical procedures. These may be concerned with the care of the patient, with investigation, treatment, or the more general aspects of ward and hospital management. No attempt is made in this book to describe the details of these procedures as there already exists a number of books that deal adequately with this. However, some general observations must be made.

Procedures Involving the Patient

The nurse must always remember that a procedure that is commonplace for her may be a unique and alarming experience for the patient. She should try to recapture her own feelings of trepidation when she first carried out the procedure, and to imagine how much worse it must be for the 'victim'.

The first step is to explain to the patient the reason for the procedure, and the actual steps involved. A patient who understands what is happening and why, is more likely to be co-operative. The explanation must be suitable for the individual patient. Do not 'talk down' to the patient, nor use incomprehensible technical terms. These days, thanks to television and magazines, many people have quite a sophisticated knowledge of the technical aspects of medicine and will not thank you for talking to them as if they had come from some primitive tribe to see the local witch-doctor. At the same time, do not be taken in by a patient's apparent understanding, as this may reflect a desire to hide ignorance rather than a real grasp of the subject. Ask them to tell you in their own words what they expect to happen, and encourage them to ask questions.

Be honest with a patient. Many procedures are to some degree painful. Admit this and warn them when the stage is reached where they may experience the pain. Before doing it, tell them that you will try to cause as little pain as possible, and that you will do it as quickly as possible. Having said this, it is the responsibility of the nurse to acquire a sufficiently high degree of skill in the procedure to be able to live up to her word. The standard reassurance that 'this won't hurt' followed by searing pain only produces a feeling of mistrust on the part of the patient. Subsequently, he is more apprehensive, and possibly uncooperative, and the resulting struggle makes the procedure even more painful.

To be proficient, the nurse must understand the purpose of the procedure and the reason for each step in it. Learning by heart from a book results either in vital steps being omitted, or pointless practices being perpetuated for ever. Remember that every procedure has a meaning for the patient beyond its immediate purpose, and that in performing it, the nurse has the opportunity for establishing a relationship with the patient. Properly exploited this can be of major therapeutic value, but if mishandled, it can result in the nurse being permanently rejected by the patient.

The Nurse as Therapist

It is the present trend to stress this aspect of the nursing role at the expense of all others. A whole new jargon has been created to describe the various aspects of the nurses therapeutic role, until there is a danger of the nurse becoming convinced that unless she has taken a degree in psychology she cannot help any patient. 'Establishing rapport', 'communication', 'therapeutic relationship', 'transference', 'group dynamics' are on every lip, like slogans at a political rally. It is important that the nurse does not take the shadow for the substance, and become so terrified of the phrases that she cannot carry out the acts they describe.

The basis of the theory is quite simple. Everyone has the need to form some close and satisfying relationship with another person. Some people as a result of inheritence and their early life experiences, find it difficult or impossible to form such relationships; others lose their ability to do so because of disease or injury. Without such relationships it is difficult to continue functioning in a normal way in the community. As a result, such people either cannot leave hospital, or if they do leave, soon break down again and have to return. To learn how to establish such relationship the patient has to be given the opportunity to experiment, and the encouragement to do so. This is the therapeutic role of the nurse. Many nurses carry it out by instinctive responses. Some are very good at it, others very bad; all can become better, by learning to understand the nature of their instinctive actions in order to develop those that are helpful and to avoid those that are not.

Care and Protection of the Patient

While the custodial role of the nurse has steadily diminished, there are still occasions when patients must be detained in hospital against their wish for their own, or society's, protection. Many such patients are detained formally under the provisions of the relevant sections of the 1959 Mental Health Act, but not infrequently a patient who has been admitted informally decides to leave against advice. Nurses are usually prepared to take such steps as are required to detain a formal patient, but there is a tendency for them to believe that they can do nothing for an informal patient. The guiding principle should be to act in the patient's best interest. If a nurse considers that a patient is likely to kill or injure himself, or to act in such a way as to harm someone else if he leaves the hospital, her first duty is to detain him until the medical officer can see him and decide what should be done. Frequently, it is sufficient to ask the patient to wait until he has seen the doctor, pointing out that to do so is only an act of common politeness. If this approach fails it may be necessary to ask a nurse to remain with the patient, or even to confine the patient to a locked room until seen by the doctor. Such steps are justified only if the patient is considered to be a real risk to himself or others, but with such the nurse is not fulfilling her duties if she merely lets the patient leave without let or hinderance.

In less dramatic ways the nurse also has to care for patients who are not fully capable of looking after themselves. While every attempt should be made to encourage the patient to do the maximum amount for himself, at times he will require special help. The kind of help necessary is discussed in the sections on nursing care that follow the descriptions of the various psychiatric illnesses in Part One.

Historical Survey

During the period of history usually referred to as 'The Dark Ages', the Church was responsible for providing care for the sick. Those who showed symptoms of mental illness were often considered to be possessed of devils. Treatment consisted of exorcism, but as the belief in, and fear of, witches increased, 'treatment' was replaced by persecution. Many thousands of people who would now be considered as mentally ill, died on the stake or by other tortures. Gradually, the attitude changed, and some religious orders began to care for the mentally ill. One such establishment was the Monastery of St Mary's of Bethlehem in London which, by 1330, was caring for a number of 'lunatics'. In 1547, Henry the VIII was dissolving the monastic institutions, and among them was St Mary's. Henry made a gift of it to the City Fathers, who formally established it as a 'House or Hospital for the Care of Lunatics'. This was the first hospital in Western Europe established to care exclusively for the mentally ill.

The males who looked after the patients were called 'basket men', from the traditional title given to monks who cared for the sick, for part of their work had been to go into the community and collect in baskets, food and alms for those in their care.

The role of the attendant, or keeper, was mainly custodial. He was responsible for seeing that the patients did not harm themselves or others, and for seeing that their bodily needs were attended to. Some found that the easiest way to accomplish this was to attach the patient to a chain and provide him with a bed of straw. Violence begat violence, and restraints were increased, so that it soon became dogma that one could not manage mad patients without an armoury of mechanical gadgets designed to limit their movements. Yet some people dared question the truth of this belief. Outstanding among them was Phillipe Pinel, who was physician to a large asylum in Paris, the Bicetre, from 1793 to 1795. He was convinced that patients need not be chained and handcuffed, and in the spirit prevailing at the time of the French Revolution the climate of opinion was such that he was allowed to put his theory into practice. A certain number of selected patients were freed from their chains and, far from attacking their liberator, they became much less violent.

Much of the credit for the success of this venture belongs to the Keeper (chief male nurse), Jean-Baptiste Pussin, and his wife. Pussin was an ex-patient who had returned to work at the Bicetre and who had gradually employed a number of recovered patients to work with him, on the principle that if they remembered their own treatment it would help them to avoid cruelty and unkindness in their handling of the patients.

Pinel's example was followed and extended in Britain by men like William Tuke who founded 'The Retreat' at York in 1796, for the specific purpose of treating the mentally ill by 'a milder and more appropriate system'.

In 1894, the nurse worked up to 100 hours a week; a far cry from the present official figure of 42 hours. In 1919, Parliament passed the 'Nurses' Registration Act', and mental nurses who had passed the appropriate examination were admitted to the supplementary part of the register. In 1946, the National Health Service Act was passed, and this reorganised the structure of medical services in Great Britain, including the hospital service. The hospitals were then administered by boards called regional hospital boards, who were responsible for all hospitals within their geographical area. Each hospital, or group of hospitals, was administered by hospital management committees. (The new structure of the National Health Service is described in Chapter 20.)

Since the end of the Second World War, not only has there been a change in the administration of mental hospitals, there has been a considerable change in attitude. This is reflected by the change in name of such establishments from asylum to mental hospital, and now to plain hospital. The barriers have been gradually dismantled, the doors opened, day hospitals, out-patient clinics, and general hospital units have been established. With this change, the nurse has come to play a more active part in the management of patients in the community from which they come, rather than in the isolation of the mental hospital. Gradually, the nurse is extending this role by running social clubs for ex-patients and by doing follow-up visits to the patient's home. As the extent of community care increases, this aspect of the nurse's work can be expected to grow more important. It is important to remember that in spite of these modifications, the basic role of the nurse has not changed, and the same personal attributes and special skills have to be learnt and developed.

The Psychiatric Hospital

This section of the book deals with the various aspects of the treatment of mental disorders, and is written largely from the viewpoint of the mental hospital. Only a small percentage of people with psychiatric disorders have to be admitted to a mental hospital or psychiatric unit. A rather greater number receive psychiatric treatment as day patients and out-patients, while the majority of milder disorders are dealt with by the general practitioner. It has been estimated that about 30 per cent of complaints dealt with by GPs are psychologically determined. The incidence of serious psychotic illness in the community is quite small, being in the order of one case per 1,000, most people suffering from severe mental disorders spend some time, at least, in the mental hospital.

Since the county lunatic asylums were built at the end of the nineteenth century, the medical services for the mentally ill have been based largely on these hospitals, which have now changed their names and much of their internal architecture. There are about 130 such hospitals in England and Wales, and they have a total number of in-patients of the order of 130,000. In addition, there are 150 hospitals for the mentally handicapped, with about 50,000 beds. Most hospitals for mentally handicapped patients have a waiting list for admission.

Reasons for Admission

The present trend in psychiatric services is to avoid admitting the patient to hospital whenever possible, and to discharge him as soon as possible if he has to be admitted. Patients are admitted only if there is a good reason to do so, and if they cannot be managed as out-patients. The reason for taking the patient into hospital may be one or more of the following:

1. *Observation* of the patient for a period of time may be necessary in order to assess his behaviour fully, and so make a diagnosis. While friends and relatives may be of help, it sometimes requires the skill of trained staff to discover the presence or absence of certain symptoms.
2. *Investigations* such as lumbar punctures, angiograms, or air encephalograms, can be performed only with the patient in hospital, if only for twenty-four hours.
3. *Protection.* When the patient is either actively suicidal, homicidal,

or so restless and confused as to constitute a danger to himself or others, admission is necessary for their own, or other's, protection.

4. *Treatment.* Most modern forms of physical treatment can be administered to an out-patient, but some require hospital facilities, e.g. prolonged narcosis, modified insulin, or intensive drug therapy. In other cases the patient has some physical disorder that makes treatment by drugs or ECT more dangerous than in the normal. Many patients do not take the drugs prescribed unless supervised, and admission is necessary to ensure this.

5. Social reasons, such as the following, may prompt the patient's admittance to hospital.

   (*a*) Cases in which the patient's illness is the result of factors in their environment that are producing acute stress. In this event it may be helpful for the patient to be away from home until events have resolved themselves.

   (*b*) Cases in which the patient's behaviour is so disturbed or anti-social that society can no longer tolerate it.

   (*c*) Cases in which friends or relatives of the patient require a rest from looking after them, and a break from the physical and mental effort involved.

As soon as a patient is admitted, all those concerned in the management of that patient should draw up at least a tentative plan of treatment and rehabilitation. This prevents the patient being 'lost' in the ward, and also avoids the danger that different members of the staff may have a different and conflicting approach to the patient.

The first minutes and hours of the patient's time in hospital can be critical in determining his attitude towards treatment both then and in the future. The way in which his relatives are dealt with may determine how much support they will give the patient in the future, and to what degree they will co-operate with the hospital staff. In a wider context, the experience of the patient and his relatives will, in part, determine the community's ideas about the hospital. It is obvious, therefore, that the nurse's dealings with the admission of a patient plays a vital part in the success of his treatment, and in the creation of a favourable impression of the hospital in the eyes of the world at large.

To perform this task well, the nurse must be aware of the patient's fears and anxieties concerning mental hospitals, that are probably shared by his relatives, and she must deal with these while carrying out the routine tasks associated with an admission. The patient's anxiety is more important than his date of birth!

The Effect on the Patient of Admission to Mental Hospital

The effect of hospitalisation on the patient will be determined in part by his personality and previous experience, but also by his attitude towards his admission. Some patients will regard the hospital in much the same way as they would regard a garage—a place in which experts will find out why they are not working properly, and put them right without much effort on their part, beyond passive co-operation. Others will look upon the hospital as a place of safety, an asylum, where they will be protected from society, or where their own destructive impulses will be controlled. Such patients may be very difficult to discharge when their more florid symptoms have subsided, because they fear the outside world. Yet other patients, especially those who do not recognise that they are ill, will regard hospitalisation as an unwarranted attack on their personal liberty, and will respond either by aggression, or by accepting that their worst fears have been realised, and reconciling themselves to permanent institutionalisation.

Whatever the patient's attitude, certain reactions are almost universal. On entering an unfamiliar environment and being separated from family, friends, and familiar places, most people experience some degree of anxiety. This may be diminished if the staff make every effort to help the patient feel welcome and 'at home'. This involves describing the physical structure of the hospital, showing him where he sleeps, eats, puts his letters, gets his hair cut, and the like, and giving him some guidance about the roles of the various staff members he will meet. In some hospitals, a booklet containing this information is issued to new patients. Another way of doing it is to introduce him to a patient who has been in hospital long enough to know his way around, but who is nearing discharge, so that the new patient does not feel discouraged by the length of time his 'guide' has been in hospital.

The anxiety arising from separation from his family may be lessened by careful explanation of the visiting arrangements, both to the patient and his relatives. Most hospitals now have almost unrestricted visiting, realising the important part relatives may play, both in causing and curing mental disorders. This provides an opportunity for involving the relatives in treatment, and perhaps helping them to modify attitudes that are damaging to the patient.

A very real problem for some patients is loss of earnings. This is much less pressing now, because of the various provisions for financial help to the ill, and the fact that treatment is free, but many patients are not aware of the benefits that are available, and how to obtain them. The nurse must be able to explain these details to the patient or his relatives, or if necessary, refer them to a member of the hospital staff who is responsible for this aspect of patient care. In some hospitals, a person is employed as Welfare Officer to deal with these problems. The nurse should know his name, when he is available, and where his office is situated.

A further source of anxiety is the unfamiliar procedures that patients undergo as part of their treatment of investigation. The names of these activities are hidden from the patient, by using mysterious initials which may even get mixed up. ECT, ECG, and EEG, sound very similar but are very different performances! Nothing should be done to the patient, from changing his ward to giving him an injection, without first explaining in appropriate terms the nature and purpose of the procedure, and allowing him to ask questions about it.

The Effects on the Patient's Relatives of his Illness and Hospitalisation

As part of their work, nurses have to cope, not only with the patient but also with his relatives, and it is necessary for the nurse to have some insight into the effect the patient and his illness has on his relatives, and also the effect they have on the patient.

Many relatives experience strong feelings of guilt about the patient and his illness. This may reflect their feeling that they are in part to blame for it, or that they are failing him by allowing him to enter hospital, or, finally, it may arise because they recognise that they are glad to see the back of him. This sense of guilt may make the relatives act in a variety of ways.

1. They may salve their conscience by trying to ensure the patient is 'properly looked after'. This sometimes leads to their being aggressive towards nursing staff, complaining about trivial or even imaginary shortcomings.
2. Some react by becoming extremely dependent on the hospital,

and constantly seeking reassurance that they 'did the right thing' in having the patient admitted.

3. Others rationalise their fears and find 'logical' explanations for their relatives' illness; reasons that do not involve *them* in any blame.

4. Some relatives project their guilt and anxiety, and blame other people (including the hospital staff) for causing the illness. Such 'explanations' may be quite irrational.

Such reactions may place considerable burden on the nursing staff, who often remark, 'the relatives are more trouble than the patient'. However, if the patient is to be helped to return home, the relatives must be handled in such a way that the difficulties he faces are not increased. Not only is the nurse's relationship to the patient's relatives important for that particular patient's future, but it also helps to create the attitude of the public at large to mental illness and mental hospitals. The nurse should try to convey, both by what she says and does, an attitude of respect for the patient and his relatives, a sense of kindness and understanding, and a willingness to help.

The nurse who is aware of the feelings of the relatives will realise the need for giving them adequate time to talk about their fears and anxieties in whatever way they choose to express them, whether it is by repeatedly asking the same question or by grumbling and complaining endlessly. She will also be concerned for the physical comfort of the relatives, making sure they have somewhere comfortable to wait, and that they are able to obtain food or drink, if necessary.

The nurse should also take the opportunity of observing the way in which the patient and his relatives behave towards each other.

Staff of Mental Hospital

A mental hospital is a small community which, in some instances, is almost self-supporting. There are usually about the same number of paid staff as there are patients. The staff all play a part in treating the patients, and no group can function efficiently without the others. A nurse in the course of her work will come into contact with people in a wide range of jobs. It is necessary for her to know something of their function in the hospital setting. Space does not permit discussion of the large number of people employed in cleaning, heating, decorating, and repairing the hospital, nor of those whose job it is to provide the food, clean the wards, and wash the clothes. However, their tasks are no less important than those of the people who play a more direct part in the patients' treatment.

Many people in mental hospitals, either as a part of their illness or as a result of institutionalisation, neglect their personal appearance. This not only has a lowering effect on their morale, but it may also make them appear different from the 'normal' population and lead to their being isolated or rejected by the community outside. A vital step in their rehabilitation is an increase in concern for their physical appearance. The hairdresser and/or beautician play an important part in this. While some patients have to have their hair cut and washed on the wards, whenever possible they should go to a separate hairdressing saloon where they can have the same range of styles and treatments that are provided in an ordinary commercial hairdressers. Apart from hair care, women patients may benefit from instruction in the use of cosmetics and the treatment of facial hair and other blemishes.

The importance of proper dental care is obvious, and most mental hospitals have regular visits from a dentist. Though it is no longer believed that mental illness can be caused by infected teeth, patients with bad teeth tend to eat less, and take a restricted diet, which may contribute to poor physical and mental health. The danger of loose or broken teeth in patients undergoing ECT has also to be considered.

In elderly patients, simple foot troubles such as long nails, corns, and bunions can lead to loss of mobility, and the services of a qualified chiropodist cannot be overvalued.

Apart from physical care, some patients require spiritual help and advice. This is provided by the hospital chaplain. Many chaplains now see their role as being much more than taking services on Sundays and distributing tracts and good cheer the rest of the week, and wish to help with the social and psychological problems of the patient.

Admission to this community is a disturbing event for the patient and his family. It can be made less frightening and confusing if the reason for the patient's admission is clearly defined, and if the effects of admission are understood by the nurse who receives him.

16 Psychological Treatments

The Therapeutic Community

Through the studies of institutions by sociologists the observations of some psychiatrists, and the development of certain 'experimental' units, a gradual awareness has developed of the effect that the social structure of a psychiatric hospital has on the patients and staff. Much of man's behaviour is determined not only by his own needs and attitudes, but by the wishes and expectations of the society in which he lives. It is reasonable, therefore, to suppose that the behaviour of a patient in a psychiatric hospital will also be influenced for better or for worse by the type of society that exists within the hospital.

The characteristic features of the traditional institution have been described by Goffman, an American sociologist. He pointed out that such institutions tend to isolate the inmates from the world outside, while at the same time encourage them to give up their personal identity. This latter aspect he called 'the stripping process'. The patient on arrival is often literally stripped, his own clothes and personal possessions are taken from him, 'for safe keeping', and he is bathed—irrespective of his state of cleanliness. He may lose his name, being referred to as 'that psychopath, or the schizophrenic in ward 1', or if elderly, as 'pop' or 'gran'. Differences in educational and social background tend to be ignored, all patients being treated in terms of the lowest common denominator. Perhaps the worst feature of all is the stripping away of the patient's right to make decisions for himself. Sometimes, as a result of their illness, patients are unable to make sound judgements and have to be prevented from acting in ways that would be harmful to themselves or others, but the vast majority are capable of making most or all the decisions that a 'normal' person makes. The institution, however, tends to deny this and to take over decision-making even in respect of the most trivial activities.

The loss of personal identity and self respect is increased by the social isolation imposed. The institution itself is often remote from the place in which the patient lives and visiting by friends and relatives may be restricted, or even disallowed. The patient may be confined to the hospital and its grounds, to the ward, or even to one room. Within the hospital the patient is isolated from the staff by the barriers of a language which, at first, he does not understand—the use of jargon, and initials, and nicknames. He is exposed to a set of rules that are not clearly stated and that do not match those of the world outside. Simple things like smoking may be regarded as an almost criminal act, and lead to disproportionate punishment or loss of privilege. In this setting, many forms of treatment such as drugs or ECT may be regarded by the patient, and some of the staff, as a form of punishment.

The patient in such an institution is concerned with two things: either to get out of it as soon as possible, or to make life as comfortable for himself as possible under the circumstances. Goffman described four different ways in which patients attempted to do this. The particular method chosen depended upon the patient's personality, illness, and previous experience: the same patient may use different techniques at different times.

1. WITHDRAWAL
The patient withdraws into himself, ignoring everything that goes on around him. The degree of withdrawal may vary from mild disinterest, to total mutism and refusal to respond in any way. Such patients are sometimes said to be 'regressed'.

2. REFUSAL TO CO-OPERATE
This involves aggressive refusal to conform in any way to the rules and demands of the institution. Such patients are usually referred to as 'difficult'.

3. COLONISATION
The patient resolves his difficulties by 'adopting' the hospital in place of the world outside. He conforms to the rules and in return for 'good' behaviour in giving up independence, is rewarded by extra privileges. Such patients often respond to the suggestion that they are fit to leave hospital, by an acute worsening of their symptoms.

4. CONVERSION

This involves the patient's adopting staff attitudes and behaviour as his own. They may help in caring for other patients, and not infrequently treat other patients more strictly than the actual staff would.

Similar patterns of behaviour also develop among the staff, who are as prone to institutionalisation as are the patients.

It can be seen that because of the authoritarian structure of the old institution the patient may be forced into two types of response— resistance, either by withdrawal or aggression, or surrender with the development of dependence on the institution. Either response is likely to make it more difficult for the patient to return to life outside the hospital.

Long before the characteristics of institutions and the response of the patient were stated in this way, people had tried intuitively to modify their structure so that it would lessen the harm to the patients and staff. The introduction of work therapy was one such move, and a great improvement was brought about by the 'open door' policy that led to greater freedom for the patient. The introduction of tranquillising drugs made this process much easier and more acceptable. The logical conclusion to these measures was to avoid admitting the patient to the institution, and this has led to the development of out-patient clinics, day hospitals, and psychiatric units in the general hospitals.

Such developments help to avoid some of the dangers of institutional life, but do not exploit the positive features of community life to eliminate undesirable behaviour. It is the attempt to do this that has led to the development of units usually called 'therapeutic communities'. This term has now been used so often and applied to such different types of units that it is almost meaningless, but its use should really be restricted to units which apply most of the following principles. There is no golden rule about how these principles should be put into practice, the detailed structure of the unit must depend on the wishes and skills of the people working, and being treated, in it.

The main aims of such 'communities' are:

1. To change the authoritarian organisation that encourages dependence and institutionalisation for one that promotes a democratic sharing of responsibility and decision-making by both staff and patients.

2. To provide an environment in which the patient can feel able to try out different ways of behaving in order that he may learn which methods are satisfactory and which are not.

The principles involved in achieving these aims tend to overlap and can be summarised as follows:

1. Joint decision making
2. Sharing of information
3. Permissiveness
4. Reality-confrontation

The application of these principles leads to units that tend to be organised in a similar way.

1. JOINT DECISION-MAKING

In order that patients may remain individuals, capable of functioning in the outside world, they must be encouraged to make decisions for themselves. Some patients tend to blame their actions on 'authority' figures rather than accept their own responsibilities. To remove their scapegoat, and to help patients take part in decision-making, there has to be some sacrifice of authority on the part of the staff. There must also be provision for the discussion of problems before decisions are made. To serve this purpose most therapeutic communities set aside time for meetings in which all the patients and staff on the unit take part. These meetings not only allow for discussion and decision-making, but also provide an opportunity for sharing information.

2. SHARING INFORMATION

It has been realised that the doctor who sees a patient for only, at most, an hour a day, cannot know what is happening to the patient during the other twenty-three hours each day. Thus, he may be unaware of events and relationships that are playing a vital part in the patient's illness or its treatment. The people most able to provide this information are the other patients and the nursing staff. In some traditionally organised wards, however, the only nurse to speak to the doctor would be the charge nurse or sister, and no one would dream of asking the opinion of a junior nurse, let alone another patient. The general community meeting provides such an opportunity, but it has to be supplemented by a series of other smaller meetings for various groups of staff. The organisation of such a unit, therefore, involves the planning of a time-table of various meetings. It is usually found that the need for particular meetings waxes and wanes and the system has to be revised from time to time.

3. PERMISSIVENESS

To enable patients to feel free to try out various forms of behaviour in an attempt to learn new techniques there must be a high degree of tolerance. If all forms of deviant behaviour are immediately suppressed by isolation, punishment, or the use of drugs, neither the patient nor the staff will learn anything of the nature of the under-lying problems. It is not, however, sufficient to be tolerant of such behaviour, it must also be discussed with the patient to help him understand more clearly the effects of his actions, his reasons for so doing, and the reasons why society at large would not tolerate it. It is important that such an examination of cause and effect should be carried out as soon as possible after the event. Permissiveness and tolerance have some limits and these in part are linked to the need for reality-confrontation.

4. REALITY-CONFRONTATION

This means forcing the patient to look at the nature of his problems, his relationships, and his actions, without using the various forms of escape such as denial, withdrawal, projection, and distortion. He must also be helped to see the needs and demands of society and how he must modify his own behaviour to the point where society is prepared to tolerate him. This does not imply a brainwashing process to produce colourless non-conformists, but the development of sufficient mutual understanding to allow of peaceful coexistence. It is the conflict between permissiveness and reality that creates many of the problems in such a community, and to achieve the correct balance between them calls for great skill on the part of the staff.

The Role of the Nurse in a Therapeutic Community

To work in such a setting the nurse must be prepared to modify some of her traditional ideas about the work she is expected to perform, and the 'status' she will have. Status will tend to be conferred in accordance with ability and experience rather than by rank, though in general, of course, higher rank reflects greater skill. The nurse, and other staff, will be less able, however, to 'pull rank' to protect themselves in situations where their lack of knowledge or personal weak points are being exposed. Instead, the nurse will have to develop her skills, and become sufficiently mature to examine her weaknesses realistically. In return, she will be given more interesting and responsible work, and less routine undemanding tasks. She will still be expected to fulfil the functions, already outlined, of observer and technician, but a greater emphasis will be placed on her relating to the patients in her care.

The therapeutic community provides a setting in which other forms of treatment, both physical and psychological, can be undertaken, not as isolated events in the patient's day to day life, but as part of a total effort to enable him to return to the world outside with the optimum chance of remaining there. The rest of this chapter describes the various forms of 'psychological' treatments that may be used.

Psychotherapy

This treatment consists of trying to help the patient see the nature of his difficulties more clearly, and to aid him in finding new and more satisfactory methods of dealing with them, so that he is better able to cope with life and its stress, and consequently derives greater and more lasting satisfaction from it. While, ideally, the aim of treatment is to provide the patient with insight, and to modify his personality, in practice both patient and therapist have often to be satisfied with something less. The methods of achieving these ends and the degree of insight aimed at vary and are best described under various headings, but the general principle remains. That is, two people enter into a relationship in which the therapist helps the patient explore the workings of his own mind and suggest new ways for the patient to deal with his difficulties.

Defining the Problem
Many people who are suffering from emotional disorders find it difficult to accept this idea. This may be because they have been brought up to think that any emotional response is a sign of weakness and implies failure on their part. It may arise as a result of their belief that the doctor, or other person that they ask for help, will

not take them seriously if they complain that they feel anxious or depressed. Some are likely to offer physical symptoms such as headaches, indigestion, or pain, in order to arouse interest and sympathy. In others, the underlying cause of their emotional state is so threatening, painful, or embarrassing, that they have to deny its existence even to themselves.

It is necessary, therefore, to be aware that when a patient complains of some symptom, mental or physical, this may not be the real problem. Often the nature of the complaint has a symbolic relationship to the actual problem. Such relationships are a common feature of everyday life. For instance, we refer to people who annoy us as 'a pain in the neck' or a difficult problem as being 'a real headache'. We must remember that not all such complaints have a symbolic function—tension can cause a headache, but so can a brain tumour! Clues that suggest there is some other problem than the one offered are: the failure of the symptom to respond to the usual method of treatment (e.g. pain not influenced by pain killing drugs); the absence of any physical cause for the symptom; or the development of a new symptom if the doctor dismisses the first one as being unimportant.

To help the patient accept that the symptoms of which he complains have an emotional basis, it is usually necessary to reassure him on three points:

1. That this does not make his complaint any less important, or less deserving of help.
2. That emotional problems do not imply weakness or failure on the part of the patient.
3. His complaints are 'real' not imaginary—it often helps to offer a simple explanation of how muscular tension can produce pressure on nerve roots, thus causing a headache, or how anxiety leads to the release of adrenaline and the physical effects this produces.

Sometimes such simple reassurance and explanation leads to the patient losing his symptoms but, more often, the patient having accepted the emotional basis for his symptoms says 'why am I emotionally disturbed'.

Underlying Causes

These fall into two groups, (a) events in the patient's early life, and (b) the situation in which the patient finds himself at present.

Some psychiatrists maintain that it is always necessary to uncover the events in early life that have led to the patient finding certain things threatening in later life. They would advocate that the patient can be really and lastingly helped only by psychoanalysis. Other psychiatrists would say that the events in the 'here and now' are more important, and by defining these and helping the patient come to terms with them, a satisfactory result, in practical terms, is obtained. Both camps agree that the patient's response to his present situation is, to a large extent, determined by his early experience, but they differ in how important these events are from the treatment point of view. All but the most superficial forms of psychotherapy are to some extent based on the theories and practice of psychoanalysis, so it is necessary to have at least an outline knowledge of this subject.

Psychoanalysis

This treatment technique and its theory evolved from the original work of a Viennese neurologist, Sigmund Freud. He became very interested in the problem of hysterical symptoms that were commonly seen by neurologists at that time, and was impressed by the alteration in these symptoms when the patient was hypnotised. He became aware that many of these symptoms had a sexual significance, and that many patients appeared to have had some frightening sexual experience in childhood that they were able to remember only when hypnotised. He also noted that those patients who recalled these childhood incidents most clearly and dramatically seemed to benefit most from the treatment. He concluded that the symptoms were caused by these childhood memories, which the patient had tried to blot out of his mind, and that the cure depended upon discovering these events and helping the patient accept them and not to try to deny them.

He began to treat patients on this theory, but soon found that many could not be hypnotised. It was necessary, therefore, to find some other way of helping them to uncover these hidden events. The technique he devised was that of 'free association'. This consists of encouraging the patient to talk about anything that comes into his head without trying to sort out the important from the unimportant. The 'analyst' intervenes only when the patient seems unable to produce more material. Freud noted that the more closely related the topic was to events that were emotionally important, the more difficult the patient found it to talk freely. Thus, in the course of many sessions it was possible for the analyst to define events and persons who had had a traumatic effect on the patient. If asked directly about these topics, however, the patient could not, or would not, discuss them.

From his experiences with patients, and from examination of the material produced in these sessions, Freud devised a theory of the human mind and its development which has profoundly altered man's ideas. Whether correct or not, it has cast light upon areas that were previously totally dark. He also studied in detail the the relationship between the therapist and the patient, and this in some ways is more important as far as treatment is concerned than the theories of the mind's structure, for it would seem likely that the way in which the therapist uses this relationship determines the result of his treatment far more than the theoretical explanations he offers to himself or the patient. The following section is a grossly over-simplified account of:

1. Freud's theory of the mind's structure and development.
2. The relationship of therapist and patient and its use in treatment.

Freud was not the first to suggest the model of the mind described below, but he amassed so much fresh material to support his ideas that the theory is usually associated with his name. He considered that the mind could be divided into three levels: the Conscious, the Preconscious, and the Unconscious. The conscious part comprises all that we are aware of at a given time, our knowledge of our immediate surroundings, sensations, ideas, and thoughts. All that part of our mind that can be readily brought into our conscious mind at will, comprises the preconscious. The unconscious mind comprises all these memories, desires and prohibitions of which we are not consciously aware and which we are unable to become aware of even by a deliberate effort of will.

Freud postulated that the unconscious processes are prevented from entering the conscious mind by some sort of mental censorship, and he further divided personality into three components. He called the basic needs and drives that act as the source of motivation, the *Id*. The part of the personality that concerns itself with compromising between the demands of the *Id* and the restrictions imposed by the 'real' world on satisfying them, he called the *Ego*. Finally, the aspect of personality that a person develops as a result of learning from his parents, those features of character and behaviour that they and society approve of, was called the *super Ego*. This aspect of personality differs from 'conscience' in that it acts not only at a conscious level, but also in the unconscious.

The Freudian explanation of anxiety is that the person developing it does so because of the conflict between the demands of his id, and the restrictions of his super ego. Normally, the person resolves this conflict by some compromise solution; e.g. a woman wanting to slim, who is tempted to eat a cream cake may partly satisfy her greed, while salving her conscience, by eating only half of it. If practical solutions are not possible, the person will try to diminish his anxiety by resorting to some form of mental mechanism (described earlier), but if these fail or have to be used excessively, the patient may then present as a neurotic illness. Analysts claim that the form the illness takes, depends on the personality of the patient, and that this, in turn, is determined by how successful the patient was in dealing with the initial stages of his development as a child. These stages have been described in the section on normal development but briefly comprise:

1. Oral erotic
2. Oral aggressive
3. Anal erotic
4. Anal aggressive
5. Phallic
6. Oedipal

The type of behaviour that the patient demonstrates, depends upon the stage to which he regresses.

In psychoanalytic treatment, although the particular model of the mind, and the theories of personality differ between the various 'schools', the basic aim is to help the patient uncover events in early childhood that were so threatening they prevented him from passing normally through that particular stage. Having discovered these events, using some form of free association, the patient has to be helped to understand the relationship between those events and his present circumstances, and to see how his anxiety is due to a re-lighting of previous fears.

Many psychiatrists feel that the proof of these theories leaves much to be desired and that in any case the technique is not a practical form of treatment for the majority of people. However, in the course of the profound and intimate relationship between analyst and patient, analysts learnt a great deal about a process that seems of crucial importance in any form of human relationship, and especially so in a relationship that is designed to help the patient. This is the process called *transference*, and an understanding of its nature and how it may be used, is of vital importance to anyone working in the field of mental health.

Transference

In every human relationship there is a tendency for those concerned to transfer some of the emotions they have previously felt for important people in their lives on to the other person. That this kind of thing happens has always been recognised, and our everyday language is full of expressions indicating the kind of situation: e.g. 'He is like a father to me', 'The way she nags, you would think we were married', 'I love him like a brother', 'She could not have done more for me if she had been my mother'.

These strong emotions are usually those felt for parents and siblings (brothers and sisters) and generally have no logical connection with the person concerned in the new relationship. While this process occurs to a greater or lesser extent in all relationships, it is most pronounced in the intimate relationship between psychotherapist and patient, and it was in the course of psychoanalysis that the great importance of this process was recognised.

The patient begins unconsciously to regard the therapist as if he were a substitute for her father. Thus, she may develop strong feelings of love and dependence—so-called *positive transference*, or, on the other hand, if her relationship with her father was poor, she may regard the therapist as threatening or rejecting and feel angry and hostile towards him—*negative transference*. As in most people there is a mixture of these feelings of love and hate towards the same person, the patient may vary between positive and negative feelings for the therapist. This mixture of emotional response is called ambivalence. The therapist is not immune to emotions about the patient, and his reaction to her is called *counter transference*, the essential difference being that because of his training the therapist should be consciously aware of the reasons for his response, and thus be able to control or modify his behaviour in spite of them. The patient, on the other hand, has to be helped by the therapist to recognise what she is doing, and then helped to understand why she continues to respond to people as if they were her father, mother, husband, or brother, as the case may be. Thus, her relationship with the therapist provides a practical demonstration of the way in which she behaves in 'real' life, and helps to illustrate how problems arise for her in the present, as a result of events in her past. When she has gained insight into her responses, it is hoped that she will be able to modify her actual behaviour in such a way that she can deal with the present in a more realistic and satisfactory way.

While this conscious use of the transference occurs to the greatest extent in psychotherapy, an understanding of it is essential to the nurse if she is to form a therapeutic relationship with her patients, and not merely a relationship that has all the faults and failures that have bedevilled the patient's previous experiences.

By understanding that the strong negative feeling a patient shows towards her may reflect the way the patient felt towards his mother, wife, or sister, the nurse may feel less rejected and, therefore, less prone to respond with hostile feelings herself. The nurse must remember that not all emotional response is due to transference—if she behaves like a tyrant, other people will hate and fear her for what she is, irrespective of how they felt about their mothers! Conversely, the patient who demonstrates great affection for, or dependence on the nurse, may be doing so less because of the nurse's qualities, but more as a result of his strong feelings towards his mother. Realising this, the nurse may feel less flattered, but more able to deal realistically with the situation.

The nurse needs to be aware of her own tendency to project emotions on to the patients, and other staff members. As this is, in part, an unconscious process, she may not always be aware of the reasons for her response, and will only become so when possible reasons are suggested by her colleagues. This is one reason why staff meetings are valuable.

With increased awareness of the patient's underlying motives and of her own responses, the nurse is able to modify her approach so that the patient can be helped to establish a relationship, even if it is largely on terms dictated by the patient. This relationship must then be consciously used by the nurse to enable the patient to learn to relate in a more mature and satisfactory way in the future.

Group Therapy

Individual psychotherapy is both time-consuming and expensive and cannot, therefore, be made available to everyone who might benefit from it. To overcome this difficulty, patients began to be treated in small groups. It soon became obvious that this form of treatment had other advantages apart from that of cost and time. Group psychotherapy is now considered as having the same status as individual psychotherapy, being more effective than it, in some conditions, and less effective in others.

The advantages are that the patient is provided with a wider range of opportunities for learning how his behaviour influences, and is influenced by, other people. Secondly, the intense relationships that develop between patient and therapist in individual therapy may prove too difficult to handle, particularly if the patient is prone to 'acting out' his emotional difficulties: in a group this relationship is spread between the members of the group and may thus be kept at a less intense level. A further advantage to the patient is that in listening to the problems of others he becomes aware that his own difficulties are not unique and peculiar to himself. This helps to lessen his sense of isolation more effectively than the therapist's reassurances.

The techniques of group psychotherapy vary enormously, depending upon the personality and training of the therapist. Most therapists agree that a group should not exceed twelve in number, the members having similar backgrounds and education and sharing similar or related problems. Group psychotherapy is employed most frequently in the neurotic and personality disorders, but it is also employed with schizophrenic and even demented patients. Some groups are called 'open groups', in which new members may be introduced to the group as others drop out. Other groups are called 'closed groups' in which no new patient joins the group during the time it functions.

The therapist may play a variety of roles in the group. Some act as a kind of teacher, doing most of the talking, and directing the comments of the patients. Others play an almost passive role, saying very little apart from making an occasional interpretation of some statement or form of behaviour, or intervening when the tension between members reaches an explosive level.

The role of the nurse in group psychotherapy will depend on the wishes of the person running the group. Her primary task will be to learn from the experience. She must learn to understand the dynamics of group pressures, the dynamics underlying individual behaviour, and must come to understand some of her own responses to the patients and the therapist.

Hypnosis

The history of hypnosis starts with Mesmer, a flamboyant character who used a hypnotic technique in treating various disorders, and gave public demonstrations. He developed a theory to explain the effects, based on an analogy with magnetism, and postulated that some form of invisible fluid passed between the subject and the hypnotist. The method fell into disrepute, and even today it tends to be considered as a rather questionable practice. Many investigations have been carried out to try to determine the nature of hypnosis, but no conclusive result has been obtained.

In essence the hypnotist uses a variety of techniques to render the patient in a state of greatly increased suggestibility. Having done this, he then uses the increased suggestibility to:

1. Encourage the patient to talk about events that have been repressed, and which the patient cannot produce in the normal state. This is similar to the analyst's use of free association to overcome repression.
2. To get the patient to 'relive', in a dramatic and emotional way, events that have been traumatic for him in the past, and are causing symptoms. This corresponds to the use of drugs to produce an abreaction.
3. To implant suggestions about the disappearance of symptoms, or other changes in behaviour that will occur when the patient comes out of the hypnotic state.
4. To 'decondition' the patient to stimuli that in every day life produce feelings of panic or anxiety. This represents one form of behaviour therapy.

The indications for hypnotherapy in psychiatry are limited, though it has many applications in dentistry and obstetrics as a way of inducing diminished pain sensitivity. It should never be carried out as a party demonstration, or by people who are not prepared or capable to deal with the emotional material that the subject may produce. The nurse has probably no role to play in formal hypnotic treatment but may well take part in various forms of relaxation techniques that are based on modified hypnosis.

Behaviour Therapy

The Russian physiologist Pavlov demonstrated that nervous activity could be considered as consisting of reflexes that were of two kinds—

unconditioned and conditioned. When food is placed in the mouth, saliva is secreted (unconditioned), but if a bell is rung each time food is presented to an animal, in time the animal will salivate when the bell is rung, even if no food is produced (conditioned). Pavlov went on to demonstrate a number of features of the way in which such reflexes can be established or suppressed, and later developed a theory about the way in which mental symptoms may arise from the establishment of faulty conditioned reflexes, or by interference with established reflex patterns. From his work has been developed a theory of learning which, in turn, has given rise to a technique of treatment called *behaviour therapy*. In an over-simplified way the theory can be stated as follows. Certain ways of behaving can be considered as being due to:

1. Failure to undergo conditioning.
2. Development of response to the wrong stimulus.
3. Persistence of response when the original stimulus has been removed.
4. Response to a potentially harmful stimulus.

Examples of the type of behaviour resulting from these are:

1. Psychopathic personality.
2. Various sexual deviations, particularly fetishism.
3. Anxiety states and other forms of neurosis.
4. Alcoholism or drug addiction.

Treatment can thus be directed at either obliterating a set of responses, or replacing the pleasant response by an unpleasant one.

The first technique is that of deconditioning, in which the patient is presented with objects or situations that get closer and closer to the thing that makes him anxious, while at the same time his level of anxiety is reduced by drugs, hypnosis, or reassurance. An example of the method is that used in treating cat phobia, where the patient is at first shown drawings, then photographs of cats, then a piece of furry material, then she holds the material, and so on, until she can tolerate a live cat.

The second technique consists of giving the stimulus that normally gives the patient pleasure (e.g. alcohol, pornographic pictures, a gambling machine) and at the same time causing him discomfort, either with an injection that makes him vomit, or with a mild electric shock. The aim is to set up a new conditioned reflex, in which the original stimulus no longer produces pleasure, but now leads to feelings of anxiety and physical repulsion. Such techniques have been used in the treatment of alcoholics, sexual deviants, compulsive gamblers, and the like. The treatment is extremely unpleasant and requires a high level of motivation on the patient's part and extreme enthusiasm on the part of the therapist.

17 Physical Methods of Treatment: 1 Drug Treatment

Physical treatment in psychiatry is based on the fact that by altering the chemical and physical environment of the brain cells in various ways, changes can be produced in the patient's mental state and behaviour. The methods employed include drugs, electroconvulsive therapy, insulin treatment, and surgical operations on parts of the brain.

The nurse has special responsibilities in regard to looking after, and giving out drugs, and has special tasks in relation to the other forms of physical treatment. However, the value and effectiveness of physical treatment is not restricted to the actual physical effects of the drug or the operation. It has often been shown that a number of patients receiving tablets that contain only inactive substances like chalk (placebos) also improve. Any form of treatment has considerable psychological significance, as well as its direct effect on the brain. The giving out of medicines provides an opportunity for the nurse to form a relationship with the patient. Many patients regard taking pills as 'proper' treatment, and think that talking about their problems is a waste of time. Such people are only prepared to examine the nature of their difficulties after they have been given the reward of a tablet.

Other patients refuse drugs or other treatments, and their refusal gives the nurse a chance to discuss with them the reasons for their attitudes. The patient may wish to remain 'ill' and in hospital, and feel that if he takes the drugs, his symptoms will go, his defence will have failed, and he must face his problems again. Some refuse because they have delusions that they are going to be poisoned. This enables the nurse to find out why the patient feels this is likely to happen, and it may help to uncover a wide range of ill-formed paranoid ideas. Yet other patients refuse their medication as a gesture of independence, a last ditch stand against institutionalisation.

215

In dealing with refusal of treatment, the staff, medical and nursing, must know clearly what the aim and purpose of the treatment is in each individual case. All refusals should be reported to the doctor, so that decisions can be made. In some instances, the patient's mental state may be so disturbed that no contact can be achieved until drugs or ECT, have been given, even if the patient resists, but in most cases a greater understanding of the patient's point of view, and explanation of the reasons for a certain form of treatment will allow of some compromise solution, satisfactory to both staff and patient.

Drugs used in psychiatry fall roughly into three groups:

1. Anti-psychotic drugs
2. Anxiety relieving drugs
3. Anti-depressant drugs.

There is a degree of overlap between the different therapeutical agents of these three groups; for instance, some of the anti-depressants are sedative and tend to diminish anxiety. Some of the anti-psychotic drugs may be used in smaller doses to diminish anxiety.

When learning about a particular drug the nurse should familiarise herself with the following points:

1. The indications for its use
2. Its normal dose range
3. Its side effects
4. Its toxic effects
5. The treatment of overdosage.

It is not possible to deal in detail with all the drugs currently used in the treatment of psychiatric disorders but some representative examples will be described.

The Anti-psychotic Drugs

The drugs of this group are sometimes referred to as neuroleptics or major tranquillisers.

In 1951, research workers in France investigated a drug that was to revolutionise the treatment of schizophrenia and manic states. The drug was chlorpromazine, marketed under the trade name Largactil. In 1952 two European psychiatrists demonstrated its value in certain psychiatric illnesses. Its main clinical effect was that it calmed and sedated the patient without making him too sleepy or confused. It also seemed to diminish the intensity of hallucinations and delusional ideas.

Research continued into a number of related compounds which were chemically composed of a phenothiazine ring. The drugs of this group are often known as 'the phenothiazines'. Chlorpromazine remains one of the most widely used of this group and will be described in detail. Other members of the group will then be briefly mentioned.

Chlorpromazine:

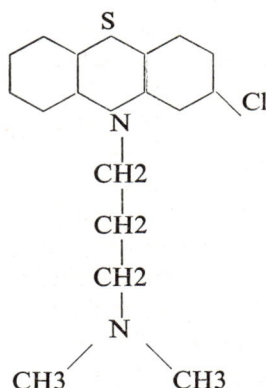

$$S$$
$$Cl$$
$$N$$
$$CH2$$
$$CH2$$
$$CH2$$
$$N$$
$$CH3 \qquad CH3$$

Chlorpromazine reduces restlessness and physical overactivity and tends to produce a degree of mental calmness and tranquility. It also tends to diminish vomiting and lowers the thermo-regulating centres.

Its chief indications in psychiatry are:

1. To reduce the mental and physical activity of patients with schizophrenia and those in the manic or hypomanic phases of manic depressive psychosis.
2. To reduce the hallucinationary experiences of patients with schizophrenia.
3. To cover the withdrawal of alcohol in patients who are physically addicted to it and in the treatment of established delirium tremens.
4. To control agitation in patients with agitated depression or anxiety states.

5. In anorexia nervosa, to overcome the patient's reluctance to eat, and to increase weight gain.

Dosage from 25 mg three times daily to up to 1 g daily. It is available in the form of tablets, syrup or intramuscular injections.

Side Effects and Toxicity

Many side effects can be produced by phenothiazine derivatives. Some are relatively trivial, others serious and may require the drug to be stopped. The side effects can be noted under the system that they effect.

Central Nervous System. One of the commonest side effects of phenothiazine drugs given in moderate to large doses is the production of symptoms resembling those described by James Parkinson in 1817 as 'the shaking palsy'. There are many causes for this condition, which is the result of interference with the functioning of the extra-pyramidal system of the brain, which regulates the tone of muscles and enables movements to be made smoothly and without jerkiness. The symptoms produced by damage to this system vary, depending on the nature and exact site of the damage, but in general there is a combination of tremor and rigidity, and the patient's ability to start voluntary movements is impaired. The face takes on an expressionless appearance, like a mask, and while the patient can still smile or frown, the movements are slowed down. Dribbling is a frequent early sign. The posture becomes abnormal, in that all the joints tend to be held in the flexed position, and the patient no longer walks in the normal way. His arms do not swing, and he takes small shuffling steps, tending to go faster and faster, as if trying to regain his balance. There may be a characteristic tremor of the fingers, that resembles the action of rolling a pill, and the patient's limbs or head may show a rhythmic tremor when he is at rest. The development of these symptoms requires the dose to be reduced, or the symptoms can be controlled by the use of drugs such as cogentin, artane, or disipal.

Although not very common with chlorpromazine, some of the other phenothiazine derivatives are liable to produce acute spasm of certain muscle groups, so that the eyes may rotate upwards and become fixed in this position for a time (oculogyric crisis). The head may be rotated to one side (spasmodic torticollis), or the whole body may be arched backwards (opisthotonus). These spasms are painful and are called dystonic reactions. (These severe reactions can often be abolished by injecting 10 mg of Kemadrin.) Other patients develop what they call 'fidgety legs', when they feel unable to stay still and keep moving about to try to diminish their sense of discomfort. This condition is called akithesia.

The Cardiovascular System. Phenothiazines tend to produce a fall in blood pressure, particularly when the patient is standing. Patients having large doses of these drugs usually have their blood pressure recorded, both standing and lying, twice a day. In older people, the fall in BP on standing may lead to a faint, and they may injure themselves in falling. Some patients on phenothiazines develop a rise in pulse rate.

Body Temperature. The temperature whether normal or raised tends to be lowered by the large doses of chlorpromazine and, thus, a patient may develop an infection without a corresponding rise in temperature. Conversely, some patients show occasional spikes of temperature while taking the drug.

Hormonal Disturbance. Some patients put on excessive weight while having chlorpromazine. The reason is not known. In some patients, however, the increased weight only represents a return to normal body weight due to improved dietary intake.

Amenorrhoea is a common side effect.

Liver Damage. One in 200 patients treated with chlorpromazine develops jaundice of an obstructive type. Stopping the drug usually leads to rapid recovery from the jaundice. The reaction seems to be due to individual sensitivity and is twice as common in women as in men.

Skin Reactions. A variety of allergic rashes occur in patients on chlorpromazine. In addition, many patients become abnormally sensitive to the effects of the sun, and in severe cases may become badly sunburnt after quite short exposure. For this reason patients are warned not to sunbathe, to wear hats that give shade to the face and neck, and if exposure is unavoidable they must use some form of ultraviolet filter cream.

Other Phenothiazine Drugs

A large number of derivatives have been synthesised that differ from chlorpromazine in various ways. It is not possible to discuss these in detail, and only a few of the better known ones will be mentioned.

Trifluoperazine (Stelazine). This drug has less sedative effect and does not produce liver damage. It is frequently used as a maintenance drug in chronic schizophrenia. It has a greater tendency to produce dystonic side effects. The dose range in psychotic illnesses is from 5 to 45 mg a day in divided doses, with an average dose of 15 mg a day.

Fluphenazine enanthate (Moditen) *and Fluphenazine decanoate.* These drugs are derivatives of fluphenazine and have the advantage of being given as an intra-muscular injection which is slowly absorbed over the course of the following fourteen to forty days. Thus, they are particularly useful in the treatment of patients with chronic schizophrenia who are unreliable in taking medicines by mouth. Many such patients refuse to continue with their treatment once they feel better, and then relapse some weeks after terminating their drugs. Others are just unreliable at taking pills so that a steady therapeutic level is not reached. Yet others find it much easier to have one injection every few weeks than to be bothered by regular pill-taking.

The disadvantages are that once an injection is given the drug cannot be discontinued if side effects are a problem. Fortunately, the major common side effect is Parkinsonism and this can generally be controlled by giving drugs such as Orphenadrine (Disipal) Benzhexol (Aartane) or Proyclidine (Kemadrin).

Many hospitals now run special follow-up clinics for patients maintained on these drugs where their progress can be monitored and the dose adjusted.

It is usual to start the patient on the drug as an in-patient. A test dose of 0·5 ml is given by deep intramuscular injection and the patient is observed for the development of extra pyramidal symptoms for the next four or five days. If these are not a problem a further 1 ml of the drug is then given. The dose is adjusted by the amount administered and the frequency of injection. It is usual to put the patient on oral phenothiazines temporarily before using the injectable forms.

Thionidazine (Melleril). This is a less-potent phenothiazine with a correspondingly lower level of side effects. It is therefore of value in elderly confused patients, who often cannot tolerate the more potent drugs.

Non-phenothiazine Derivatives

Flupenthixol (Fluanxol; Depixol). This is a potent non-sedating drug of the thioxanthene series. While it has a marked anti-psychotic action it is alerting rather than sedating and is, therefore, of value in those schizophrenic patients who show marked apathy, withdrawal and inertia. It is not indicated in patients who have been overactive or aggressive.

This drug is also available as a depot injection and, as with fluphenazine, an initial test dose is given of 20 mg followed five to ten days later by a further 20 mg.

The major side effects are extra pyramidal symptoms.

Haloperidol (Serenace). This is a butyrophenone derivative. It is probably most often used in the treatment of mania and hypomania but is also used in schizophrenia and organic psychoses. It can be given by mouth or by injection in doses varying between 1 and 200 mg per day.

Its main side effect is the development of extra pyramidal symptoms.

Anti-depressant Drugs

The drugs used in the treatment of depression were discovered as a result of chance observation, but subsequent investigation has led to the formulation of a tentative explanation, in terms of brain biochemistry, of the changes that occur when a person becomes depressed. The following account is grossly over-simplified but helps to illustrate how the anti-depressant drugs may work.

Nerve cells consist of the cell body containing a nucleus, and a long extension called an axon, which ends in a number of branches. These may end on another nerve cell body or, in motor nerves, on a specially adapted muscle fibre. There is a minute gap between the end of the axon and the cell on which it ends, so that when a stimulus passes along the axon it has to be transmitted across this gap. This is done by liberating at the nerve ending minute amounts of a chemical. In the neuromuscular junction this has been shown to be acetylcholine, but in the brain cells it is probable that a number of different chemicals may act as transmitter substances. These chemicals are adrenaline, nor-adrenaline and 5-hydroxytryptamine, all of which belong to the group of chemicals called amines. Almost as soon as they are released from their storage sites they are either destroyed by an enzyme called mono-amine oxidase or are restored. It is thought that a person's mood is in some way related to the level of amines that are in a free, active state in his brain. The higher the level of free amines the higher the mood: thus, drugs that raise the level of amines should also raise the mood. There are two ways in which this can be brought about; first, by preventing the amines being re-absorbed into their storage sites, and secondly, by preventing the enzyme, mono-amine oxidase, destroying them. The anti-depressant drugs can be divided into two broad groups depending on the way in which they act.

Group I—The Tricyclic Antidepressants

Imipramine (Tofranil). The forerunner of this group of drugs imipramine is still widely used It has very little sedating properties, which may be an advantage at times, but in cases where there is anxiety and agitation as well as depression it has usually to be given in combination with a tranquillising drug.

The onset of its action does not usually occur for ten to fourteen days after the patient starts taking the drug.

The side effects inherent in the nature of the drug are dryness of the mouth, sweating, constipation, disturbance of accommodation; postural hypotension may also be noted.

Toxic doses may cause coma, convulsions and cardiac arrest.

It is given with caution to patients known to have ischaemic heart disease and to those patients who have epilepsy.

Amitriptyline (Tryptizol). This is usually regarded as the anti-depressant drug against which new drugs are compared. It is used in most forms of depression and, because it has a fairly marked sedative effect, it is particularly useful in depressive states with anxiety. Some people find it too sedating to tolerate during the day and for that reason is often given in a single dose at bed time, which not only avoids daytime drowsiness but also helps overcome the sleep disturbance so often a distressing feature of depressive illnesses. It is available in a slow form which allows a therapeutic level to be maintained in the blood over twenty-four hours from a single night-time dose. The dose range is from 30 to 200 mg daily.

Side effects are the same as for all members of this group of drugs.

The rate of onset of improvement is claimed to be more rapid.

Nortriptyline (Aventyl) and *Protriptyline* are similar in their effects and side effects.

In general, the tricyclic drugs are not given at the same time as drugs of the monoamine inhibitor group, nor for a period of about three weeks after treatment with MAOI drugs has ceased because of the danger of hyperpyrexia, convulsions and subarachnoid haemorrhages occurring.

Some psychiatrists, however, do use these drugs in combination and claim success in cases that have failed to respond to any other form of treatment.

Group II—The Monoamine Oxidase Inhibitors

A number of these drugs were introduced but abandoned because of their serious side effects, particularly on the liver. The following continue to be used in selected cases. They are regarded as being more successful in reactive and neurotic depressions but there is evidence to suggest that people respond better to tricyclic or MAOI, depending on genetic factors rather than the nature of their illness.

All patients taking these drugs must avoid certain articles of diet and have to be warned about this in advance. They must also be advised not to take any other drugs without first checking with a doctor that it is safe for them to do so.

Foods that must be avoided are: cheese (in any form), Oxo, Bovril, Marmite, pickled herrings and broad beans. Alcohol should also be avoided. The reason for these prohibitions is that the foods listed contain tyramine, and when monoamine oxidase is inhibited, taking tyramine can produce severe hypertension, which may lead to cerebral haemorrhage.

Phenelzine (Nardil). This drug is often used in the treatment of phobic anxiety states when there is an element of underlying depression. The dose is in the order of 15 mg three times a day.

Apart from the serious side effect mentioned above, there are minor ones such as dizziness, fatigue and gastro-intestinal disturbance. These tend to wear off after a few days on treatment.

Tranylcypromine (Parnate). This is similar in action to phenelzine and has the same side effects. As it may cause difficulty in getting to sleep, the last dose is usually given not later than 3.00 p.m.

Lithium Salts

This drug, which was originally tried in cases of hypomania, has also recently become widely used in cases of recurrent depression with or without a history of hypomanic episodes.

Lithium is not found normally in the body and it has a number of side effects and toxic effects. Its mode of action is not at present understood. To limit the serious toxic effects of the drug it is necessary to monitor the dosage at regular intervals by measuring the serum level of lithium. This is expressed in milliequivalents (mEq) per litre. At first, samples are taken once a week; when a stable level is achieved estimations are performed less often but may be ordered if the patient shows any symptoms of overdosage.

Mild side effects are common at the start of treatment but usually disappear after three or four weeks; if they persist or worsen, however, they may indicate the onset of toxic levels. Harmless side effects include nausea, loose stools, find tremor of the hands, polyuria and polydipsia.

Signs of impending intoxication are: vomiting and diarrhoea, coarse tremor of the hands, sluggishness and sleepiness, vertigo, dysarthria.

Concentrations above 2 mEq/litre indicate intoxication. Severe intoxication mainly affects the central nervous system. Impaired consciousness leads into coma. Attacks in which the limbs are hyperextended may occur, fits may also be produced.

Patients with poor kidney function are more prone to develop lithium intoxication because lithium is excreted in the urine. If, therefore, it is decided to treat a person with poor kidney function the serum levels should be checked more frequently.

Drugs Used in the Treatment of Anxiety

These drugs are sometimes referred to as anxiolytic drugs and are also commonly called minor tranquillisers. In general, they do not possess antipsychotic properties but clinically there is an overlap between the minor and major tranquillisers. Some of the most popular and widely prescribed of these drugs belong to the group of benzodiasepine derivatives. Three examples of this group are:

Chlordiazepoxide (Librium). Members of this group not only have a tranquillising action but are also muscle relaxants and anticonvulsants. They are used in anxiety states, obsessive compulsive neuroses, organic illnesses with anxiety features: e.g. peptic ulcer, skin diseases, etc., and with antidepressant drugs in mixed depressive anxiety states.

Chlordiazepoxide can be given by mouth or by intramuscular injection, the dose range varying from 10 to 100 mg daily in divided doses. In larger doses it may produce drowsiness and ataxia and patients should be warned not to drive until they are certain that their ability is not impaired on the drug. It would seem to have almost no serious side effects in normal dosage, and even massive overdoses, unless taken in combination with other drugs, do not usually cause death in treated cases.

Diazepam (Valium). While similar in action to chlordiazepoxide, diazepam is more potent. It is now widely used as a premedication for minor surgical procedures.

The dose range is from 2 mg three times a day up to 30 mg daily. In acute cases i.m. injections of 10 mg may be given. It is also used in the treatment of status epilepticus.

Side effects are usually of drowsiness and ataxia and indicate that the dose should be reduced.

Nitrazepam (Mogadon). Although chemically closely related, and having tranquillising properties, nitrazepam is used almost exclusively as an hypnotic. The dose is from 5 to 20 mg. It is particularly useful in the elderly.

Another anxiolytic drug is *chlorazepate* (Tranxene) which can be given as one capsule (15 mg) at night, which produces a twenty-four hour calming effect.

Chlormethiazole (Heminevrin). This sedative drug is used extensively in the management of alcoholic withdrawal. It is also of use in agitated or restless geriatric patients. It has a very low toxicity, the commonest side effect being a tingling sensation in the nose, and sneezing. It is potentiated by some phenothiazine drugs.

18 Physical Methods of Treatment: 2 Electroconvulsive and Other Therapies

Electroconvulsive Therapy

In 1933, a Hungarian doctor, Von Meduna, began treating a group of schizophrenic patients by injecting camphor intramuscularly, and thus producing an epileptic fit. The reason for trying this treatment was the observation of another Hungarian, Dr Nyiro, that very few patients suffered from both epilepsy and schizophrenia (an observation not supported by subsequent investigations). Von Meduna thought that epileptic attacks might, therefore, relieve the symptoms of schizophrenia, and put his belief to the test. Some of the patients improved, though more cynical observers suggested that this was due to the treatment being so terrifying, rather than to any direct effect of the fit. Camphor was soon replaced by drugs that could be given intravenously such as metrazol (cardiazol) and picrotoxin, which acted more quickly and certainly. It was then noted that those patients who had evidence of depression or who were stuporose, showed the most marked improvement.

In 1937, following experiments on animals, two Italian psychiatrists demonstrated that convulsions could be safely induced by passing an electric current through two electrodes applied to the patient's head, just above the temples. In the early days, the patients were conscious until the current passed through their brain, and the resulting convulsions were so violent that they not infrequently broke arms or legs, or injured their spines. Nowadays, the patient is first given a short-acting anaesthetic, followed by a drug that temporarily paralyses the voluntary muscles, so that the convulsion is modified and reduced to a mild jerking of some muscles. The muscles of the jaws, however, still contract strongly, because they are directly stimulated by the current, without their nerve supply playing any part. For this reason a gag may have to be used to prevent the

226

patient damaging his teeth. Oxygen has to be given to the patient before and after treatment because the respiratory muscles are paralysed as long as the effect of the muscle relaxant persists.

Indications for the Use of ECT

The use of convulsive therapy on its own did not produce good results in schizophrenia, except in catatonic stupor or excitement. Since the introduction of the phenothiazine drugs, the results have been more encouraging, especially in those patients who have marked affective symptoms. It may help to relieve the lack of interest, retardation, and depression.

Depressive Illness

The best results from ECT are obtained in patients suffering from agitated depression occurring for the first time in middle life, some 70–80 per cent of such patients recovering when given ECT. ECT is still probably the first choice for severe endogenous depression at any time of life, especially if there is marked retardation or if there is a high risk of suicide. It has to be remembered that the severely retarded patient may attempt suicide after two or three ECTs because the treatment has lessened the degree of retardation, but not yet improved the mood. When the depression is atypical, or has a considerable element of reaction, the results of ECT are not always satisfactory, and may even lead to a worsening of symptoms.

ECT is sometimes used in states of acute mania, though less often since the discovery of the major tranquillisers. Sometimes, a patient who has both depressive and manic episodes may swing from depression to mania following ECT.

ECT has been tried in almost every condition known to psychiatry, and good results are claimed for it, but the above conditions constitute the major indications.

Preparation of Patient for ECT

The preparation of the patient begins the night before treatment is due, when the patient should be told that he is to have ECT the next morning. When it is the patient's first treatment, a simple explanation of the procedure must be given, and the patient is then asked to sign a form, stating that he agrees to undergo it, and that he has been told what it entails. If the patient refuses, and it is considered essential that he has ECT, the forms should be signed by his nearest relative, even if the patient is detained under the 1959 Mental Health Act. The patient is reassured about the very slight risk involved in the treatment, and told that he must not have anything to eat for at least four hours before treatment, though he may have a drink, not less than two hours before.

On the morning of treatment, the patient is again reassured if he is anxious, and may be given some form of premedication. This may include some form of sedative for very apprehensive patients, but usually consists of either atropine or some related drug, that is intended to reduce bronchial secretions. Sometimes, atropine is given intravenously during the induction of anaesthesia. The patient awaits treatment, out of sight of patients who are having, or recovering from their ECT. He is asked to empty his bladder and bowels prior to going to the treatment room.

In the treatment room, the patient is asked to lie on the bed, having removed his shoes or slippers. The nurse makes sure that his mouth is empty, removing any false teeth. Tight clothing that is liable to restrict breathing is loosened, and the doctor then gives the injection of short-acting anaesthetic, followed by a muscle relaxant. Often, the patient is given oxygen by positive pressure at this stage, before the electrodes are applied. When the doctor is satisfied that everything is in order, he presses the button and the current passes through the patient's brain. Although the patient's muscles are paralysed, the effect is not always complete, and to avoid the risk of a sudden movement it is customary for a nurse to hold the legs and arms of the patient lightly. As soon as the fit has ceased, the patient is given more oxygen, as at this stage his respiratory muscles remain paralysed, and he is unable to breathe for himself. As soon as voluntary breathing has returned, the patient is turned on to his side and carefully observed, until fully recovered.

Nursing Aspects of ECT

For most people, any form of operation involving an anaesthetic is frightening, and the nurse must try to ensure that any anxiety the patient may have is reduced to the minimum. This may be done by explanation and reassurance, not only from the nurse, but also from a patient who has had ECT and no longer fears it. Prolonged waiting often induces a state of anxiety. The nurse should try to ascertain when treatment will start, and if there is some delay, she should try to keep the patient occupied rather than merely waiting.

Talking to the patient about subjects unrelated to illness or treatment may help.

Following ECT, some patients are confused for a varying length of time. In this state, they may lose or mislay items of value such as rings, wrist watches, or handbags. For this reason, it is usual to ask them to put them in a safe place before treatment.

The patient who is confused and disoriented, with no memory for recent events, can be helped by the nurse to re-orientate himself. She should speak slowly and clearly, and answer his questions however many times he asks them. Out-patients should not be allowed to leave the hospital until all confusion has cleared. Another important aspect is the patient's ability to walk. Some feel unsteady, and are liable to fall if not assisted. Most patients are very thirsty after treatment, partly as a result of the atropine, and it is customary to give them a cup of tea or other drink after they have come round.

Modified Insulin

In a number of mental illnesses there is a tendency to lose weight, and the patient's recovery seems to be delayed until their normal body weight is restored. For such patients modified insulin therapy may be used in addition to the specific treatment of the underlying disease. Insulin lowers the level of glucose in the blood, and in large doses produces a state of stupor or coma and, eventually, death, but in smaller doses it has the effect of producing mild sedation, reducing tension and increasing the appetite. Patients with good personality suffering from anxiety states tend to do best on this treatment. It is also used to increase weight in certain schizophrenics, and combined with phenothiazines it is used in the treatment of anorexia nervosa.

Technique

Treatment is carried out in a darkened and quiet ward, the patient having been kept without food from 8 p.m. the previous night. At 7.30 a.m. he is given an intramuscular injection of 20 units of soluble insulin, and the dose is increased by 10 units each day until a level of 80 to 100 units is reached, depending upon the response. The patient is carefully observed, to avoid coma developing, and if he appears to be getting stuporous he is given a glucose drink. If he is unable to take this by mouth, treatment is interrupted by giving intravenous glucose, or by the intramuscular injection of 1 mg of glucagon. If treatment has to be interrupted in this way, the next day 10 units less insulin is given. Three hours after the injection the patient is roused and given a large breakfast with a high carbohydrate content, and is encouraged to eat as much as he wants during the rest of the day, during which he is kept under supervision because delayed hypoglycaemic reactions can occur. Treatment is continued until the patient's normal weight level is restored.

Nursing Care

The nurse must be able to recognise the signs of hypoglycaemia, in order to know when to give glucose drinks to interrupt the treatment. These signs differ from patient to patient, but tend to be constant for a particular patient.

The early signs include palpitations, sweating, tremor, restlessness, and excitability, and thus resemble the physical signs of anxiety. As the blood level falls, the patient may become confused, or there may be a marked change from his normal pattern of behaviour. Thus, he may become violent, abusive or noisy or give the impression of being drunk. Speech may become slurred, and other movements are unsteady or incoordinated. At this level, it is usually possible to get the patient to take a glucose drink by mouth.

If the patient becomes stuporous, that is, responding to painful stimulus with meaningful movements, it is necessary either to give glucose via a nasal tube, or for the doctor to give an intravenous injection.

During treatment the patient tends to be more susceptible to suggestions, so that the treatment is more effective if the opportunity is taken for the nurse to encourage and reassure the patient both directly and indirectly by her own enthusiasm and optimism.

Continuous Sleep Treatment (Prolonged Narcosis)

This form of treatment is used extensively in Russia, possibly because it fits in well with Pavlovian theory, but in Western Europe, since the advent of more specific treatments such as the anti-depressant drugs, it is used less often. It is mainly employed in the treatment of patients of previously good personality who have broken down as a result of severe and acute stress, and have developed anxiety, depression, or hysterical symptoms.

Sleep treatment requires a high degree of skill by the nursing staff if its risks are to be minimised. These risks are due in part to confining the patient to bed, and in part to the effects of the sedative drugs employed. The risks are: bronchopneumonia, respiratory failure, heart failure, urinary retention, dehydration, vitamin deficiency, and toxic confusional states.

An attempt is made to keep the patient asleep for twenty hours a day by the use of a combination of chlorpromazine and sodium amytal. He is nursed in a quiet, darkened, warm room, but he may be walked to the lavatory once a day. Fluid intake and out-put charts must be kept. Fluid intake must be kept at a high level (at least five pints every twenty-four hours) and any failure to achieve this should be reported. Blood pressure is also measured and recorded twice a day. The drugs are given at times arranged so that when meals are due the patient is beginning to wake up. The actual dose used has to be varied in the light of the patient's response.

Any evidence of cardiovascular collapse, fall in blood pressure, or rise or fall in pulse rate calls for interruption of treatment. The bed should be raised on blocks at the foot end, and it may be necessary to give intravenous glucose. Signs of bronchopneumonia (shortness of breath, pyrexia, flushed face or noisy respiration) require treatment to be terminated and antibiotic therapy started. When it is decided that treatment has gone on long enough, the drugs must be gradually reduced in order to avoid withdrawal symptoms such as epileptiform fits.

Psycho-surgery (Leucotomy)

History

Attempts at relieving the symptoms of mental illness by operations designed to allow evil spirits to escape from the skull date back to pre-history, but modern psycho-surgery dates from the work of Egas Moniz and Almerda, who performed an operation on patients with severe mental illness, in which the connexions between the frontal lobes of the brain and deeper structures were severed. As a result of studying brain injuries and patients from whom tumours had been removed from this area, it was known that damage to the frontal lobes could cause personality changes without severe memory loss or impairment of memory. The aim of the operation was to make the patient less anxious, tense and pre-occupied.

Present Methods

Techniques have been modified from the original operation so that it is now designed to sever, on both sides, the fibres that connect the frontal cortex to the dorso-medial nucleus of the thalamus. Such operations are performed through trephined openings, and the fibres are cut with a sharp instrument. The fibres may also be destroyed by implanting radioactive yttrium, or by using electrical current to coagulate them.

Patient Selection. Even with random selection of patients, the operation often produced good results, but sometimes it also led to disastrous consequences. It is now possible to define those patients likely to benefit more exactly, and thus the results are more rewarding.

Indications

Although the operation has been tried in almost all psychiatric illnesses, it is now limited mainly to those in whom tension and anxiety are leading features. The best results are obtained in patients who have a good stable personality prior to the onset of the illness, as shown by their capacity for forming stable relationships, and by an adequate work record. Conditions most often considered for leucotomy are now chronic depression that has not responded to adequate treatment with drugs and ECT, and severe obsessional states.

Pre-operative Preparation

It is essential to obtain a detailed history from the patient and his relatives, supplemented by information from nursing staff, occupational therapists, social workers, and others who have had close contact with the patient, before a decision to operate is made. The relatives must understand clearly the risks involved, the aim of the operation, and the part they must play in the patient's consequent rehabilitation. They have to accept that a person who for many years may have been dependent and an object of pity, may return to them confident and perhaps a little tactless. This sometimes results in the relatives unconsciously attempting to cast the patient once more in the role of invalid.

Post Leucotomy Management

The patient returns from operation not infrequently in a state of relative inertia, and the immediate task is to stimulate him into activity. He may tend to stay in bed, or sit about the ward, but he must not be allowed to drift into a state of chronic apathy. As soon as possible, he must graduate from in-patient care to day attendance, and then back to full-time employment. Intensive follow up care by social workers, and attendance at patient social clubs and the like are essential, if full benefit is to be derived from the operation.

Complications of the Operation

There is a definite mortality associated with the operation, and in the immediate post-operative period the greatest risk is of cerebral haemorrhage. The delayed complications seem to be that (*a*) some patients develop incontinence that may require intensive habit training, and (*b*) there is a possibility of post traumatic epilepsy, when the patient may be started on anticonvulsant drugs.

Undesirable Personality Changes

These may take the form of excessive apathy and lack of concern, or more commonly, a release of inhibition so that the patient becomes restless, over-active, talkative, with a tendency to make foolish jokes, tactless, and lacking in social judgement, impulsive, emotionally blunt, and aggressive if frustrated.

19 Sociology and Psychiatry

Sociology is an attempt to apply the methods of scientific investigation to Society; that is, the study of the various groups, institutions, organisations and cultures in which man has his being. The scientific method has yielded enormous gains in knowledge in the field of physical phenomena and to a lesser extent in the biological sciences. Social science has yet to prove itself in the same way but already large amounts of data have been established and some unifying theories advanced. Students should read some introductory text-books of sociology as part of their training.

In this chapter a very restricted look is taken at the areas where sociology and psychiatry overlap.

'No man is an island' and no man can be fully understood without examining him in the context of the society in which he lives. Much of our notion of mental disorder is based on a person's disordered behaviour. This behaviour is, in part, determined by the beliefs, expectations and reactions of those people who form the patient's immediate society, whether as members of his family, his work-mates or his religious order. Not only is it determined by them but it is judged by them. Thus, to some extent, our judgement of mental disorder in an individual is a social judgement.

Sociologists and psychiatrists can study the effect of social factors on mental disorders in a variety of ways. As a result of their studies they may suggest social methods of treating or preventing mental disorders. They may also examine the present institutions concerned with the treatment of mental disorders and suggest ways in which these may be improved, or alternatives that might be tried in their place. The subject of the present social arrangements for treating mental disorder will be discussed in the next chapter.

In this chapter some of the social factors that seem to influence mental disorders will be considered.

Some of the first questions that come to mind are:

1. Do mental disorders occur equally frequently in different groups in a society?
2. Do they occur with different frequency in different societies?
3. What is their frequency and are they getting commoner?

The study of such questions is called epidemiology. It can be defined as the study of the distribution of diseases in space and time and the factors that account for these distributions. This technique has yielded some very important advances in organic medicine; for example, a recent study showed that deaths from coronary artery disease were much more frequent in areas where drinking water was 'soft'. This finding has given rise to a number of projects and any future theory of the causation of coronary artery disease must take this aspect into account.

The aims of epidemiology can be listed as follows:

1. To measure the amount and distribution of an illness in a community and thus to demonstrate health problems that need tackling.
2. To identify sections of the population most at risk and thus suggest preventive measures.
3. To clarify the natural history of the disease without which it is impossible to assess the effects of treatment on its course.
4. To measure the effectiveness of health care provided by the various medical services.

Two terms constantly used in epidemiological studies must be defined:

Prevalence: The proportion of a given population who are suffering from a particular disease at a given time.

Incidence: The number of new cases of a disease that occur during a specified period of time in a specified unit of population.

A number of studies have shown that various forms of mental disorders occur with different frequency in different sections of the population and between different societies.

Thus, one would expect that epidemiology would help to sort out the factors that produce this difference in distribution. To date, the majority of such studies have highlighted our ignorance rather than illuminated our knowledge.

One primary difficulty has been in defining those of the population who are actually suffering from the condition. Our criteria for making psychiatric diagnoses are often extremely vague; many are based on value judgements which depend on, and reflect, certain social attitudes of the patient and the psychiatrist.

We are also surprisingly ignorant of the natural history of many psychiatric disorders. When we try to estimate the frequency of such disorders we discover that many people have symptoms similar in nature and degree to those of our patients yet neither they nor their medical advisers regard them as being ill. Indeed, the decision to regard them as patients and treat them, to regard them as delinquent and punish them, or to regard them as heroes and reward them may be determined by social considerations rather than by the nature of their disorder.

In spite of these and other difficulties many interesting and worth-while studies have been carried out and if not always providing answers, they have at least posed fresh questions and suggested new ways of looking at old problems.

One way of subdividing a complex industrial society such as ours is on the basis of social class. Up to the First World War (1914–18) the class structure in Britain was fairly clearly defined and also fairly rigid. Most people were born into a particular position in society, recognised it and remained within it. Since then, social mobility both in a geographic and in a class sense has vastly increased. Some of the concomitants of social class such as earning capacity, education and status have changed markedly in the years since 1945. However, the classification of society, largely on the basis of occupation, still serves some useful purpose. The General Register Office which analyses census returns divides the population of England and Wales into five classes:

Class 1: Higher professions; commissioned officers; company directors; etc.
Class 2: Minor officials in public administration; clerks; farmers; teachers; etc.
Class 3: Skilled workers
Class 4: Semi-skilled workers
Class 5: Unskilled workers

The best-known study of the relationships between social class and mental illness is the one carried out by Hollingshead and Redlich in New Haven, Connecticut in 1958. It was published as a book called *Social Class and Mental Illness* and describes in detail the problems of carrying out such a study and the methods used to try and overcome these.

They concluded from their study that the incidence of psychotic illnesses, particularly schizophrenia, was much higher in social class five. This finding has been repeated in a number of other studies.

A number of theories have been put forward to account for this excess of psychotic illness in social group five. One explanation is known as the 'downward drift' which postulates that either the patient or his parents have failed at their occupation because of their mental illness and have 'drifted down' into the lower social group. Another theory is that the social, economic and psychological stresses found in economically underprivileged areas tend to produce psychotic breakdown more frequently in those genetically predisposed than do the different stresses found in more well-to-do families. The evidence for or against these and other theories is such that at present the verdict must be 'not proven'.

The Family

Most people are born into a social group known as a family. Their early rearing is almost exclusively performed by members of this group and, in due course, the majority of individuals form a continuing sexual relationship with a member of the opposite sex, have children and form a new family group of their own. The effect of the family group on its various members is likely to be a critical factor in whether or not they develop some form of mental disorder.

The main functions of the family are:

1. To provide a stable setting for having and rearing children.
2. To socialise and educate its children.
3. To provide support and care for its dependent members.
4. To provide roles and duties for its members.

In examining family life it is important to distinguish between events and activities in the family and the feelings and emotions that these events produce in the various individuals taking part. The former are relatively easy to record and measure, the latter are much more difficult to quantify and many studies have not paid sufficient attention to this aspect of validity and reliability.

In industrial societies families composed of parents and their children tend to live in separate households. This residential isolation of the 'nuclear' family is characteristic of our society. The quality of social life in such societies has greatly improved since 1900 as a result of technological advances. Working hours are much shorter and most jobs much less physically demanding. People expect much more from life and are less inclined to be satisfied with things as they are. Women have achieved an increasing degree of equality with men and, with efficient methods of birth control, they are no longer burdened by constant child-bearing. Thus, women now often contribute substantially to the family finances. The family is not a static arrangement but undergoes a cycle of development, starting with the marriage, continuing with the children maturing and becoming independent, and finishing with the death of the parents.

The choice of a marriage partner seems in Western societies to be a very personal, private matter as compared to the arranged marriages of some Eastern societies. In fact, the choice of partner is not all that haphazard. Most people's choices are affected by religious, educational and class factors. Thus, people tend to marry partners with similar levels of education, a common religion, similar social background and of the same race. This is referred to as assortive mating.

The fact of being married or not correlates with the chance of needing psychiatric hospital treatment. The lowest risk is for married people and increases through the single, the widowed and divorced. This could be due to the fact that people who have or develop mental illness are less able to establish or maintain a married relationship or it could be a reaction on the person's part to relative social isolation.

Conjugal Roles

In pre-industrial Britain the roles of men and women in a marriage were quite distinct. The woman's place was in the kitchen producing meals and in bed producing children. The husband worked and provided for the family. Many forms of work were physically too demanding for women to do but with the development of machines this is much less true and there are now few occupations closed to women. Men and women have changed in their expectation of marriage and tend to feel that the union should provide equal satisfaction for both partners. This can create problems when both partners' expectations are different or when one partner's expectation changes but the other partner cannot or will not compromise.

In a 'normal' family there is a triangular relationship between mother, father and child. Each parent is able to play specific roles and the child learns to identify with the parent of the same sex. Circumstances may lead to one or other parent being unable to fulfil his or her role through absence, illness or death and the remaining parent may have to try to fulfil both roles, which at times may be conflicting.

Studies have shown that delinquency is more frequent among boys who have lost their fathers in childhood.

When a family loses the mother even greater disruption occurs, the children often having to be placed in institutions or foster homes. It is difficult to study the effect of loss of the mother figure in isolation as it produces so many other changes in the pattern of upbringing of the children. Some studies have suggested that loss of the mother by death has less consequent effect on the children than loss by divorce or separation. It is possible that this reflects the disturbance within the family preceding the mother's departure.

A number of studies have been made of family relationships in families of patients suffering from various forms of mental illness in an attempt to demonstrate abnormalities in the way the members of the family relate, which might cause the patient to develop symptoms. One of the best known of these is the one carried out by Laing and Esterton published under the title *Sanity, Madness and the Family*. In this they describe a process which they call 'mystification'. This seems to consist of the parent(s) saying one thing while doing another and expecting the child to do what is said rather than what is done. This is claimed to be particularly common in families in which a child develops schizophrenia—but it is difficult to qualify it in a way that allows comparison with 'normal' families. It would seem to be a pretty common technique. Further research is needed to clarify this and other questions before judgement can be passed.

Families form the building bricks of communities—groups of people near each other, working together, sharing facilities for education and leisure. In industrial societies the majority of people live in large conurbations, often travelling considerable distances to work. The centres of such towns and cities tend to be dominated by shops and offices with relatively few people living there. These few are often either very wealthy and live there from choice or very poor and have no option.

Such communities obviously differ from those in suburban areas and even more so from rural communities.

One might imagine, therefore, that the incidence and even the nature of mental disorders might differ between these very different environments. Studies of mental illness in people moved from old slum areas to new town housing estates have failed to discover any 'suburban neurosis', or indeed, any increase in neurotic illness. It is possible, however, that in a situation where family support is no longer present—where the young mum cannot ask Gran's advice when little Willie comes out in spots or when husband keeps coming home in the early hours—that people seek and need more professional help.

The increase in social mobility, both in a class and in a geographical sense, has highlighted problems of dependency. The ability of a family to support its dependent members both in a financial and in an emotional sense can be a major factor in the outcome of an illness. Caring for Grandma when she becomes demented is a different proposition when the family lives in a fairly large house, has other relatives close by, and is relatively well-to-do, from when the family is poor and lives in overcrowded conditions.

The 'Sick' Role

When a person becomes ill, societies' attitude to him changes to some extent. He is no longer expected to fulfil his normal social responsibilities, e.g. go to work. He is no longer expected to look after himself entirely and must be cared for. He is expected to want to get better and he is supposed to seek help and follow the advice he receives from his doctor or whomever he consults. This sick role is in the majority of cases a temporary state of affairs. In primitive societies there is no such thing as 'chronic sick', though chronic diseases are widespread. The sufferer must resume his responsibilities quite quickly, however he feels, for the community cannot long support non-productive members.

In technologically more advanced societies such chronically ill people can be supported and in most civilised societies it is considered right that they should be.

One group of people who have a high level of dependency are the very aged, who are also socially underprivileged. Their income levels are low, they are socially isolated and often poorly housed. Apart from social problems they have more physical diseases and more than their fair share of mental illness. They now form the majority of patients in mental hospitals. It is important to remember, however, that the vast majority of old people are not sick, isolated or poverty stricken.

One task of social science is to examine the ways in which health care and social support can best be provided. This assessment of medical and social services is a comparatively recent development. Most such services in this country have developed on an *ad hoc* basis. Many specialist services have started as a result of a few people's enthusiasm, rather than as a result of a scientific assessment of the needs and resources of a community. This has led to considerable discrepancy in the standard and availability of services in different parts of the country. It has also led to disproportionate amounts of money and staff being invested in the more glamorous branches of medicine an surgery with relative neglect of the mentally ill and handicapped.

Recently, both the Social Services and National Health Services have undergone a reorganisation of structure and management. The present structure and the services available to the psychiatric patient are described in the next chapter.

20 Rehabilitation and Community Services

The aim of rehabilitation is to return the patient to a normal home life, and to a job that matches his needs and abilities. To achieve this aim, it is necessary to assess the degree to which the patient is likely to be handicapped and to plan a programme of treatment that will minimise the handicaps, and develop to the full such assets as the patient has. This treatment will require the use of physical and psychotherapeutic methods of treatment. The importance of the social setting in which treatment takes place has been described under the heading of the Therapeutic Community.

This chapter considers the part played in rehabilitation by occupational, industrial, and recreational therapy. Enforced idleness and boredom have a detrimental effect on the personality and may lead to anti-social behaviour, withdrawal, loss of self respect, or increased preoccupation with symptoms. Part of the purpose of occupational therapy is to prevent this, and to stimulate the patient to fresh interest and activity.

Occupational Therapy

The particular form of occupation chosen depends on a number of factors. In most hospitals there is a trained occupational therapist in general charge of the department, but the nurse still plays an important part, either on the ward or in the special buildings set aside for occupational therapy. Working with the patients in this way provides an opportunity for observing their behaviour under work conditions, which may differ greatly from their behaviour on the ward or at group meetings, and may be very important in determining how well they will adjust to life in the community. The nurse also has the chance to form a close relationship with the patient, by working alongside him. The nurse who remains detached and aloof, offering advice but not getting her hands dirty, will have less success than the nurse who takes off her coat, and gets involved.

She must encourage and help the patient, but should resist the temptation to take over the task and do it herself.

The patients doing similar occupations form a natural group; and an important aspect of occupational therapy is the use of such groups to provide the patient with a chance to develop his social skills, and to see how he can perform in tasks that resemble those he must perform in the world outside the hospital. Thus, if patients are being paid for the work they do, the amount each receives can be determined by the group on the basis of an assessment chart, which can be devised so that not only output, but punctuality, concentration, speed, reliability, and general behaviour can be taken into account.

No patient in the hospital should be left without a job. Those who are not able to attend the special departments must be given suitable work in the wards. This may involve domestic work on the ward, but it must always be remembered that such activity is for the patient's benefit, and not the hospital's. Often a patient who has performed such tasks well becomes too valuable, and ward staff resist her discharge or transfer through self interest. To avoid this a 'domestic group' can be formed from patients on different wards. The group are then responsible for cleaning, bedmaking, dishwashing and the like, on a number of wards. Another duty they might perform is to prepare meals for other patients. This provides an opportunity for a housewife who has had difficulty with domestic jobs to relearn how to shop for a family, and to prepare and serve a meal. It is important that patients in the group should take turns in doing the more interesting and pleasant jobs, as well as the chores.

The particular work given to the patient must be designed to lessen his symptoms, provide a means of self expression, an outlet for repressed energy, while training memory and concentration, and boosting self confidence. Although the choice must depend on the needs of the particular patient, some general guidance can be given.

Neurotic Illnesses
Many patients with neurotic illnesses are not admitted to hospital, but may attend as day patients. The aim of occupational therapy with such patients is to help them gain confidence, reduce their anxiety, and develop their ability to be concerned with, and for, other people.

The patient should start in a small group, gradually taking on more responsibility and moving on to a larger group. Activities that are beyond the patient's ability, take a long time to finish, or can be performed in isolation should be avoided. With hysterical patients it is important that other members of the group should be able to accept dramatic 'acting out' by the patient without showing too much sympathy or distress. The patient must be encouraged to seek attention by doing well at the task she is given, or by taking on responsibility instead of developing symptoms.

Psychotic Illnesses

Manic patients require activities that involve a moderate amount of physical effort and do not take long to complete. Such work should be done in a comparatively quiet environment to limit the amount of distracting stimulation. The nurse must be prepared to tolerate the patient's argumentativeness without being drawn in, and accept verbal hostility without becoming annoyed.

Depressed patients require an occupation that distracts them from their morbid ideas while allowing them to express some of their feelings of guilt and aggression. The tasks should not be so difficult that the patient fails to do them, nor should they involve rapid movements or decisions. He must be drawn into a group of quiet but fairly cheerful patients, who are not too noisy or overactive. Within the group he may be encouraged to undertake tasks that help other members, thus enabling him to compensate for some of his feeling of guilt and worthlessness.

With schizophrenic patients the aim is to keep them in contact with reality, thus avoiding their withdrawal into fantasy. This is best achieved by not putting such patients into work groups composed entirely of schizophrenics, but including patients who have good contact with the 'real' world. Schizophrenic patients require constant stimulation, and repetitive, automatic tasks should be avoided as these may encourage retreat into fantasy. Tasks that involve co-operation between two or more patients also help to avoid isolation and withdrawal.

The aim with patients who have organic brain damage may be to preserve as long as possible their capacity for looking after themselves, while preventing institutionalisation. Tasks that require the learning of new skills, and involving judgement and initiative should be avoided. As least some of the time should be devoted to activities that require gentle exercise, especially of the joints of the hands and wrists.

Industrial Therapy

The aims of industrial therapy differ somewhat from occupational therapy, in that the tasks undertaken more closely resemble those by which people can earn their living. An attempt is made to train the patient to perform a job that will enable him to work outside the hospital and to develop habits that are essential if his work performance is to be satisfactory.

Few hospitals are equipped to train patients in skilled or semi-skilled trades, but suitable patients with satisfactory work habits may be referred for such training to Government Training Centres.

Recreational Therapy

Many patients find it difficult to take part in social activities in the community. They feel awkward, shy, and self-conscious, or have never learnt the skills involved in dancing, playing games, or even in making conversation. As a result, their lives have been lonely and restricted, and this may have increased their sense of isolation or rejection to the point where they could no longer tolerate it. For such people, the provision of a range of recreations in the hospital may provide them with the first opportunity for learning new skills and gaining confidence in a sheltered setting where they know a number of people, and where their attempts at 'joining in' are sympathetically helped.

For those patients who have previously led a full social life before coming into hospital, the provision of such activities helps to prevent boredom, apathy, and frustration. Apart from the mental stimulation, recreational activities provide an opportunity for the patients (and staff) to have some physical exercise.

The organisation of such activities may be the responsibility of one person, the recreational therapist, or it may be shared among the nursing staff, but in either case, the most important thing is for the patients themselves to have the largest say in the type of programme they want. This can be done at ward level, or for the whole hospital, by getting the patients in each ward to elect a representative to attend a Patients' Activity Committee responsible for drawing up a plan of events. Medical, nursing, and occupational therapy staff should be represented on the committee, as should a member of the hospital's League of Friends.

The programme should be a balanced mixture of artistic and educational activities, such as music groups, play-reading, typing classes and the like. Social activities such as dances, films, bingo, concerts, and outings, and sporting activities ranging from darts to soccer, and from chess to cricket. The more intellectual pursuits help the patient to learn new skills and widen his horizons, while the more active sports provide an opportunity for getting rid of excess energy and working off aggressive feelings.

Community Services

Every person leaving hospital is faced with a variety of problems, and their capacity to deal with these and the amount of help they receive will determine whether or not they are able to survive in the community. The number and severity of the difficulties will vary from patient to patient, so that an attempt must be made to decide how much, and what kind of, support is required in each case. To do this it is necessary to know what type of help is available. The aim of this help is not to take over the patient's life but to provide temporary support while he or she learns to adjust to the demands of personal, family, and social responsibilities. The major areas in which help is required may be summarised as, (a) money and work, (b) accommodation, (c) medical supervision, and (d) family and social relationships.

The basic needs of the patient with regard to financial help, employment, and accommodation are covered by the provisions of various Acts of Parliament. These have laid down rules that have to be carried out, either directly by Government departments, or by departments organised by local authorities. This chapter summarises the various agencies available to assist in helping the patient to remain in the community. At present the mental nurse plays only a small part in the community care of patients, but this aspect of her work is growing in range and importance all the time. In many ways, the nurse who has known the patient in hospital and has formed a good relationship with him is the ideal person to continue his supervision in the community.

The services outlined have been divided into *statutary* and *volun-*

tary; it is obvious that the two tend to overlap to some extent but, in general, the statutory services provide a kind of safety net to try to make sure that no one has to exist below a certain financial level, and that medical services are available to all in need. The voluntary services attempt to improve the *quality* of the life open to the person rather than merely helping to keep the patient well and out of hospital.

Statutory Services

These are provided by central government departments and by local government authorities. Central government departments are mainly concerned with (*a*) financial support of the sick, aged or unemployed, (*b*) placement in, or training for, employment, and (*c*) medical services. Local authorities have a duty to provide a wide range of services as part of their health, welfare, education, and children's departments.

The following section outlines the provisions available and indicates the training and particular skills of the people involved. For a more detailed description readers are recommended to consult, *Welfare Services*, published by the British Red Cross Society.

Financial

In 1966, the functions of the Ministry of Pensions and National Insurance, the National Assistance Board, and the Ministry of Labour were amalgamated into a new Department of Health and Social Security. The range of services remained unchanged.

National Insurance Benefits. Everyone who has left school, and has not reached the age to qualify for a retirement pension, pays a contribution towards a national insurance scheme. This money is supplemented by employers, and the government. In return for their contribution, insured people are entitled to the following benefits, subject to various provisions. The amount paid varies from time to time and is, therefore, not quoted here.

Sickness Benefit. This is payable during incapacity for work due to illness, on the basis of a medical certificate. It is not paid for the first three days of an illness, or for isolated days. The rate of benefit is reduced after a certain length of time spent in hospital. The majority of patients under the age of sixty-five in hospital qualify for this payment, and, it may enable those who have no dependants in the community to save a small 'nest egg' against the day they are discharged.

Unemployment Benefit. This is payable only when a person is unemployed and not receiving wages. He must be both capable of work and prepared to do it. Thus, it is only available to patients who are not in hospital.

Retirement Pensions. At the age of sixty-five for men and sixty for women, a retirement pension is payable, subject to their not earning more than a set amount. Above the age of seventy (men), sixty-five (women) the pension is payable irrespective of earnings. If the patient is in hospital, the pension is reduced after eight weeks, and again after one or two years.

Employment

To remain in the community it is almost essential that the patient has a job, not only because of the financial benefits but also because of the boost to morale that regular work gives. It has been demonstrated that prolonged unemployment can, in the absence of any primary psychiatric illness, lead to deterioration in personality and ability. Various agencies exist to help a patient find work and, if necessary, to train him in a new job.

Employment Exchanges. These offices are run by the Ministry of Labour (now Social Security) and apart from paying out unemployment benefits it is their task to keep a register of all jobs available in the area, and to arrange for the unemployed person to be placed in a suitable vacancy. Special arrangements are made to help disabled or handicapped people, whether the handicap be physical or mental.

Disablement Resettlement Officer. Every local labour exchange has one official whose special concern is finding work for the disabled. He will visit patients while they are still in hospital, if requested. Some hospitals employ a rehabilitation officer, who carries out a similar function but, in addition, finds contract work for patients to perform within the hospital.

Industrial Rehabilitation Units. A major problem for many psychiatric patients is that they have lost, or never acquired, work habits. Thus, they find it difficult to get to work on time, they tend to leave work unfinished, work slowly or carelessly, and in general do not perform as adequately as their workmates. To help with such problems there are a number of Industrial Rehabilitation Units.

The patient attends a centre for six to eight weeks during which time he works in an industrial atmosphere and is encouraged to achieve a maximum level of proficiency. He is also assessed to decide what type of work would best suit him. The units do not train people in new occupations. Those who need to learn a new trade may attend either of the following:

1. Government training centres where courses are run covering a variety of trades, lasting twenty-six to fifty-two weeks. The training is provided free, and maintenance allowances are paid. When a course is completed satisfactorily the person is accepted as qualified by the particular Trade Union concerned—a most important fact in obtaining future employment.
2. Sheltered workshops have been set up by the Government and local authorities as, for the more severely disabled, work in normal competitive employment may be impossible. Here the patient can work at suitable tasks at a rate that is within his capabilities.

Accommodation
Many patients who have been in hospital for a long time will no longer have homes to return to. Some will have been rejected by their relatives, while for others to return to an emotionally charged household may be detrimental. Elderly patients may no longer require hospital facilities, yet be unable to manage a house and look after themselves without considerable help. There are a number of different kinds of shelter provided to help with such problems, though the actual number of places available falls far short of the need.

Hostels, Halfway Houses, etc. Various religious organisations run hostels that provide cheap accommodation for people who would otherwise be homeless.

Many hospitals now own houses that are used to provide temporary accommodation for patients while they demonstrate their ability to return to society, or until normal lodgings or homes are found for them. In some, patients are entirely self-supporting; in others, a nurse acts as housewarden. There must be free movement from such hostels, otherwise the population becomes static, and all that has happened is the establishment of a chronic ward some distance from the main hospital.

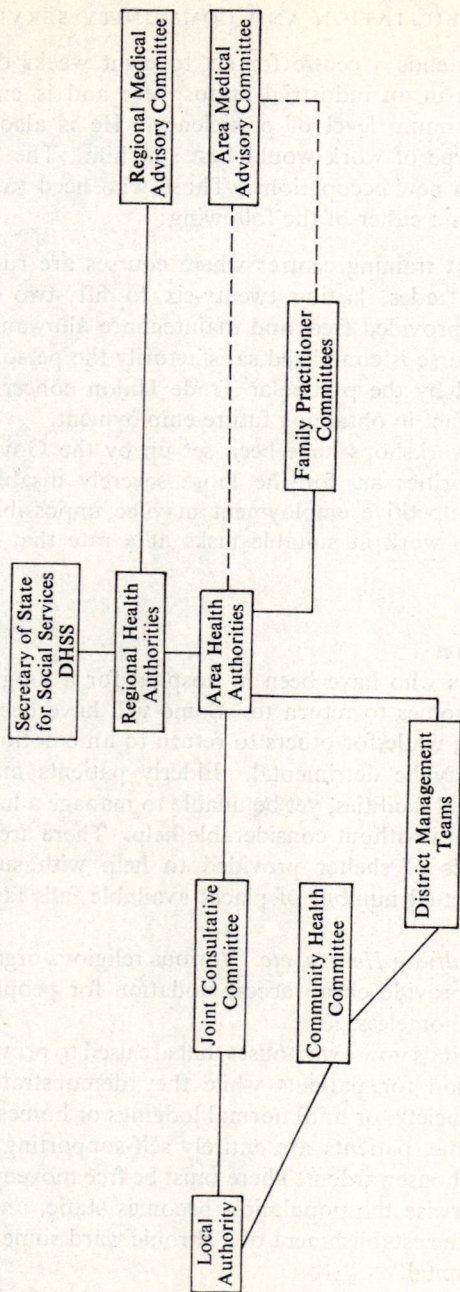

FIG. 2 Administration Structure of the Department of Health Social Services

- Regional Medical Advisory Committee
- Area Medical Advisory Committee
- Family Practitioner Committees
- Secretary of State for Social Services DHSS
- Regional Health Authorities
- Area Health Authorities
- District Management Teams
- Joint Consultative Committee
- Community Health Committee
- Local Authority

Part III Accommodation. Under Part III of the Mental Health Act of 1959 the provisions of Part III of the 1948 National Assistance Act were extended to cover patients who have or have had mental disorders. Under this section, Local authorities have a duty to provide residential homes for such persons.

Lodgings, 'Foster Homes', etc. Some hospitals now keep a register of landladies who are prepared to take discharged patients. Their board may be paid in part by local authorities or the Ministry of Social Security. Having overcome their initial anxiety, many landladies find that patients who have been in hospital for long periods make ideal lodgers, and will take them in preference to 'normal' tenants. Some families are prepared to 'adopt' a patient so that he becomes part of the family, and not merely a lodger. This arrangement has long been a feature of patient care in Holland and Belgium.

Meals on Wheels

Some people especially the aged, can manage in their own homes, but either cannot or will not prepare adequate meals for themselves. In time they develop some degree of malnutrition that may prove a critical factor in precipitating their admission to hospital. To combat this, local authorities are empowered to help finance voluntary organisations providing a service that delivers ready cooked meals to the patient's home.

National Health Service

In 1948, The National Health Service came into operation. Its aim was to provide a comprehensive health service, covering every branch of medical and related activities, which would be available to all, irrespective of their financial means. The Service is financed by general taxation supplemented by a small contribution that is paid with the National Insurance Contribution.

The service, which was administered by the Ministry of Health, consisted of three branches, (1) General Medical Services (family doctor), (2) Hospital and Specialist Services, and (3) Local Health Authority Services. This arrangement with its three divisions was often criticised for leading to demarcation disputes and wasteful reduplication. Plans were drawn up to try to unify the administration, and on 1st April 1974 a reorganised National Health Service came into effect (*see* Fig. 2). On that date the existing 15 regional hospital boards, 36 boards of governors of teaching hospitals, all hospital management committees and local health authorities were replaced by 14 regional health authorities, 90 area health authorities and 205 districts. The regional health authorities cover roughly the same areas as the hospital boards used to.

The Family Doctor
The general practitioner or 'family doctor' is the key person in the community care of patients, and to obtain free medical attention a patient must be registered with a general practitioner. The family doctor undertakes to provide care for his patients twenty-four hours a day, seven days a week, and it is he who decides whether the patient needs to be referred for specialist treatment or opinion. When a patient leaves hospital, he returns to the day-to-day care of his family doctor. By virtue of his knowledge of the patient, his family, and social situation, the family doctor is in a unique position to assess the problems the patient has or creates. The vast majority of patients, suffering from milder forms of mental illness are treated by the GP and are never seen by a psychiatrist.

Hospital and Specialist Service
Every kind of hospital care is given under the National Health Service, both in-patient and out-patient. Most of the hospitals in Britain were taken over by the National Health Service although a few private hospitals remain.

There are about 130 hospitals in England and Wales that take mental patients. The majority of them were built between 1850 and 1914, and they vary in size from a few with 3,000 beds to some with fewer than 500 beds, the average being about 1,000 beds. Thus, at any time in England and Wales there are about 130,000 patients in hospital being treated for some form of mental illness. Most of the hospitals were built by local authorities as 'County Lunatic Asylums'. In 1930 the Mental Treatment Act changed the name to Mental Hospital, and in 1959, the word 'Mental' was dropped in order that these hospitals should be regarded as any other hospital—a place for the treatment of the ill. The specialised treatment of mental illness is carried out very largely by the medical staff of these hospitals, with the aid of nursing and other professional staff. In addition to in-patient care, the staff usually work at out-patient clinics, day hospitals, and day or night hostels.

Out-patient Clinics. These may be held at the general hospitals in the district served by the mental hospital or at the hospital itself. At these clinics new patients are seen for diagnosis and treatment, having been referred there by their family doctor. In addition, patients who have left hospital may be seen if it is considered they require a more intensive follow up than their GP can provide. This enables the psychiatrist to check on the patients' symptoms, their response to medication, and the difficulties they are experiencing, and to modify their treatment, both physical and psychological to enable them to avoid relapse and readmission.

Day Hospitals. Some hospitals have separate buildings that patients attend by day, returning home in the evening. In other hospitals, day patients share the same facilities with in-patients. The purpose of day attendance is twofold: first, to provide extra support for the patient by way of group therapy, social contacts, occupational therapy, and supervision of medication, and, secondly, to provide relief for the patient's family. This relief may often be crucial in deciding not only whether the patient can remain out of hospital, but, also, the degree of stress he is exposed to when at home. By avoiding full admission the patient is enabled to keep in contact with his everyday life, thus avoiding some of the risks of institutionalisation.

Night Hostels. Some patients can manage at work during the day, but cannot tolerate the nights. Others require more support than out-patient attendance, yet cannot or will not attend the hospital by day. Such patients may be managed in a night hostel. They arrive in the early evening, are given medication, if prescribed, and take part in group psychotherapy and social activities. They sleep in the hostel, and before leaving for work they may be given the morning dose of their drugs. Such provisions are particularly valuable for alcoholics, helping to keep them out of public houses, and also for chronic schizophrenics who tend to lapse into a state of social isolation, and who may have difficulty in getting up and off to work in the morning. Those who tend to stop their drugs if not constantly supervised are also helped by this kind of arrangement.

COMMUNITY CARE

For some time now, the declared policy of the Ministry of Health is gradually to reduce the population of mental hospitals and to develop alternative community services care for the mentally ill.

The success of this policy depends on adequate organisation of services in the community and on availability of suitably trained workers.

In England and Wales, bed occupancy in hospitals for the mentally ill has been steadily declining since 1955. On a national scale, the ratio has decreased between 1954 and 1964 from an average of about 3·4 to 2·8 beds per 100 population. For planning purposes, now only 0·7 beds per 1000 population are recommended for the mentally ill. This dramatic decrease of in-patient population has been accompanied by:

(a) A steady increase in admissions and re-admissions to the traditional psychiatric hospital and to psychiatric units attached to the District General Hospitals.

(b) Patients are being discharged after a much shorter stay in hospitals.

(c) New out-patients seen at clinics have almost doubled.

(d) Treatment and care for the mentally ill on 'day-patient' basis has been developed by nearly all hospitals.

(e) Aftercare has been developing more effectively with psychiatric nurses taking a more prominent part.

The Concept of Community Care

Community psychiatric care might be defined as the extension of the psychiatric services of an administrative area to patients outside the psychiatric hospital and the development of an appropriate organisation for doing this. A good community care service embraces prevention, care and after-care of those who are particularly vulnerable to further breakdown. Such a service would provide a wide range of facilities, which must, of course, include the traditional psychiatric hospital or a psychiatric unit as integral parts of the total community. Total community facilities can be summarised as follows:

(a) Psychiatric hospitals or units, out-patient clinics, day hospitals, special units for children and adolescents, specialised centres for the treatment of drug dependency and alcoholism, health centres, family doctors with a team of social worker, health visitor and, more recently, psychiatric nurses making their contribution.

(b) Social services departments of the local authorities provide hostel type accommodation, training centres, sheltered employment, in some cases, and social workers' expertise. Social workers give advice to patients and to their families regarding various services and the financial help available as part of social security.

(c) Voluntary organisations contribute in many ways as free agents in promoting a better understanding and acceptance by the community of the mentally ill. Several voluntary organisations have central national committees with local branches other voluntary organisations are exclusively local, e.g. League of Friends. The work of voluntary organisations varies considerably: the majority raise funds for national or special local projects; others concentrate on providing opportunities for individual friendship, social activities for groups of patients and other rehabilitative pastimes.

Community care is more than the substitution of care in the community for care in the hospital. It is a broader consideration of both the patient and his environment. He is a member of a family unit as well as a member of the larger community, and the best psychiatric care is that which embraces the whole family. The criteria of success of community care cannot be judged by the extent to which hospital admission is avoided. The effects of relationships within the family must also be taken into account.

It is now particularly stressed that the psychiatric hospital should no longer be considered merely as an in-patient treatment centre but as an important part of a comprehensive psychiatric service. Such a view should represent a fundamental change in organisation and in attitude of hospital staff to their role.

The Case for a Community Psychiatric Nurse

Before the days of mental hospitals, it must be assumed that all psychiatric nursing and care took place in the community. It is only since the war that it has become widely recognised that patient care needs to continue in the community. Many agencies are concerned with after-care and it is inevitable that nursing skills will be required as an integral part of total care.

Domiciliary nursing care for the physically sick has been organised in this country for many years, yet no such provision has been made for the mentally ill. This absence of psychiatric nurses' work in the community was a result of a hospital-orientated psychiatric treatment, separate administrations of hospital, local authorities and general practitioner services and lack of special skills and training of psychiatric nurses. Perhaps the most important factor was that the responsibility for community services rested with the local authorities.

The psychiatrists began extending their role outside mental hospitals thirty or forty years ago by means of steadily expanding out-patient clinics, domiciliary consultations and community care schemes. Participation of psychiatric nurses in the community care began as pilot schemes only about twenty years ago and these were initiated by mental hospitals. At Wokingham Park Hospital, Surrey, psychiatric nurses have been seconded to extra-mural duties in the Borough of Croydon since 1954. Moorhaven Hospital, Devon, pioneered a similar scheme in 1957. At the beginning, the main duties of psychiatric nurses in Croydon included:

(a) Supervision of patients not requiring hospitalisation.
(b) Follow up and support.
(c) Supervision of out-patient clinics.
(d) Organisation and running of out-patient clubs.
(e) Job and accommodation finding.

During the past few years the role of these nurses has been modified. Nurses remain on the establishment of the hospital and they are now an important part of Croydon's integrated psychiatric service. The nurses work exclusively with out-patients and have no hospital duties. Each nurse has a list of regular patients, and weekly meetings take place in the centre under the psychiatrist co-ordinating community care. Social worker and other interested doctors attend this meeting. Each nurse reviews the patients on her list and decisions about further actions are taken at this meeting. The function of the nurse is primarily clinical. Informal contacts between the nurse and social workers are frequent and the weekly meeting ensures that overlap is avoided. This service is available to patients discharged from the hospital and from the psychiatric unit, from day hospitals and from out-patient clinics.

The scheme pioneered by Moorhaven Hospital concentrated from the beginning on discharged patients with some special problems that needed nursing help. The decision to use a nurse for after-care was arrived at by discussion between the medical, nursing and social work staff. The following considerations were borne in mind:

(a) The patient was still suffering from a psychiatric illness which limited the capacity of other services to provide the necessary care and attention.

(b) A special relationship between nurse and patient as already existed was necessary for the patient.

(c) A supporting link between the patient and the hospital was considered to be necessary. This is reassuring both to the patient and to the family.

This scheme has gradually expanded and, in recent years, the General Nursing Council approved an experimental nurses training scheme enabling psychiatric student nurses to qualify as Registered Mental Nurses with a Diploma in Community Psychiatric Nursing. Other psychiatric hospitals started various schemes enabling a few nurses to work in the community. By 1967 an analysis given by the Royal Medico-Psychological Association showed that forty-two hospitals throughout England and Scotland used their psychiatric nurses for varying work in the community. A breakdown of their main roles was as follows:

Hospitals	Main Nurse's Role
35	for follow up of patients
19	for social work
22	for drug supervision
12	for drug administration

Since the above survey, in the past few years the majority of psychiatric hospitals have developed varying schemes enabling nurses to use their skills and knowledge for the benefit of patients and their relatives.

One of the problems that has frustrated the advance of the psychiatric nurse into the community is the possibility of demarcation disputes arising among the various professional workers involved. Since the reorganisation of the National Health Service it is anticipated that the work of psychiatric nurses in the community will be facilitated. A revised syllabus of 1974 for mental nursing includes a section on fundamentals of community care and on aspects of sociology. In this revised syllabus advice is given that techniques of community nursing must be explored.

For the past ten years numerous articles have appeared in the *Nursing Mirror*, *Nursing Times* and in other professional journals describing in some depth the initiation and success of psychiatric nurses' work in the community in various parts of the country. Although there is a considerable variation in the nurse's role and most of the schemes are limited in scope, nevertheless the most convincing argument in favour of a community role for the psychiatric nurse is that such a policy works. The hospitals operating such schemes are satisfied that the results justify their existence and expansion.

Administrative and Training Aspects

Before any scheme for involving the psychiatric nurse in the community is embarked upon, it is essential that the Department of Social Services of the local authority should be taken into the confidence of the hospital from the beginning. The duties of the nurse would need to be defined as well as the communication systems. Ideally, systematic communications regarding the patient and his needs should cover the consultant in charge, patient's family doctor, social worker and the nurse. Administratively the nurse is a member of a psychiatric division providing comprehensive care.

The majority of nurses working in the community concentrate on after-care of patients. A few nurses are attached to a team headed by a consultant psychiatrist. The time spent by these nurses should be equally divided between work in the community and in their wards, day hospitals or psychiatric units to which they are allocated. This administrative arrangement enables the nurse to know her patients before their discharge and to establish a meaningful relationship. Administration of drugs and observation of symptoms is easier with this type of arrangement. The nurse can periodically report on the progress of patients in her care to the doctor in charge. Referrals for out-patient consultation or even for re-admission are thus facilitated.

In other schemes the nurse works exclusively in the community but is a member of the staff of the psychiatric division. The nurse in this case is based at out-patient clinics, day hospitals, psychiatric units or health centres. Patients for after-care are referred to this nurse who may have opportunities to visit the patient in the hospital prior to discharge. In some parts of the country the psychiatric nurses work in close liaison with the patient's general practitioner.

It is important that periodic reviews of the nurse's work should be carried out and new developments should be considered jointly by medical, social and nursing staff. In most schemes there is a nursing officer designated responsible for the psychiatric nursing community care. Planning of patients' visits in their homes is an important factor to be taken into account as well as distances, journeys and frequency of visits to the patient. Training in the community work of selected nurses is essential. This can be achieved by series of study days and discussions organised locally or by seconding nurses to other hospitals with already established schemes. Pre-discharge case conferences are helpful as part of the preparation of the nurse for this new role. Periodically, various hospitals organise conferences on psychiatric nurses' work in the community. These conferences or symposia are well advertised and they provide opportunities for increasing and sharing the knowledge of community care of the mentally ill.

The Faculty of Health and Social Studies at Chiswick Polytechnic, London, offers a twelve weeks community psychiatric nursing course. The aims of this course are as follows:

1. To provide a comprehensive education and training that will equip the Registered Mental Nurses and Registered Mental Nurses Subnormality working from hospital or community health centre to provide continuity of nursing care and treatment for the psychiatric patient outside hospital 'in-patient' situation.
2. To develop the special skills required to fulfil their extended role, e.g. skills in perception, assessing need, adaptic practical skills. counselling, reporting.
3. To develop within the nurse an understanding of the total environment and its effect on the individual and the family.
4. To help the nurse gain insight into family relationships and the effect of mental illness on family functioning and to assess the best means of providing support.
5. To equip the psychiatric nurse with knowledge of the skills of other disciplines working in the community, available resources and methods of referral.
6. To enable the psychiatric nurse to carry out appropriate health education.

This course consists of a theoretical part and practical work including field placements in the hospital and community. The syllabus of the course includes sociology, psychology, social policy and social services, principles and practice of community psychiatric nursing.

It is anticipated that either courses will be available as part of post-registration education approved by the Joint Board of Clinical Studies.

Nurses Role in the Community Care

There is no standard pattern for a community psychiatric nursing service. Each hospital has an individual approach depending on its needs. A brief guide is given to selected nurses, who develop their role gradually, using their knowledge and understanding of the mentally ill and their own initiative. The aims and functions can be summarised under the following headings:

Health education and preventative aspects.
Continuation of treatment and support.
Establishment of patients in the community.
Communications and research.

Health Education and Preventative Aspects

1. Education in community care to junior members of the team.
2. Education of positive mental health aspects in the community: members of the family, patients' schools, clubs and societies. This role is only in its infant stages and selected nurses will require a special training. Social clubs exist outside hospitals regularly attended by ex-patients, their relatives and other interested members of the society. Several of these clubs make a regular provision for educational activities on topics of positive mental health.
3. Noting any deterioration of the patient and recommending referral for medical attention.
4. Observing the family situation and advising its members on the best methods to cope with environmental stresses or how to seek medical advice.

Continuation of Treatment and Support

1. Maintaining a continuous therapeutic relationship with the patient for as long as it is necessary.
2. Counselling and supporting both patient and relatives and dealing with crisis situations.
3. Trying to ensure that the ordered medication is taken. This medication can be ordered by a doctor to be taken regularly or,

in some forms of mental illness, given by injection at longer lasting intervals.
4. Noting and dealing with side-effects of treatment. Immediate contact with a doctor in charge is necessary.
5. Taking part, where appropriate, in group methods of treatment.

Establishment of Patients in the Community
1. Encouraging the patient to become an independent individual as far as possible.
2. Advising on aspects of employment or seeking help and expert advice of a social worker.
3. Teaching the patient how to cope with various aspects of life in the community. This applies especially to patients who have spent many years in hospitals or to groups of patients living in homes or hostels with a regular support from a psychiatric nurse.
4. Noting special requirements in the home situation and advising how to seek additional help as part of social security. Very frequently a social worker is requested by a nurse to deal with social services or with social security departments.

Communication and Research
1. Giving a periodic overall report on the patient's progress to the doctor in charge or to the social worker on any special problems requiring expert attention.
2. Making special arrangements or communicating needs for special consultations with medical or paramedical members of the health service.
3. Taking part in the multidisciplinary team discussions and reviews of patients under psychiatric care.
4. Taking active interest in the work of voluntary organisations and encouraging their helpful activities.
5. Taking part in the evaluation of psychiatric nurses' work in the community and participating in research projects on community methods of treatment and care.

21 Legal Aspects

The first act dealing with the mentally ill in England was passed in the time of Queen Elizabeth 1, and dealt mainly with the disposal of the estates of the insane. In 1601, The Poor Relief Act, created the post of Parish Overseer, who was responsible for arranging the admission of 'pauper lunatics' to asylums.

The question of property remained the main preoccupation of the law until an act in 1774, which regulated the licensing and inspection of 'madhouses'. In 1853, thanks largely to the efforts of the seventh Earl of Shaftesbury, three acts were passed. These were modified by a number of further Acts, until in 1890 they were all replaced by the provisions of the Lunacy Act. This Act remained the basis of the treatment of mental illness until the Mental Health Act of 1959. In 1930, the Mental Treatment Act, modified the previous legislation to allow patients to enter mental hospital of their own free will, and to provide a method of detaining patients who required, but refused, treatment for a short period, without them being certified.

The history of the legislation concerning the mentally ill and the subnormal reflects the attempts of society to reconcile two conflicting needs, i.e. the protection of society against forms of behaviour that appear threatening, while at the same time protecting the individual from being deprived of his liberty and property by the malicious acts of people who might benefit as a result. This led to a situation in which a patient would be admitted to a mental hospital only when so gravely ill that his madness could be recognised by a lay person, namely a justice of the peace. Having been 'certified' insane, the person lost all civil rights, and found it difficult to obtain his discharge even when he recovered. This state of affairs had several effects. First, it meant that, in general, the patient with a milder illness, or someone in the early stages of a severe illness, could not be admitted for treatment. Secondly, that the emphasis in the mental hospitals was on custodial care rather than treatment.

Thirdly, it increased the stigma attached to mental illness and its treatment.

These features were modified to some extent by the Act of 1930, but after the Second World War, the climate of public opinion was such that the time was ripe for redrafting the legislation to bring it into accord with modern knowledge and society's changed attitudes.

The Act of 1959 was based on the recommendations of a Royal Commission which gathered extensive evidence before publishing its report in 1957. The Act had two main aims, first, to make admission to mental hospitals as simple and as informal as admission to a general hospital (though it provides powers of compulsory detention, it stresses that these should be used only in exceptional circumstances) and, secondly, to change the emphasis from institutional care to support of the mentally ill in the community. The Act is divided into nine parts and each part is sub-divided into sections. It is not proposed to deal in detail with the provisions of the Act, apart from those that most directly concern the mental nurse.

Part I
This deals with the repeal of previous acts, and the dissolution of the Board of Control, whose function was taken over by the Ministry of Health. Section 4 defines and classifies mental disorder for the purposes of the Act, as follows.

(Part I, Section 4)
Definition and classification of mental disorders.

1. In the Act, 'mental disorder' means mental illness, arrested or incomplete development of mind, psychopathic disorder, and any other disorder or disability of mind.
2. In the Act, 'severe subnormality' means a state of arrested or incomplete development of mind which includes subnormality of intelligence, and is of such a nature or degree, that the patient is incapable of living an independent life or of guarding himself against serious exploitation, or will be so incapable when of an age to do so.
3. In this Act, 'subnormality' means a state of arrested or incomplete development of mind (not amounting to severe subnormality) which includes subnormality of intelligence, and is of a nature or degree that requires or is susceptible to medical treatment, or other special care or training of the patient.

4. In the Act, 'psychopathic disorder' means a persistent disorder or disability of mind (whether or not including subnormality of intelligence) which results in abnormally aggressive or seriously irresponsible conduct on the part of the patient, and requires. or is susceptible to, medical treatment.
5. Nothing in this section shall be construed as implying that a person may be dealt with under this Act as suffering from mental disorder, or from any form of mental disorder described in this section, by reason only of promiscuity or other immoral conduct.

Section 5 states, in effect, that a patient who is not unwilling to be admitted and for whom treatment is available may, on medical advice, be admitted to any hospital that is prepared to receive him, without any kind of formality. This includes children over the age of sixteen who are capable of expressing their own wish, even if their parents or guardians object.

Part II

This deals with the local authority services, and requires them to make the following provisions:

1. Residential accommodation for persons who are, or have been, suffering from mental disorder.
2. Centres, staffed and equipped for their training or occupation.
3. The appointment of officers to act as mental welfare officers.
4. The exercise by the local health authority of their functions in respect to persons under guardianship.
5. The provision of any ancillary or supplementary service which might be of benefit.

Part III

This deals with the registration and conduct of nursing homes and residential homes.

Part IV

This deals with compulsory admission to hospital and guardianship. This part of the Act is of particular importance to the nursing staff, as they are often expected to make sure that a patient being admitted compulsorily is accompanied by the correct documents.

Section 25 refers to the application for admission for observation, which may be made on the grounds that the patient is suffering from a mental disorder which warrants his detention in hospital for observation, with or without other medical treatment, for at least a limited period; and that he ought to be so detained in the interests of his own health or safety, or with a view to the protection of other persons. The application is made on the written recommendation of two medical practitioners, one of whom must be approved by the local health authority as having special experience in the diagnosis or treatment of mental disorder. The application is made by the patient's nearest relative, or in certain circumstances by the mental welfare officer. If the application is accepted by the managers of the hospital (usually the hospital management committee), the patient may be detained for up to twenty-eight days beginning on the day on which he is admitted.

The doctors signing the recommendation must have seen the patient together or within seven days of each other, and the person making the application must have seen the patient within fourteen days of the date of the application.

Section 26 applies to an application for admission for treatment which may be made in respect of a patient on the grounds that he is suffering from mental disorder, being either:

1. in the case of a patient of any age, mental illness or severe subnormality;
2. in the case of a patient under the age of twenty-one years, psychopathic disorder, or subnormality;

and that the disorder is sufficiently severe to merit detention, and that such detention is necessary in the interests of the patient's health or safety, or for the protection of others.

The application is based on the written recommendation of the doctors, as for Section 25, but each recommendation must include a description of the type of mental disorder the patient is thought to have, the grounds for the doctor holding this opinion, and a statement why other methods of dealing with the patient are not considered appropriate.

Section 29 states that an emergency application may be made by any relative of the patient, or by a mental welfare officer supported by the written recommendation of one medical practitioner. The patient may be detained for seventy-two hours from the time of admission, unless during that time a second medical recommendation is given and received by the managers, detaining him for a further period of twenty-eight days from the time of admission (Section 25), or for one year (Section 26).

Section 30 enables an application to be made under Sections 25, 26, or 29, in respect of a patient who is already in hospital on an informal basis and who demands to leave but whom, in the opinion of the responsible medical officer, requires to be detained while application for formal admission, as above, is made.

In order to safeguard the interests of the patient, and prevent wrongful detention, the Act makes provision for the discharge of patients detained under the above sections as follows:

1. Patients admitted for observation (Section 25) can only be discharged by the responsible medical officer or the managers of the hospital—but not by the nearest relative.

2. Patients on Section 26 can be discharged at the request of the nearest relative, if the relative gives written notice to the hospital managers seventy-two hours prior to the patient leaving hospital. Should the responsible medical officer feel that the patient is a danger to himself or others he must make a report to the managers during this seventy-two hours, who must then inform the nearest relative that his application has been refused, and no further application can be made for the next six months. The relative can appeal against this decision to a Mental Health Review Tribunal, within twenty-eight days of being so informed.

3. Three or more members of the hospital management committee can consider an application for the patient's discharge, and order it if they think fit.

Part V

This is concerned with the admission of patients involved in criminal proceedings, or serving sentences. Section 60 enables the court to order the admission of a person to hospital and his detention there. The provisions correspond to those outlined in Section 25, except that the nearest relative does not have the power to discharge the patient. Should the court consider that there is a risk of the offender repeating his crimes, if not restricted to hospital, he may be committed under Section 65, in which case only the Secretary of State can (a) grant leave of absence, (b) transfer the patient, and (c) order the patient's discharge.

In the case of a person who is already serving a prison sentence, and who is then found to be suffering from mental illness, psychopathic disorder, subnormality or severe subnormality, of a degree that warrants detention in hospital for medical treatment, the Secretary of State can order his transfer to hospital under Section 72.

Part VI
This deals with the transfer of patients within the United Kingdom, the removal of alien patients to their own country, and for the return of patients who are absent without leave.

Part VII
This contains the regulations concerning special hospitals, providing treatment under conditions of special security.

Part VIII (The Management of Property and Affairs of Patients)
This part defines the function of the Court of Protection, which consists of one or more judges of the Supreme Court, nominated by the Lord Chancellor, a Master and Deputy Master, and other officers also nominated by the Lord Chancellor. The court can exercise its powers when the judge is satisfied, having considered the medical evidence, that a person is incapable, by reason of mental disorder, of managing and administrating his property and affairs. It does not matter whether the person is in hospital informally, under a Section, or not receiving treatment at all. The judge may appoint someone to act as receiver, who is then responsible for managing the affairs of the patient as the judge directs.

The Lord Chancellor also appoints Visitors, who are either medically or legally qualified, whose duty it is to visit patients in the care of the court and to investigate matters relating to the capacity of the patient to administer his affairs. The Visitor has the right to interview the patient in private, and in the case of medical visitors, to examine the patient, and any relevant medical records.

Part IX
This contains miscellaneous and general regulations.

Mental Health Review Tribunals

Under Part I, Section 3 of the Act, each Regional Hospital Board area has a Mental Health Review Tribunal, which consists of legal members and lay members appointed by the Lord Chancellor after consultation with the Minister of Health. One of the legal members is appointed chairman.

A patient detained in hospital on Section 26 may apply to a Tribunal within six months of the day of his admission. He cannot make another application during the twelve months beginning with the date of his admission. Application can also be made by a near relative who has been prevented from discharging the patient as previously described. The Tribunal will order the patient's discharge if at the time they consider he is not suffering from mental illness, psychopathic disorder, subnormality or severe subnormality.

Offences

The Act defines various offences and lays down punishment for those who commit them.

Offences include:

1. Forging of documents required or authorised by the Act.
2. Ill treatment of patients.

    Any staff found guilty of ill treating or wilfully neglecting a patient are liable on summary conviction to imprisonment for up to six months, or to a fine not exceeding £100, or both, or on conviction or indictment, to a term of imprisonment not exceeding two years, or to a fine, or both.

3. Sexual intercourse with patients.

    Any man employed in a hospital or mental nursing home who has unlawful sexual intercourse with a woman who is receiving treatment for a mental disorder in that hospital or home, knowing or having reason to suspect that she is a mentally disordered person, is liable on conviction to imprisonment for a term not exceeding two years.

Correspondence of Patients

These provisions apply to both informal patients and those detained on section. Any letter or parcel addressed to the patient can be withheld from him if, in the opinion of the medical officer, the receipt of it would interfere with the treatment of the patient or cause him unnecessary distress. Such packets shall be opened, and if the sender's name and address can be discovered, must be returned to him by post.

Letters or parcels sent by the patient may be withheld from the Post Office, if:

1. The person to whom they are addressed has written to the hospital asking that any communications addressed to him by the patient be withheld.
2. The medical officer considers that the contents would be unreasonably offensive to the recipient, if it is defamatory of other persons (except people on the staff of the hospital) or would be likely to prejudice the interests of the patient.

Letters addressed to anyone who might play a part in safeguarding the patient's freedom or safety are excluded from these provisions and must be posted. This applies to letters addressed to:

1. The Minister of Health.
2. Any member of the House of Commons.
3. The Master or Deputy Master or other officer of the Court of Protection.
4. The Managers of the hospital.
5. To any other authority or person having power to discharge the patient.
6. At any time when the patient is entitled to apply to a Mental Health Review Tribunal, to that tribunal.
7. Solicitor acting for the patient.

The medical officer is entitled to open postal packets from patients only if he is of the opinion that the patient is suffering from mental disorder of a kind calculated to lead him to send communications that are offensive, defamatory or likely to damage his own interests.

22 'What have you learnt?'

Learning and Examinations

This chapter is intended for nurses who are coming towards the end of their training. We hope that during that time you have used this book to help you to clarify some of the problems you have met, and that it has provided some of the factual basis necessary for an understanding of the patients and their disorders. Learning is not confined to memorising facts from books; the nurse learns from her daily work in the wards, and from the ideas and examples of her colleagues. At the end of her training, the nurse should have developed her own philosophy of nursing as part of her general maturing. In this book we have tried to imply a nursing philosophy without spelling it out in detail. It might now be helpful to try to express it in as short and simple a way as possible.

Mental nursing demands above all *respect*—respect for the rights and dignity of the individual human being. This respect must apply to all our patients, however disturbed, dirty, anti-social, demanding, tiresome, ungrateful, or lost they may seem. From this basic respect can develop the next essential, *understanding*. This understanding involves not only intellectual understanding, but also emotional understanding, not in a sentimental way but in the kind of way that enables one to enter into the patient's world, to see as he sees, and feel as he feels. The nurse who has respect and understanding must also have *awareness*. She must be aware of the reality of the situation in which the patient finds himself, and she must be aware of her own responses to the patient and his needs. Such a nurse can play her full role, for as a result of her respect, understanding, and awareness, she can provide the patient with both the emotional support he requires and the guidance he needs to resolve his difficulties. A nurse who develops her capacity for this work will enjoy the satisfaction of being of service to others. This gives truer and more lasting happiness than any of the presently popular ambitions for wealth, status, or excitement.

The nurse, before being rewarded by having full responsibility for the care of patients, must, however, pass a qualifying examination. For many nurses, good though they may be in their daily work, this hurdle assumes nightmarish proportions. Most examinations demand a certain verbal skill, and tend to place those who lack this skill at a disadvantage. However, passing exams is a skill that can be acquired with a little hard work and practice. Teaching a subject like mental nursing in a way that is aimed only at passing exams is to be deplored, but it is equally foolish to pretend that exams do not matter. We wish to end this book by providing advice on preparing for, and taking the final examination. To this end, some specimen questions, which can be used as a test of how much you have learnt, are included.

Preparing for the Examination

During the last few months of training, the nurse should begin to organise her knowledge for the purpose of passing the final examination. From the detailed syllabus she should plan a revision course that covers all topics, and draw up a rough timetable for revising. The amount of time devoted to study in the plan should be realistic and should allow a certain latitude for days lost to study through unforeseen accidents. It is probably best to select one textbook to work from at this stage. No textbook is complete or entirely satisfactory, and during the training period the nurse should have read widely, from textbooks, articles, and monographs on specific topics. In this last stage of training, time is too short to do this: find a textbook that suits you and stick to it. There is no point in merely reading or rereading a book from cover to cover. Knowledge must be tested. Take a chapter and find a number of questions on the topic with which it deals. Try to answer the questions *before* reading the chapter. Read the chapter and check your answers. This method also provides opportunity for practising examination techniques.

The Written Papers

The questions on the written paper are set by the examiners after much hard work. Each word has been discussed and agreed on; therefore, the candidate should be prepared to pay close attention to the question. The first step in attempting the paper is to read the instructions with extreme care. Note exactly how many questions have to be tackled, whether there is a choice, and how much time can be given to each question.

Having understood the instructions, read through *all* the questions. The shocked feeling that one cannot answer any of them will give way in a few minutes, unless you really have done no work at all in the previous three years! When there is a choice of questions, decide which you are going to do, and the order in which you are going to tackle them. Take the easier ones first—but do not spend more time on them than you have allowed yourself. It is better to have some extra time in hand to tackle the questions you find more difficult.

Now reread the question, noting any special points. For example, if the question includes the age of a patient, this suggests the examiners have something special in mind—you wouldn't expect puerperal illness in a woman of sixty-five or presenile dementia in a girl of eighteen.

Having reread the question, jot down any facts that seem relevant on your rough working sheet. It is surprising how even well-known facts such as normal body temperature, or the dose of morphine, can suddenly leave the mind in the course of writing an answer. Only now are you ready to put pen to paper as far as the answer paper is concerned. The minutes have ticked by, and at least one candidate will have already asked for an extra answer book! Console yourself with the thought that nothing is easier to write quickly than nonsense. Having finished your answer to the first question, repeat the process for each question in turn. Make sure that you have answered all the questions and all parts of each question. No marks can be awarded for questions not answered—nor for little notes saying, 'I know the answer, but didn't have time to do it'.

When the paper is finished, read through your answers, correcting any spelling mistakes, errors of punctuation and the like. The examiner is not supposed to deduct marks for poor writing, or spelling errors, but being human, he is more likely to look with favour on a script that is neat, well set out, easy to read and shows a certain level of literacy. It is very tiring marking papers that give the impression of being written by a demented spider using an ink-filled poker!

The Viva Voce
All too often the candidate opens his mouth and puts his foot in it. This is a contortion that leads neither to audibility nor success.

A viva is like a game of chess. The examiner has the benefit of the first move, but after that the candidate has every chance to dictate what he is asked. Remember that the examiner is probably as hard pressed to think up questions, as is the candidate for answers. Examiners will usually welcome a lead from the candidate, so if there are certain topics about which you feel particularly confident, you will almost certainly be able to direct the conversation round to them.

Never use technical words unless you can give their exact definition. When the candidate says, 'the patient has delusions, is hallucinated', or the like, few examiners can resist asking, 'What is a delusion, hallucination, etc. etc.'. You will score marks if you know the answer, but lose face if you don't. Do not try to teach the examiner—he thinks he knows it all and will only feel hurt. However, if you disagree with something he says, do not be afraid to say so. The general impression created by the candidate can be very important. Examiners prefer candates who seem pleasant and polite, but above all else, they like a candidate who gives the impression that she is interested in her work, keen, and receptive to new ideas. A student who has become institutionalised in the course of three years' training is a depressing and discouraging candidate.

Finally, here are some specimen questions. Attempt to answer them, then consult the relevant chapter—rewrite your anwer in the light of your new knowledge, and keep it for a final read through in the last few days before the examinations.

Questions on all Chapters

Chapter 1

(a) Mention some of the psychosomatic symptoms that may be complained of by the patient in a state of anxiety.

(b) What are the main principles in the treatment of neuroses?

(c) A patient in your care complains of being in a state of panic.
   (i) What may be the reason for this?
   (ii) How would you help such a patient?

(d) What do you know about the nature of hysteria?

(e) Describe the symptoms of a patient suffering from obsessional neurosis, indicating the treatment and the nursing care.

Chapter 2

(a) What do you understand by 'psychopathic disorder'?

(b) Give an account of the possible causes of psychopathic personality development.

(c) Explain the provisions in the Mental Health Act concerning psychopathic disorders.

(d) Discuss the treatment problems of the psychopathic patient in the psychiatric hospital.

(e) Discuss the sexual deviations in relation to mental disorder.

(f) What types of individuals are likely to experience sexual difficulties?

(g) Discuss the problems of sexual deviants in a psychiatric hospital.

Chapter 3

(a) Discuss the main causes of alcoholism and drug addiction.

(b) How may excessive drinking affect the physical, mental, and social wellbeing of the individual?

(c) Describe two examples of alcoholic psychoses, indicating treatment and nursing care.

(d) Discuss the prevention and treatment of drug addiction.

Chapter 4

(a) Describe a depressed patient you have helped to nurse, indicating your part in the treatment and the nursing care.

(b) Compare and contrast endogenous and reactive groups of depression. What are the main lines of treatment?

(c) What observation would indicate that a patient should be regarded as a high suicidal risk, and how should the care of such a patient be organised?

(*d*) Give a comprehensive account of the nursing aspects of depressed patients.

(*e*) Discuss the nursing care of a patient with mania.

Chapter 5

(*a*) Describe the behaviour of a patient whom you have nursed, who was disturbed by delusions and hallucinations, indicating the measures taken to help this patient.

(*b*) How may the following aspects of personality be disturbed in schizophrenia:
  (i) thinking,
  (ii) emotions,
  (iii) volition?

(*c*) What measures are adopted in psychiatric hospitals to prevent the deterioration of schizophrenic patients?

(*d*) Discuss the role of the nurse in trying to establish a therapeutic relationship with a schizophrenic patient.

Chapter 6

(*a*) What observations and reports of the nurses may be useful to the doctor in establishing the diagnosis of acute *organic* brain disturbance?

(*b*) Describe fully the nursing care of acutely ill and restless patients.

(*c*) What factors may be responsible for a sudden deterioration of the functions of the brain?

(*d*) Discuss the treatment of the patient suffering from acute brain syndrome.

Chapter 7

(*a*) Describe the main features of a patient suffering from senile dementia.

(*b*) What may be the causes of chronic dementia?

(*c*) Explain the possible mental changes following head injury.

(*d*) Give a full account of the nursing care of patients who are showing signs of chronic dementia.

Chapter 8

(*a*) What precautions should be taken with epileptic patients?

(*b*) What would you do for the patient during a major convulsion?

(*c*) Explain the nature of epilepsy.

(*d*) Give an account of the drugs used to treat epileptics.

(*e*) Indicate how your understanding of epileptic personality may contribute towards a therapeutic relationship.

(*f*) How would you differentiate between epileptic and hysterical fits?

Chapter 9

(*a*) Discuss the difference between mental subnormality and mental illness.

(*b*) What may be the causes of mental subnormality?

(*c*) What common disorders of behaviour may occur in children?

Chapter 10

(a) What observations would indicate that a withdrawn patient may be suffering from physical illness?

(b) Why is fluid balance important for the maintenance of normal body functioning, and in which conditions may the patient become dehydrated?

(c) Discuss the importance of accurate charts and records when nursing the physically ill.

(d) Explain the 'psychosomatic' concept of body functioning.

(e) Give examples of psychosomatic conditions and describe one more fully, including treatment and nursing aspects.

(f) Explain the nursing measures taken to ensure that the physical health of the mentally ill patients is maintained, and the early discovery of any physical illnesses is reported to the doctor.

(g) give an account of the observation and the methods of collection of the following specimen:
  (i) sputum
  (ii) vomit
  (iii) faeces
  (iv) urine.

Chapter 11

(a) Describe the nursing care of an unconscious patient.

(b) Discuss the reasons why sufficient exercise is important for elderly patients.

(c) Describe the 'ideal day' for a group of elderly patients.

(d) What are the dangers of prolonged bed rest?

(e) Discuss the problems associated with bed sores and incontinence of urine.

(f) What are the responsibilities of the nurse concerning the care of the dying?

Chapter 12

(a) What do you think is important to observe in a patient who is frequently aggressive?

(b) Discuss the possible reasons of aggression in a psychiatric hospital.

(c) A patient with aggressive tendencies may be well behaved with one team of nurses on duty and may be very truculent with other nurses. Discuss the possible reasons for these two varying patterns of behaviour of the same patient.

(d) Describe the patient's day during 'closed group' methods of care.

(e) Discuss the measures taken to minimise incidences of aggression in psychiatric hospital.

Chapter 13

(a) Discuss the normal and abnormal patterns of human behaviour.

(b) Compare and contrast the neurotic and psychotic groups of mental illnesses.

(c) Explain the terms 'delusion' and 'hallucination', illustrating with examples from the patients you have helped to nurse.

Chapter 14
(a) Give a brief account of the emotional stresses in childhood and adolescence.
(b) Give a brief summary of the causes of mental disorders.
(c) It is suggested that unconscious processes influence human behaviour. Discuss this, illustrating your answer with examples from every-day life, and as may be seen in the mentally ill.
(d) Discuss the psychological stresses of old age.

Chapter 15
(a) What are the main reasons for observing a patient?
(b) What are the main principles of good observation?
(c) What guidance would you give to a junior nurse concerning nursing procedures involving the patient?
(d) Explain the role of the nurse in relation to:
  (i) psychotherapy
  (ii) care and protection of the patient.
(e) Discuss the reasons why a patient may require admission to a psychiatric hospital.
(f) How can the nurses help the patient during his stay in the hospital?
(g) How may relatives be affected by the patient's illness and hospitalisation?
(h) What observations would you make on a newly admitted patient, and how may your observations be useful in the total care and treatment of this patient?

Chapter 16
(a) Discuss the concept of a therapeutic community in a psychiatric hospital.
(b) Discuss the nursing problems arising from the transference situation indicating the desirable attitudes to be adopted by nurses.
(c) Write short notes on the following:
  (i) group methods of treatment
  (ii) group psychotherapy
  (iii) hypnosis
  (iv) behaviour therapy.

Chapter 17
(a) Enumerate the physical methods of treatment of the mentally ill and describe one more fully.
(b) Explain the use of major tranquillisers in the treatment of the mentally ill.
(c) What observations would you make on patients who are treated with (1) tranquillisers, (2) anti-depressant drugs?

Chapter 18
(a) Describe the nurse's responsibilities in relation to Electroconvulsive Therapy.
(b) Write short notes on the following treatments:
  (i) modified insulin
  (ii) prolonged narcosis
  (iii) leucotomy.

Chapter 19
Discuss the difference in incidence of mental disorders in different social classes.

Chapter 20
(a) What attitudes should the nurses maintain so that the patients could benefit from occupational therapy?
(b) Give a brief account of the National Health Service and the part your hospital takes in it.
(c) What do you think are the most important points concerning the rehabilitation of mentally ill patients?
(d) What do you know about the provisions available for the mentally ill in the community?
(e) Discuss the role of the Day Hospital in the treatment of the mentally ill.
(f) Explain the roles of the following:
  (i) psychiatric social worker
  (ii) mental welfare officer
  (iii) child care officer.
(g) Discuss the advantages and limitations of occupational and industrial therapies.
(h) Discuss briefly the concept of 'community care' of the mentally ill.
(i) What changes are required in the attitudes and training of psychiatric nurses to enable them to work effectively in the community?
(j) Discuss briefly the main aims and functions of a psychiatric nurse in the community.

Chapter 21
(a) Outline the main provisions in the 1959 Mental Health Act for the admission of patients to hospital.
(b) What explanations would be given to the relatives concerned about the Mental Health Review Tribunals?

Books for Further Reading

The topics dealt with in this book cover almost every aspect of psychiatry. It is obvious that to keep the book within reasonable limits, many topics can only be outlined. The following books will be found useful for more detailed treatment of various subjects. Most are available in cheap editions.

Barton, Russel: *Institutional Neurosis*. (John Wright and Sons, Bristol)

Stengel, Erwin: *Suicide and Attempted Suicide*. (Pelican, London)

Clark, David: *Administrative Therapy*. (Tavistock Publications, London)

Cleckley, Henry: *The Mask of Sanity*. (C. V. Mosby Co.)

Freud, Sigmund: *Introductory Lectures on Psycho-analysis*. (Penguin, London)

Heaton-Ward, W. Alan: *Mental Subnormality*. (John Wright and Sons, Bristol)

Hays, Peter: *New Horizons in Psychiatry*. (Pelican, London)

Welfare Services. (British Red Cross Society, London)

Berne, Eric: *Games People Play*. (Andre Deutsch, London)

Valentine, C. W.: *The Normal Child*. (Pelican, London)

Storr, A.: *Sexual Deviation*. (Penguin, London)

West, D. J.: *Homosexuality*. (Penguin, London)

Stafford-Clark, D.: *What Freud Really Said*. (Penguin, London)

Lynn, Gillis: *Human Behaviour in Illness*. (Faber and Faber, London)

Crowcroft, A.: *The Psychotic*. (Penguin, London)

Kessel, N. and Walton, H.: *Alcoholism*. (Penguin, London)

Walker, K. and Fletcher, P.: *Sex and Society*. (Penguin, London)

Hinton, J.: *Dying*. (Penguin, London)

Argyle, M.: *The Psychology of Interpersonal Behaviour*. (Penguin, London)

Leech, K. and Jordon, B.: *Drugs for Young People*. (Religious Educ. Press, Oxford)

Schwartz, M. S. and Stockley, E. L.: *The Nurse and the Mental Patient*. (John Wiley and Son, New York)

Singh, M. M.: *Mental Disorder*. (Pan Books, London)

Mitchell, Ross: *Depression*. (Penguin, London)

Wells, Brian: *Psychedelic Drugs*. (Penguin, London)

Ransome, Arthur: *Introduction to Social Psychiatry*. (Penguin, London)

Index